Waiting To Be Heard

The Polish Christian Experience
Under Nazi and Stalinist
Oppression

1939-1955

Compiled & Edited by

Bogusia J. Wojciechowska

With a Foreword by The Hon. Ryszard Kaczorowski

AuthorHouse™
1663 Liberty Drive
Bloomington, IN 47403
www.authorhouse.com
Phone: 1-800-839-8640

First published by AuthorHouse 9/2/2009

ISBN: 978-1-4490-2183-2 (e)
ISBN: 978-1-4490-1371-4 (sc)
ISBN: 978-1-4490-1370-7 (hc)

Library of Congress Control Number: 2009908750

Printed in the United States of America
Bloomington, Indiana

This book is printed on acid-free paper.

DEDICATION

To my parents, Celina Kabala Wojciechowska and Bolesław Wojciechowski. This book is an expression of my love, respect and admiration for you, and gratitude for everything you did to raise your family so that we felt secure and loved, and free of the hunger and suffering you experienced in your lives.

**Figure 1.   Celina Kabala Wojciechowska,
Bogusia Wojciechowska, and Bolesław Wojciechowski,
Fairford Polish Hostel, England, 1955**

TABLE OF CONTENTS

INVASION

CHAPTER 1

CHAPTER 2

RESISTANCE

CHAPTER 3

CHAPTER 4

CAPTIVITY

CHAPTER 5

CHAPTER 6

LIFE IN TRANSIT

THE NEW POLISH DIASPORA

GLOSSARY

1 dekogram (dag)	0.1 kilogram, about 3½ ounces.
1 hectare (ha)	2.47 acres.
1 kilometer (km)	0.6214 miles.
1 stone (st)	14 pounds.
10 °C	50 °F.
Amnesty	In August 1941, Poles who had been deported were granted an 'Amnesty' and were free to join the new Polish Army that was forming in the south under General Anders.
Armia Krajowa (AK)	The Home Army, the Polish Resistance.
Babcia	Grandma.
Cichociemni	'The quiet and dark ones', Special Operations Executive.
DPs	Displaced Persons, mainly Eastern European slave laborers, POWs and concentration camp inmates, who found themselves outside their home countries as a result of World War II.
Drugi Korpus	Second Corps, 1943-47, created from the deportees who escaped the Soviet Union after the 'Amnesty' of 1942. It was commanded by Lieutenant General Władysław Anders.
German Luftwaffe	German Air Force.
Herrenvolk	In Nazi ideology; the ideal and pure race.
Kapo	A prisoner who had an administrative and/or supervisory role in a Nazi camp.
Karpacka Brygada	Carpathian Brigade. The Polish Independent Carpathian Brigade (*Samodzielna Brygada Strzelców Karpackich*) was a Polish military unit formed in 1940 in French Syria and comprised of the Polish

soldiers exiled after the Invasion of Poland in 1939 as part of the Polish Army. It was commanded by General Stanisław Kopański.

Kipiatok	Russian form of tea.
Kolkhoz	Soviet collective farm where workers were compensated with food.
Kresy	Eastern Poland: homesteads given to Polish servicemen after the Polish victory over the Bolsheviks in the war of 1919-20.
IRO	International Refugee Organization, 1947-52.
Łapanki	Round-ups of the Polish population.
Matka, Mama	Mother, Mommy.
NKVD	Narodny Komissaryat Vnutrennikh Del, the Soviet secret police, the precursor of the KGB.
Osada	Settlement or estate.
Posiolek	Family work camp.
Powstanie Warszawskie	Warsaw Uprising, August 1 – October 5, 1944.
Sohoz	Soviet collective farm where workers were compensated with money.
Szare Szeregi	The Grey Ranks, the Polish Scouting Movement, which was part of the Polish Resistance; they had grey uniforms.
Tato, Tatuś	Dad, Daddy.
UNRRA	The United Nations Relief and Rehabilitation Administration, 1943-47.
UPA	The Ukrainian Nationalist Organization.
WP	Wojsko Polskie, the Polish Army.

MAPS AND PHOTOGRAPHS

FOREWORD

I belong to the generation fortunate enough to have spent its youth in a Poland which, in 1918, was freed after 123 years from under the yokes of conquerors such as Russia, Prussia and Austria. We grew up in a sovereign state aware that everything around us was the result of 1,000 years of Christian culture, the work of generations and a sea of blood and tears shed in wars for freedom and independence.

The ideals presented to us by our mentors, such as our teachers and national leaders, emphasized selfless and dedicated service to Poland.

Principles accepted in youth prepared the Nation for the greatest challenge; that of the occupation of our Homeland by German and Soviet invaders during World War II. A generation of older friends, peers and, also, those younger, who lived during the War, passed the test of loyalty to the Polish State and exemplified the values that had made it great. These loyalties were expressed by the mottos on our military standards: *"God, Honor and the Homeland."* In staying faithful to these principles, these generations paid an enormous price in the fields of battle as well as in places of German and Soviet enslavement. Due, also, to the treachery of the Western Allies, they were condemned to live outside the Homeland for over 50 years and maintained a commitment to serve the great cause that was Poland.

After the September 1939 curse of an unequal battle with two aggressors, the Polish political emigration in France, and, subsequently, Great Britain, took upon itself the honorable role of guardian of Poland's sovereignty. Six successive Presidents of the Polish Republic living outside Poland, a country enslaved by the Soviets following the War, vowed to *'God Almighty and the Holy Trinity... to protect the true laws of the State...'* in keeping with the Constitution of 1935. On December 22, 1990, in the Royal Palace in Warszawa, I handed the original manuscript and the Presidential Insignia to my successor, Lech Wałęsa, a President freely-elected by the Polish Nation and, by this act, ensured the continuity of our Homeland.

Dr. Bogusia Wojciechowska's book presents the losses suffered by Polish Christians during and after World War II. It is a chronicle of the *'resolute'* who did not come to terms with the Yalta settlement which had dictated the placing of Poland under the rule of Stalin, and who stayed in a foreign land after the War so they could continue, though now unarmed, the battle for the freedom and sovereignty of Poland.

We cannot give them any award for their service, but we must remember the timeless ideals of their actions.

The Primate of Poland, Cardinal Stefan Wyszyński, writing during the most repressive years in Communist-occupied Poland, was able to give a perfect summary. *"After God, our greatest love is Poland! After God our love, above all, belongs to Poland, her language, achievements and culture, from which we have grown on Polish soil. Even if they were to hang banners telling us to love all people and nations, we would not be opposed to this, but yet demand that we can live, above all else, in the spirit, achievements, culture and language of our Polish land, achieved over the course of centuries by our ancestors."*

These words are the key to understanding *Waiting to be Heard: The Polish Christian Experience under Nazi and Stalinist Oppression, 1939-55*, as well as a familiarity with the history of the Polish nation; a nation whose past, present, and desired future, was, is, and always will be characterized by the battle for her independence.

Hon. Ryszard Kaczorowski

Former President of the Republic of Poland

London, February 2009

(Original Polish Text of Foreword)

Należę do pokolenia, które miało szczęście przeżywać młodość w Polsce wyzwolonej w 1918 roku spod 123-letniego jarzma zaborców: Rosji, Prus i Austrii. Wzrastaliśmy w suwerennym kraju w świadomości, że to wszystko co nas otacza to efekt tysiącletniej kultury chrześcijańskiej, praca pokoleń i morze krwi oraz łez przelanych w walce o wolność i niepodległość.

Ideały jakie stawiali przed nami nasi wychowawcy, nauczyciele i przywódcy narodu, podkreślały służbę Polsce, bezinteresowną i ofiarną.

Przyjęte w młodości wzorce wychowawcze przygotowały Naród do próby największej, jaką była okupacja naszej Ojczyzny przez niemieckich i sowieckich najeźdźców w drugiej wojnie światowej. Pokolnie starszych kolegów oraz moich rówieśników i młodszych, dorastających już w czasie wojny, zdało egzamin wierności Państwu Polskiemu i tym wartościom, które składały się na jego wielkość. Wyrażały je hasła na sztandarach wojskowych: *"Bóg, Honor i Ojczyzna."* Za wierność tym wzorcom wychowawczym pokolenia nasze zapłaciły ogromną cenę na polach bitew oraz w miejscach niemieckiej i sowieckiej kaźni. Także ta część Narodu, która przez wiarołomstwo zachodnich sojuszników, została po drugiej wojnie światowej skazana na życie poza Ojczyzną, miała przez ponad 50 lat poczucie służby tej wielkiej sprawie, jaką jest Polska.

Po klęsce wrześniowej 1939 roku w nierównej walce z dwoma napastnikami, polska emigracja polityczna we Francji a następnie w Wielkiej Brytanii przejęła zaszczytną rolę strażników suwerenności Polski. Sześciu kolejnych Prezydentów Rzeczypospolitej Polskiej rezydujących poza krajem, zniewolonym po drugiej wojnie światowej przez Sowietów, przysięgało *"Panu Bogu Wszechmogącemu, w Trójcy Świętej Jedynemu... praw zwierzchniczych Państwa bronić.."* zgodnie z Konstytucją z 1935 roku. Oryginalny rękopis tej Ustawy wraz z insygniami prezydenckimi wręczyłem 22 grudnia 1990 roku na Zamku Królewskim w Warszawie Prezydentowi Lechowi Wałęsie, swemu wybranemu przez Naród następcy, spajając tym aktem ciągłość hisotryczną naszej Ojczyzny.

Książka Pani doktór Bogusi Wojciechowskiej przedstawia losy obywateli polskich światopoglądu chrześcijańskiego w drugiej wojnie światowej i po jej zakończeniu. Jest też kroniką *'niezłomnych'*, którzy nie pogodzili się z dyktatem jałtańskim, oddającym Polskę pod władzę Stalina i pozostali po wojnie na obcej ziemi, aby dokumentować tym dalszą, choć już bezorężną walkę o wolność i suwerenność Ojczyzny.

Żadnej nagrody dać im za tę służbę nie możemy, ale trzeba przypomnieć ponadczasową ideę ich działań.

Nadzwyczaj trafnie sformułował ówczesny Prymas Polski, pracujący w najtrudniejszych latach komunistycznego zniewolenia narodu. Kardynał Stefan Wyszyński napisał przed laty: *„Dla nas po Bogu, największa miłość, to Polska! Po Bogu więc nasza miłość należy przede wszystkim naszej Ojczyźnie, mowie, dziejom i kulturze, z której wyrastamy na polskiej ziemi. I chociażby obwieszczono na transparentach najrozmaitsze wezwania do miłowania wszystkich ludów i narodów, nie będziemy temu przeciwni, ale będziemy żądali, abyśmy mogli żyć przede wszystkim duchem, dziejami, kulturą i mową naszej polskiej ziemi, wypracowanej przez wieki życiem naszych praojców."*

Słowa te są kluczem do zrozumienia książki, *Waiting to be Heard: The Polish Christian Experience under Nazi and Stalinist Oppression, 1939-55*, oraz poznania historii narodu polskiego, którego przeszłość, teraźniejszość i przyszłość taka, jaką pragniemy, była, jest i będzie zawsze naznaczona walką o jego tożsamość.

Pan Ryszard Kaczorowski

b. Prezydent Rzeczypospolitej Polski na Uchodźstwie

Londyn, luty, 2009r.

PREFACE

For the past 19 years I have been involved in teaching the Holocaust of WWII. I have spoken in schools and universities, both private and public, synagogues, churches, civic organizations, and libraries in the USA and abroad. I must say that I learned more than I had anticipated. Teaching the Holocaust is mandated in many schools, but it has become the teaching of the six million Jews and 'others', and only rarely do students learn about the five million 'others'. The United States Holocaust Memorial Museum in Washington, DC, recognizes and receives Federal Funds for 11 million victims of the Holocaust, yet our schools' curriculum has not caught up to that.

We Poles bear some of the responsibilities for that omission. In one private school, when I asked a student to tell me what he knew about the Holocaust, he answered, *"It was the destruction of six million Jews"* and, turning to his friends, he continued *"but we don't have to worry. We're not Jewish."* Another time a student wrote me an answer to the question *"Had you lived then and there* (during the Holocaust), *would you have saved another person's life at the risk of your own?"* He wrote, *"Yes, if he was one of my own."* He signed it, even though it was not a requirement, revealing a Jewish name.

As a Polish Catholic Holocaust survivor and speaker I can truly say that our students and teachers are hungry for the whole story. The non-Jewish community must get more involved in their schools' teaching curriculum and provide written and visual material to support their story. I met teachers who proudly showed me *Maus*[1] and *The Painted Bird*[2] as teaching tools on the Holocaust. Christian private schools are much more apt to invite a non-Jewish survivor as a Holocaust speaker. Some public schools are not as willing to speak about the five million 'others', as if it would be disloyal to the six million Jewish victims. Non-Jewish parents want the full story told because it will unite in strength the students and provide 'good will' among them. By not showing our children the ramifications of hate, we deprive them of growing up in love and respect for each other. To feel empathy for one group and ignore the 'others' is not an option in teaching our future generations of children about the shared tragedy of the Holocaust of World War II.

When we separate the story, we separate the people. When we separate the people we minimize the enormity of the Holocaust. By showing our shared suffering, we are united as people in respect and human dignity. Yes, we are our brother's keeper.

Bożenna Urbanowicz Gilbride

USA, 2008

---

1   Spieglman, A. (1996). *Maus: A Survivor's Tale.* New York, Pantheon Books.
2   Kosinski, J. (1976). *The Painted Bird.* New York, Houghton Mifflin Co.

When my family got to the USA in 1951, we arrived as DPs[3], country-less refugees, who had lost our parents and grandparents, our families and our homes, our churches, and our names. Everything had been left behind, buried in the great European graveyard that stretched from the English Channel to the Urals and from the Baltic Sea to the Mediterranean. Coming to start a new life in America, we could not have imagined what we would find and what we would become.

After settling in the Humboldt Park area of Chicago, an area where many Poles, DPs, refugees, survivors, and immigrants settled, we soon found out who we were. We weren't Poles and we definitely weren't Polish Americans. I never heard those words. What I did hear in the streets and in the schools and in the stores was that we were DPs and that stood not for 'Displaced Persons' but for 'Dirty Polacks'. We were the people who nobody wanted to rent a room to or hire or help. We were the 'wretched refuse' of somebody else's shore, dumped now on the shore of Lake Michigan, and most people we met in America wished we'd go back to where we came from, and that we'd take the rest of the 'Dirty Polacks' with us.

My father fought against this attitude with all his strength. He was a man who believed in Polish honor and he struggled to tell people what had happened to us and other DPs. In the stores and the taverns along Chicago's Division Street he would talk with storeowners, mechanics, plumbers, and anybody who would listen about the War and what had happened to the Poles. He would talk about the way the Nazis took millions of Poles to the concentration and slave labor camps in Germany, and he would talk about the hunger and brutality he experienced and saw. He would talk about the great Polish generals of the Second World War, Sikorski and Anders, and how the Polish soldiers, fighting alongside the Allies, took revenge on Hitler and the Germans for what they did to Poland and Warsaw, and how they had leveled both like they were wooden outhouses.

He also carried around a picture of a gallows in Germany where five or six Poles were hanging. He would show it to whomever he could, and he would start talking about what happened to these men and the others in the concentration and slave labor camps he had been in. The photograph finally got so ragged from being passed around that there was nothing left of it but tatters. After my father died, I looked for that photo in the shoebox of old pictures my mom kept under the TV set. I couldn't find it. He must have been carrying the

3 Displaced Person, DP: the term was first widely used after World War II in reference to Eastern Europeans such as Army personnel, former concentration camp inmates and slave laborers who found themselves outside their homeland.

tatters around in his old age. But losing that old gallows picture didn't matter to him, because he could also talk about the scar on his head, and he could point to his dead eye, the one that never closed. He would tell strangers about how he was clubbed by a Nazi guard for refusing to eat soup that was so inedible that even a starving man, which he was, would have to think twice before spooning that stuff into his mouth.

And, sometimes, my father would sing the songs that came out of the War, especially the one about the red poppies that covered the battlefield of Monte Cassino where so many Polish soldiers died, fighting up that mountain in the middle of the boot of Italy. I can still hear his voice getting deeper and quieter as he sang about those poppies and how the blood of the Poles can still be seen in those red flowers.

My father wasn't the only Pole who struggled to make people aware of what happened to Poland and its people during the War. There were other men and women I also heard telling their neighbors and friends they made here in America about what had happened in the War and why they had come to America as DPs, not as 'Dumb Polacks' but as Displaced Persons. Doing this was valiant and important but, sometimes, I think that it wasn't enough. When I go to the libraries and look for books about the experiences of the DPs, I find only one or two. When I talk to people about what happened to my parents and their generation of Poles, I find that people don't have any idea who the Displaced Poles were and what had happened to them in the War. This is why Bogusia Wojciechowska's book is so important. It carries on the work of that first generation of Poles. Her work helps people understand who those displaced Poles were and what their lives were like during and after the War. It does something else; when we arrived in the United States as DPs, we felt displaced, isolated, and alienated from our homes and families because, to a great extent, we never really understood what had happened to us. We had so many questions that we couldn't answer. Dr. Bogusia Wojciechowska's book helps us to answer so many of these questions, not only by giving a historic context for our experiences but, also, by giving the voices that shared this experience, the opportunity to be heard in ways that they have not been heard before.

John Guzłowski
USA, 2008

ACKNOWLEDGMENTS

Ryszard Kaczorowski *(Foreword)* was born in 1919, in Białystok, Poland. When Eastern Poland was occupied by the USSR, he became a member of the Scouts and liaison officer between this organization and the Polish Resistance. In 1940 he was arrested by the NKVD[4] and sentenced to death, a verdict which was commuted to ten years of detention in the Gulag of Kolyma.

With the German invasion of the USSR, Kaczorowski, like other imprisoned and deported Poles, was pardoned under the 'Amnesty'.[5] He enlisted in General Władysław Anders' Army which was forming on Soviet soil. He eventually traveled to Britain with the Polish troops and settled in London, where he continues to reside. He was President of the Republic of Poland, the sixth President-in-Exile, 1989-90. He was succeeded, in Poland, by Lech Wałęsa to whom he passed the insignia of state on December 22, 1990.

Zosia Hartman Biegus, with *www.northwickparkpolishdpcamp.co.uk* has established a website that documents the histories of Polish camps in England. Born in 1943 in Germany where her parents had been slave laborers, she arrived in England with her family in 1948 as a Displaced Person (DP).

Bożenna Urbanowicz Gilbride *(Preface)* was born in Leonówka, Poland, in 1933. She and her family were taken as slave laborers to Germany. She is recognized by the New York State Board of Education as an outstanding lay teacher on the Holocaust.

Hania Kaczanowska's poetry has enriched this book. Her father was taken to a Siberian prison camp, and her mother was in Germany as a slave laborer. After the War, neither of her parents felt they could return to Poland.

Martin Stepek's *(Afterword)* father, Jan Stepek, was 17 when his family was deported to the Soviet Union. By the end of the War Martin's father was an orphan; his home, the family farm, was now part of the Soviet Union, and the newly re-bordered Poland was under Soviet occupation, so he stayed in Britain.

---

4   NKVD (Russian - Norodny Komissaryat Vnutrennikh Del): the leading secret police organization of the Soviet Union, responsible for political repression during the Stalinist era. The NKVD was the precursor of the KGB.

5   With the German invasion of the Soviet Union in June 1941, Poles who had been deported were granted an 'Amnesty' in August 1941, and were free to join the new Polish Army that was forming in the south under General Władysław Anders.

Elżunia Gradosielska Olssen is a co-founding member of the Kresy-Siberia Group which has given much encouragement and assistance to this project. Elżunia's mother was deported to Siberia, and her father was a POW in Komi, Russia. Elżunia's parents traveled to England with the Polish Army in 1946.

Marek Janota Bzowski, my husband, gave valuable assistance in the proofing of this work.

The Polonia Aid Foundation Trust, London, England, helped fund the research for this book.

ABOUT THE AUTHOR

Bogusia Wojciechowska is the daughter of two Poles who met in England in 1948. Her father, who had been in the Polish Army, did not want to go back to his home, near Lwów, as it was no longer a part of Poland. Some of his family had been deported to Siberia and had perished there. His own father, forcibly moved from the land inhabited by the family for generations, was living in Poland in poverty. Bogusia's mother, meanwhile, had lived in Warszawa until the end of the Uprising in 1944. Like so many of her family, she was taken to a concentration camp in Germany and, then, as slave labor to Austria. Some members of her family perished in concentration camps in Germany. Having arrived in Britain with nothing, her father, nevertheless, completed a Bachelor's degree at Edinburgh University, while her mother completed her high school education by the age of 22. Their love of Poland and their Catholic religion sustained them through the War and in the post-War era.

Born in Oxford, Bogusia and her parents eventually moved from nearby Fairford Polish Hostel to London where she grew up. Their world was a microcosm of the lost Homeland in which friends were addressed by former rank and title, such as 'Judge' or 'General.' Parents such as these constantly reminded their children that they were not English but Polish, that the Allies had betrayed Poland, and that it was their role to continue to fight for Poland's freedom. This was quite a burden for a child or teenager who simply wanted to enjoy their country of residence. Every Saturday, while English friends spent mornings in bed, Bogusia, like so many others, had to get up early and go to Polish School. Some of her peers rebelled against these values and abandoned their Polish heritage; some embraced their parents' teachings; some sought to find their own comfort level.

Left with the question as to where she actually belonged, Bogusia began to see that her own generation had a unique 'Anglo-Polish' nationality. She pursued an interest in social history at university, and completed a doctorate in the study of migration patterns and migrant communities during the English Industrial Revolution.

However, there remained a nagging sense of incompleteness and this body of work is the realization of her calling. It is a labor of love fueled by Bogusia's determination to give recognition to the suffering of her parents' generation, a generation that had been marginalized in history for the sake of political expediency and because others have clamored for recognition with a louder voice. The website, *www.PolishDiaspora.net,* was created in 2006 by Dr. Wojciechowska as a forum designed to enable those remaining to record their own voices and to write their own history. The immediate and international deluge of interest and commentary in the project convinced her of her goal; it was that the surviving witnesses to unspeakable hardship and social destruction during the middle years of the twentieth century were owed a more tangible and fitting record of their resilience in the face of a tragedy. This book is both tribute and testament to that unheard generation.

INTRODUCTION

Waiting to be Heard is the voice of the persecuted, the brave, the hopeful, the betrayed and the determined. It is a testament to the strength of the human spirit and to a generation that did not see itself as 'victims,' but as 'survivors.' To those who trusted me and shared their most personal and often very painful experiences with me, I have to say that listening to you was a privilege and a very humbling experience. Sometimes you spoke through tears, sometimes through laughter, yet there was a common thread in your voices; it was a love of your homeland which enabled you to survive the horrors of the War and difficulties of the post-War years.

Studies of the War and post-War years have traditionally focused on political and military history. In recent years there has been a greater interest in the social consequences of the War. Nevertheless, discussions relating to the displacement of the Polish-born usually focus on the Holocaust interpreted as a Jewish-only phenomenon. Yet, in the years 1939-45, Poland lost 6,029,000, or 22%, of its total population, including approximately three million of its Christian residents.[6]

In addition, there were those who survived the War yet, at its conclusion, were scattered all over the world; by the end of 1945, 249,000 members of the Polish Armed Forces were under British command, with 41,400 dependants in the United Kingdom, Italy, East and South Africa, New Zealand, India, Palestine, Mexico and Western Germany; *"123,000 of the Polish Armed Forces refused to return to Poland."*[7] In September 1946, 330,731 Poles remained in the US, French and British Zones in Germany; by late 1948, *"171,759 had not returned to Poland."*[8]

The creation of this Diaspora is, therefore, a significant displacement of population in modern times but, also, one that has received very little attention. While this project is a contribution towards the burgeoning historiography on the subject, it is primarily a vehicle to give the Diaspora a voice, to record the experiences of the Prisoners of War, (POWs), members of the Polish Armed Forces, deportees, Displaced Persons, slave laborers, and concentration camp

---

6   Lukas, R. ed. (2005). *Forgotten Holocaust. The Poles under German Occupation 1939-44.* New York, Hippocrene Books, pp. 38-39.

7   Ostrowski, M. (n.d.). Retrieved May 2006, from *To Return To Poland Or Not To Return - The Dilemma Facing The Polish Armed Forces At The End Of The Second World War.* Unpublished PhD, www.angelfire.com/ok2/polisharmy/chapter1.html, pp. 1-2 & 7, and abstract, p. 1.

8   Ostrowski, ibid., Chapter 8, pp. 8-9. Between 1945 and 1948 it is estimated that over 2 million Poles returned to Poland from various European countries.

inmates.[9] Needless to say, with the numbers in this group decreasing with every passing year, there is an urgency to record their stories.

The refugees themselves have long sought a voice for their experiences, with an increasing number of self-published biographies becoming available. In the words of Stella Synowiec-Tobis, writing about her family's deportation to Russia: *"The story of almost two million Polish people was not written about in newspapers, or in history books, not even in Poland. That is why my friends and acquaintances are surprised by what I have been through in my life."* [10]

Indeed, I was surprised by how many people thanked me for giving them the opportunity to share their experiences. While some had talked and written about their experiences before, the majority had not discussed their experiences with anyone outside their immediate social circle. Time and again the 'second generation,' (those born to refugees, but outside Poland), mentioned that their parents were reluctant to discuss the War with them. Recounting their experiences to a stranger such as me was, perhaps, easier than sharing painful memories with their children. And the memories are still painful, as exemplified by one participant who said, *"God, I ask you; allow me to forget those days and weeks when I lay on piles of corpses in the hope of finding a tiny bit of warmth; allow me to forget the licking of ice from the walls of the cattle wagons; allow me to lose my memory of those years, my God!"*

This study does not claim to present a scientifically valid sample of émigrés. The participants were chosen or volunteered at random, usually as a result of referrals. However, the hope was that there would be a wide representation in terms of family background, sex, age, and place of residence; this turned out to be the case.

When reading this book, I hope the émigrés will be assured that their history will be known and understood. When they read of their children, the 'second generation', I hope they will see that these children have embraced 'Polishness' in their own, unique way, and that they continue to promote Poland's cause.

Bogusia Wojciechowska, USA, 2009

---

9   There were additional displacements of the Polish population as residents of the former eastern Poland, now taken over by the Soviet Union, were evicted from the their land and forced to move west, to the 'Regained Territories'. Approximately five million Poles settled in these Territories by 1950. However, Poland lost 20% of its pre-War land as a result of the new borders. Those who found themselves on the non-Polish side of the border were usually destined to become members of a new Diaspora.

10   Synowiec-Tobis, S. (2002). *The Fulfillment of Visionary Return.* Chicago: ART-POL Printing, Preface.

PARTICIPANTS

(in alphabetical order)

Adam Szymel - Aleksandra Sobkiewicz Łaskiewicz - Alicja Świątek Christofides - Andrzej Sławinski - Andrzej Zdanowicz - Aniela Bechta-Crook - Anita Paschwa-Kozicka - Anonymous (1) - Anonymous (2) - Barbara Kocuba Bik - Barbara Gryszel Masgula - Bolesław Biega - Bożenna Urbanowicz Gilbride - Celina Kabala Wojciechowska - Charles Lesczuk - Danuta Banaszek Szlachetko - Danuta Wojcik - Danuta Mączka Gradosielska - Danuta Suchecka Szydło - Emilia Kot Chojnacka - Franciszek Herzog - George Hayward (Jerzy Maciej Siennicki) - Halina Bartold Poślinska - Hania Kaczanowska - Hanka Piotrowska Orłowska - Helena Jopek (Jopeck) Zasada - Henryk Franczak - Henryk Jopek (Jopeck) - Jadwiga Krzysztoporska Piasecka - Janie Suszyńska Micchelli - Jerzy Kozłowski - Jerzy Zubrzycki - John Guzłowski – Józef Wardzala - Józef Kałwa - Józef Pankiewicz - Józef Poślinski - Józef Szkudłapski – Julek Płowy - Julian Ciupak - Jurek Biegus - Kazimiera Miara Janota Bzowska – Kazimierz Bączyński - Kazimierz Rasiej - Kazimierz Szydło - Krysia Bargiel - Lech Hałko - Lilka Trzcinska Croydon - Mari Czeczerska Sutton - Maria Pawulska Rasiej - Maria Zak Szklarz - Martin Stepek - Mieczysław Juny - Peter Tatrzyński Fleming - Rita Miller - Rita Wolf Robinson - Roma Michniewicz King - Romuald Lipiński - Stanisław Milewski - Stanisław Sagan - Stanisław Szuttenbach - Stanisława Robaszewska Woźniak - Stefa Kowalczyk Bączkowska - Stefan Mączka - Stella (Stanisława) Synowiec-Tobis - Tadeusz Król - Tadeusz Mączka - Teresa Stolarczyk Marshall – Wacław Jędrzejczak - Walter Orłowski - Wanda Larkowski - Witold Mazur - Wojsław Milan-Kamski - Zbigniew Haszlakiewicz - Zdzisława Bilewicz Korniłowicz - Zosia Hartman Biegus - Zygmunt Kopel

Figure 2. The hands of Hania Kaczanowska's father, Kazimierz Kaczanowski, and her son, Curtis, Canada, 2004

"Dziadek,[11] did you have a gun?"
The old man sat in his rocker with his grandson at his feet
As he told stories from his youth, many left incomplete.
The young boy played with the medals, tokens from the war
And with childhood innocence, wanted to hear more.
"Dziadek, were you a soldier? Dziadek, did you have a gun?"
Dziadek, Dziadek, did you ever have to kill anyone?"
The old man nodded and let his thoughts drift back
To a time when his country was heavily under attack.
Instead of enjoying autumn leaves and warm September nights
He was handed a gun and volunteered to fight.
Gone were his dreams of a future, love and romance.
Every day now could be the last dance.
He stared into the face of death and searched deep within his soul
And asked God for answers of why this senseless toll?
He had quickly become a man inside a boy
And his youth was robbed of love and joy.
He could still hear the roar of cannons that filled the air
As naked evil spirits brought misery and despair
Broken dreams and shattered lives kaleidoscope the earthly floor
As spirits soared amidst the smoke leaving behind the bloody war

---

11   *Dziadek* (Polish): Grandfather.

He tried not to relive the sadness and the pain
But to forget all this would mean his comrades died in vain.
He felt a hand on his shoulder and heard a whisper of a long-lost friend,
"I would tell your story, if your grandson to me you would lend."
Looking down into the eyes of his grandson it all became very clear
As he again had to become a proud soldier and wiped away a tear
His gnarled old hand brushed back the hair of the tiny little face
It was his duty to teach this boy and to hide the truth would be a disgrace
"Yes, my child, your dziadek was a soldier and, yes, I had a gun
But my war was not a game and I never shot for fun.
When you are older you will understand the job I had to do
And now I understand what I gave up, I did for you.
I had dreams of a family, a home, remember the stories we shared
But my life was taken away from me and yours was spared."

"Dziadek, Dziadek, did you have a gun?
Dziadek, Dziadek, did you have to kill anyone?"

© Hania Kaczanowska, 2004

Figure 3. Kazimierz Kaczanowski, Italy, 1944
Figure 4. Maria Dobrzańska Kaczanowska, Canada, 1949

Figure 5. **Map of Poland, 1939, showing the locations of participants in this study**

INVASION

CHAPTER 1

The Western Front

Figure 6. *"Whether people, gasoline, bombs, or bread, we bring Poland death."* **Painted on a German Ju-52 transport plane fuselage during the 1939 invasion of Poland**[12]

> *"I have issued the command and I'll have anybody who utters but one word of criticism executed by firing squad - that our war aim does not consist in reaching certain lines, but in the physical destruction of the enemy. Accordingly, I have placed my death-head formations in readiness - for the present, only in the East - with orders to send to death mercilessly and without compassion, men, women, and children of Polish derivation and language. Only thus shall we gain the living space that we need."*
>
> **Adolf Hitler**[13]

---

12   http://en.wikipedia.org/wiki/Image:Ger_Ju52_Sept.jpg

13   Allegedly said by Adolf Hitler, August 22, 1939, according to reports received by the Associated Press Bureau Chief in Berlin, Louis Lachner. Inscription in the United States Holocaust Memorial Museum in Washington, DC, USA.

Nazis on the Western Front

Contextual Timeline

- By 1939 Germany had identified, for extermination, 'undesirable' or 'racially inferior' groups: Poles, Serbs, gypsies, Communists, Jews, Catholic clergy, Jehovah's Witnesses, Freemasons, trade unionists, the handicapped, homosexuals, and political dissidents.

- Hitler's pretext for expansion eastward was the 'need' for more *Lebensraum*, or living space, for the German nation.

- The *Generalplan Ost* concluded that 31 million people would have to be deported in the course of 25 years. However, in 1942, Dr. Erich Wetzel, the director of the Central Advisory Office on Questions of Racial Policy at the National Socialist Party, revised this figure and arrived at a total of 51 million.

- Prior to the outbreak of WWII, 2,000 Poles living in Germany were exterminated in concentration camps.

- The *Zentralstelle*, or Central Office, prepared a special list of 61,000 Polish leaders called *Sonderfahndungsbuch Polen*, or *Special Prosecution Book Poland*, prior to the German attack on Poland on September 1, 1939.

- On March 31, 1939, the British Government assured Poland that it would provide support if Polish independence was threatened.

- On August 23, 1939, the secret German-Soviet agreement concerning the partition of Poland, the Molotov-Ribbentrop Pact, was signed. Ironically, Hitler had devoted much of his book, *Mein Kampf*, to his belief in the menace of Communism. Nazism was against everything that Communism stood for.

- On September 1, 1939, Germany invaded Poland.

- In the first days of September 1939, 20,000 randomly captured non-Jewish Poles were killed in Warszawa. The bodies, mostly of women and children, were heaped in the square outside the Cathedral Church in central Warszawa. It is estimated that 50,000 civilians were killed during the siege of Warszawa.

- On September 3, 1939, Britain and France declared war on Germany.

- The Germans began building extermination camps, concentration camps, and slave labor camps. The infamous Oświęcim (Auschwitz) Camp was established in late 1939 specifically for Poles; of the first 611 people who died in Oświęcim, 591 were Poles and 20 were Jews.

- Within the first few months of the War, all the Poles on the *Zentralstelle* list were killed outright or sent to concentration camps to die. They included the nobility, priests, university professors, teachers, doctors, lawyers, other community leaders, and even a prominent sportsman who had won the gold medal in his category at the Berlin Olympics in 1936.

Wacław J. Jędrzejczak
b. 1927, Toruń
1942-50, Germany
1950-present, Australia

It was that fateful summer when peace in Europe and our family's peace were about to be shattered. Towards the end of August 1939 it was certain that war was going to break out at any moment and final preparations for it were being made. In my home town of Toruń, in the northwest of pre-War Poland, mobilization of men for the army was in full swing. My father,[14] Franciszek, a tall, handsome, always immaculately dressed senior Sergeant in the quartermaster's office of the Toruń Artillery Officers' School, was one of the mobilization officers in the Mokre suburb. I took lunches to him and witnessed the hustle and bustle of men being registered, issued with uniforms and organized into units. The orderly process of enlisting the men filled me with confidence and all the mobilized men were also of good spirits and certain that they would defeat the Germans and save Poland; *"We will beat them with just our army caps and drive them out!"*

At night, windows had to be blacked out as a precaution against German air raids. It was still the school summer holidays. We had returned from the village of Czerniewice where we spent part of the summer, but none of my school friends had yet returned home. I was bored without their company and was looking forward to being with them again in September. As it happened I never

---

14 Throughout this book, the use of "mother, mom, mommy, father, dad, daddy", reflects the speakers' use of "*matka, mama, mamusia; ojciec, tato, tatuś.*" (Polish).

saw them again because we left Toruń before they returned.

Although the official evacuation of armed forces' families was to take place in the near future, my mother, Maria, decided not to wait for that. So, at the end of August, my mother, my brother Czesiek (who was two years my junior), and I went to Krzykosy, in the country, to my paternal grandfather, Marcin. We thought that the German Air Force was probably going to bomb the Polish cities and that it would be safer for us in the country. All our belongings, except the furniture, were packed in wooden chests and sent separately by rail to my grandfather's house. Nobody else appeared to be leaving Toruń at this time.

Figure 7. Maria, Czesław, Wacław and Franciszek Jędrzejczak, Toruń, Poland, c1939

On that summer afternoon, through the window of the train carriage, I looked out at the city of Toruń, where I had been born and where I had lived with my family at ul.[15] Jagiellońska nr. 9,[16] in the first floor flat, No. 3, its balcony with flower boxes full of geraniums in summer, and a hung hare in the frosts of winter. I wondered, *"Dear old Toruń, will I ever see you again?"*

Normally, Father would have accompanied us, but he could not leave because of his service duties. He was to move out in a few days, along with the personnel of the Artillery Officers' School, and proceed to Włodzimierz in the east of pre-War Poland. This was our first train journey without Father and we missed him right at the start because he had always taken care of all the travel arrangements. Our train was filled with young men brimming with confidence and ready to fight the enemy.

It was dusk when we arrived at Kłodawa station. Uncle Ignacy, a tall, thin man, was waiting there with horse and wagon to take us to the Krzykosy Estate, another 5 kilometers away. We were there soon and, after a welcome from my

---

15   *ul., ulica* (Polish): street or road.

16   *nr., numer* (Polish): house number.

grandfather and Aunt Stanisława, we sat down to the evening meal at a table lit by the mellow light of a kerosene lamp. We talked, mostly about the imminent war, and went to bed with the knowledge that next day we might wake to its sounds.

In the morning, Mother and I went to the railway station to see whether our luggage had arrived. To our great disappointment it hadn't arrived that day, nor would it arrive the next, or ever. We went to the station several times; we tried to telephone Toruń to find out whether our luggage had left there, but it wasn't possible to get a connection as all lines were for the exclusive use of the military. The loss of all our possessions was a bitter blow, as we were left with practically nothing. All we had was what we were wearing: light summer clothing, light shoes, and a small case with things needed for a short journey. Although there were three large chests at my grandfather's house which we had sent there a month earlier, they contained things such as our fine china, glass, and father's better uniforms, but no clothing for us.

The first bombs fell on September 1, 1939, on the Barłogi railway station 7 kilometers from us. My brother and I were at my aunt's farm in the village of Krzykosy nearby when we heard a series of explosions. Startled, we ran outside and saw a great, ominous, dark, grey cloud of smoke. In the following days, the bombardments came several times a day. We moved from the estate, where my grandfather was a supervisor, to our aunt's farm. It was further away from the main road, the target of the German bombs. One day the raid was particularly heavy. A dozen or so twin-engined bombers flew low over the area and bombed the road, the Krzykosy Estate, the people assembled there, and the horses being mobilized. A few of the planes flew directly above us at the village. With hearts pounding we sought cover alongside felled tree-trunks as machine-gun bullets whistled nearby and the earth shook from exploding bombs.

In spite of the heavy bombing, no one on the estate was killed. Many of the bombs missed the road and fell in the fields and meadows, killing cattle and horses which lay there with grotesquely distended abdomens and legs pointing in all directions. Two bombs fell near some houses on the estate, destroying fences, breaking roof tiles and windows, and damaging walls. At the neighboring village, Borysławice, the blacksmith's house next to the main road was hit and burned to the ground.

Our troops were passing through the village, stopping at times for a rest. Continuous lines of refugees moved along the main road with wagons and hand-carts loaded with their possessions. They were going in the direction of Warszawa, fleeing from the Germans in the hope that they would be safe in the capital, under the protection of our Army. They also came to us looking for food. Mother made soup in a huge pot and offered it to them.

That the defeat of our forces was a fact we found out soon enough when we saw the Germans with our own eyes.[17] Along the main road, they moved in motor vehicles, in their grey uniforms. They were foreigners; even their vehicle exhaust smelled differently. The proud, greedy, confident *Herrenvolk*;[18] we could feel their might. It distressed us terribly that they had overcome our courageous, smaller forces with their massive material advantage and that they were driving on our roads where, not so long ago our Polish uniforms had held sway. Polish troops were also passing through, here and there in small groups on horseback and on foot in the confusion, trying to avoid capture and to return home. We searched for Father among them and asked a passing artillery group about him. No, they did not know him. We were very worried. Was he still alive?

Stefa Kowalczyk Bączkowska
b. 1924, Baby
1942-45, Germany
1945-46, Italy
1946-present, England

We lived at Baby railway station, where my father was the station master. It was September 1, and the next day it was my father's Saint's Day (he was called Stefan), and mine. At 7 AM we heard on the radio that the Germans had crossed the Polish border and had started attacking and bombing Wieluń. We went onto the platform where there were two policemen, some railway workers, my father, and some other people. Suddenly a plane flew over the station and started shooting at us. We hid in the waiting room.

A feast had been prepared at home for our Saint's Day. There was a lot of food as we were a large family; there were seven children, aged 8 to 15 (I was the eldest). On September 2, we took things out of the rooms, such as bedding and clothing, and locked them in the cellar, to ensure that they did not get stolen (which they did). We wrapped the food in the tablecloth and got on a train to leave Baby and get to safety.

We only got as far as Koluszki, 25 kilometers away, as the railway tracks had already been bombed. We fled the train into the nearby forest as bombs were

---

17   German troops arrived in this area about September 6; they were the 10th, 17th, and 24th Infantry Divisions.

18   *Herrenvolk* (German): in Nazi ideology, the ideal and pure race.

falling and so our wanderings began. In all the confusion we were separated from my father. By then, German soldiers were everywhere so I went up to a one and asked, *"Where is my daddy?"* Of course, he didn't know what I was talking about.

My memory has gone blank as to what happened next. There are many episodes from the War that have been wiped from my memory. What I do remember is that we found ourselves in a small, deserted village, and that there was a small house where we found potatoes and cooking pots. We boiled and ate the potatoes. I next remember that when we left the house the Germans started talking to us and someone translated that they were telling us to go home. On the way back to Baby we went through Tomaszów Mazowiecki, where I saw Hitler and his entourage. We were going home by horse and cart, all his soldiers were riding their motorbikes and were saluting *"Hiel Hitler"* and we were pushed into a ditch. We were hurt, but not badly.[19]

We got back to our home in Baby and found that the house had been totally ransacked; the rooms had been stripped bare. Even the locks to the cellar had been broken and everything had been stolen. I have another gap in my memory here, but I remember that we stayed in the house and somehow managed to live. My father continued working at the station, but the Germans were bringing in their own people and, eventually, my father was thrown out and replaced by a German.

We stayed in Baby until 1942 and survived by selling vegetables. I used to go to Warszawa with a heavy sack of potatoes to sell. On one of these trips during the journey home, the Germans stopped the train at Radziwiłów and a German soldier started shouting at me, *"Raus, raus!"*[20] There were lots of German soldiers in the station; they got us off the train and started segregating us into groups. We had to show our German-issued identity cards. Since I was 18 years old, I was taken as a slave laborer to Germany.

---

19   Hitler visited the 19th Infantry in this area during the first week of the War.

20   *Raus* (German): abbreviation for *'Heraus'*, meaning 'out'.

Stanisław Sagan
b. 1926, Anin
1945-46, Germany
1946-56, England
1956-present, Canada

Figure 8. Stanisław Sagan, Anin, Poland, 1939

My family, which consisted of four children and my parents, lived in the south-eastern suburb of Warszawa called Anin. This was only 20 kilometers away from Warszawa's center, so most of our neighbors commuted to the city daily. At the end of August 1939, I was anticipating starting a new school year on September 4.

On the morning of September 1, my brother, Zbyszek, and I walked into our front garden. We had an extensive property with numerous, tall, pine trees, and bushes. The garden was in its natural, wild state and a great place for us to play. This was the last day of our school holidays and we wanted to have as much fun as possible. The weather was beautiful with not a single cloud in the sky. Suddenly we heard the drone of aircraft overhead. We looked up and saw two or three planes flying at a very high altitude, but not in any formation; they seemed to be circling around each other with a rising or diminishing roar, as if they were engaged in a dogfight.

In the last few weeks the threat of war had become very real and, even as a young boy, I was aware of this. We read the newspapers and knew of the Molotov-Ribbentrop Pact[21] and of British and French promises of help to Poland in case of German attack. In Warszawa's public parks and squares, trenches had

---

21   Molotov-Ribbentrop Pact: The Treaty of Non-Aggression between Germany and the Union of Soviet Socialist Republics signed in Moscow on August 24, 1939. It remained in place until Germany attacked the Soviet Union on June 22, 1941.

been dug by volunteers to provide shelter in case of air raids. We had also dug a zigzag-shaped trench in our front garden[22] and prepared one room in our house as a shelter from possible gas attack by insulating the windows and doors. Gas warfare had occurred during the First World War, and the memories of this were vivid in many people's minds. I remember visiting a display organized by the Air Raid Defense League which showed gas masks, what poisonous gases could do, and how you could protect yourself against them. We protected the window panes in the house from falling out by pasting paper to the glass in a crisscross pattern.

The only radio in our villa was owned by our landlords who, on September 1, were at work in Warszawa. Neither we nor the other two families occupying the apartments in our villa had any access to the radio and, therefore, had no immediate knowledge of the German invasion. Quite frankly, watching the airplanes high in the sky, my brother and I were sure that we were seeing some training exercises as we had seen in previous weeks. I do not remember when we finally learned that war had started but, as soon as we knew, our mother immediately told us to hide in the insulated room. We were in the room for an hour or so and, when we found that nothing had happened outside, we emerged cautiously. There was no bombing in our area that day or during the next few days.

Saturday's newspapers spoke of the German attack on Poland. On the front page there was a declaration from the President of Poland, Professor Ignacy Mościcki,[23] confirming that the eternal enemy of Poland had attacked our country without any formal declaration of hostilities. And then came the euphoric Sunday. Around 11 AM, we heard that Great Britain had declared war on Germany, as did France later on that day. We heard, on the landlord's radio, a transmission from the streets outside the British and French embassies in Warszawa where thousands of Poles were demonstrating their appreciation of these declarations by singing the British and French national anthems. My brother and I were given the task of sitting by the radio and reporting any new developments to the grown-ups in the house.

The Polish press, and Polish radio too, were optimistic before the outbreak of hostilities; they supported the official government version of Polish readiness and some, less-informed friends of mine, even welcomed a German attack because, *"we will show those bastards where to get off..."* (I do not remember if I shared that opinion but, most probably, I did.) My age group was extremely patriotic and

---

22   The zigzag shape was to prevent bomb splinters from penetrating all sections of the shelter and, also, to obstruct the movement of tanks.

23   Ignacy Mościcki, (1867-1946), President of Poland, 1926-39.

believed in our Commander-in-Chief Marshal Śmigły-Rydz.[24]

On September 8, we heard an army colonel on the radio advising Warszawa's population to leave the city and go east. In retrospect this was unfortunate advice because this caused clogging of the roads leading from Warszawa and provided an easy target for German planes which started to shoot at the fleeing population. Even though the colonel had called mainly on men of military age to leave, whole families with children and pets took to the roads.

My mother was no exception. She decided that all of us would flee east as well. We heard that trains were still running and walked with some hand luggage to the nearby railway station in Wawer. We were not the only ones; hundreds of people were already at the station waiting for any train going east. While we were waiting, the *Luftwaffe*[25] flew over us and started dropping bombs and opened up with machine-gun fire. My family hid in a small space under the overhang of the concrete platform. Thankfully, the bombs missed the station by a considerable margin.

Finally, a train arrived; it consisted of open platforms on which were carried steel pipes. We climbed onto such a platform and sat on the pipes. Some of the other Polish travelers were Polish soldiers whose outfits had dispersed and who were going east where they were supposed to regroup and return to battle. We sat on this platform for hours until it got dark and then the train started to move east.

I dozed during the journey and remember waking up every time the train stopped, which it did many times during the night. By morning we had traveled less than 40 kilometers from Wawer. With daybreak there was the danger of German bombing (during this time the *Luftwaffe* was not active after dark). We all needed to wash but even though there were some houses in the area, no one wanted to leave the train lest it left during their absence.

The journey continued very slowly. Finally, my mother had had enough. When we reached a village called Karczew we got off the train and went to a small house where we bought soup. I remember seeing Polish foot-soldiers rushing through Karczew in an eastward direction. When asked what was happening at the Front they refused to give us any information, saying that we could not imagine the force of the German onslaught on the western side of the River Wisła.

We were stuck, but my mother was an energetic woman and soon made the acquaintance of the wife of a high executive in a privately-owned narrow

---

24   Edward Śmigły-Rydz, (1886-1941), Commander-in-Chief Marshal of Poland, 1936-39.

25   *Luftwaffe* (German): German Air Force.

gauge railway company. Her husband had decided to abandon the seemingly hopeless trek eastwards and they were returning to Warszawa. They had a private railway car and invited my mother and us to join them if we wanted to return to Anin. This was exactly what my mother wanted. After dusk the little train headed west, and, in the early hours of the next day, we threw ourselves into our beds at home.

In the next few days the news from the Front was bad. It goes without saying that the start of the new school year was postponed. In a small community like Anin, store supplies were dwindling and new ones were not arriving. It was dangerous to travel in search of food during the day, as the *Luftwaffe* was everywhere. Anin was bombed but only one four-story residential building burned down, not far from where we lived. During such raids (the air raid alarms were no longer operational), all of the inhabitants of our villa would go down to the cellar and wait until we no longer heard aircraft overhead. Somehow, the shelter we had dug in the front garden was abandoned. I was afraid when I realized that the bombs could fall on the house we lived in.

The first time German soldiers appeared in our village was the day we heard about the Soviet Union's attack on Poland; it must, therefore, have been September 17. Three or four frontline soldiers with powerful flashlights came down the steps into our cellar and noisily demanded to be conducted through the house in search of hidden Polish soldiers and Jews.

My mother was restless. She thought that we should move to Warszawa where life might be easier. My sister, who worked in the city, found us a one-bedroom apartment. We were lucky as, with the heavy bombardment of Warszawa prior to its surrender on September 27, apartments were hard to find. Five of us lived in this one-room apartment, with a niche for a kitchenette and a bathroom. It was always dark in our room as the apartment had only a tiny glass window. The large window opening was boarded up with plywood; indeed, there was not enough glass in Warszawa to glaze all the damaged windows. We were, however, compensated by having central heating which, with the days getting colder, was very important. We also had an electric stove and power. Later on, the use of power by Poles would be severely curtailed and janitors had to disconnect power under threat of the death penalty.

I was 13 years old. How different Warszawa looked. Bricks, stones, glass, and furniture were piled almost two stories high. Some apartment buildings looked like dolls' houses: you could see every room in the interior on every floor including the bathroom fixtures, but the front wall was missing. Other buildings were burned to the ground. Every green space along the streets was occupied with the graves of Polish soldiers and civilians. The soldiers' graves had helmets placed on top of rough wooden crosses. Some had pieces of cardboard attached to the crosses with handwritten names. There were many horse carcasses in the streets, with the best pieces of meat removed. Wounded Polish soldiers stood in the streets begging. German patrols were everywhere but, at this time, had not yet begun stopping civilians.[26]

We had a sad Christmas that year, but we did manage to get a small Christmas tree which we decorated with cheap tissue paper in red and white, the Polish national colors.

Aleksandra Sobkiewicz Łaskiewicz
b. 1929, Poznań
1944-45, Germany
1945-46, Italy
1946-present, England

Some weeks prior to the start of World War II my father, who was an officer in the Army, was called up and sent to defend Silesia in the event of a German attack. On September 1, a lot of noisy airplanes appeared in the sky and started bombing our home town of Poznań. We all went out of the house into the garden and our mother said that, because the sirens were blasting and the airplanes were dropping bombs, the war had started. This was soon confirmed on the radio. I had no idea what it implied. My fear was that our father would never come back and that our mother might get killed and we, five children aged seven to 11, would be left on our own.

Within the next few days, our mother made the decision to pack our bags and we set off east, out of Poznań, to escape the German Army which was rapidly approaching from the west. This turned out to be a badly thought-out plan. We arrived at the main railway station full of hope that we could get away from the front lines and the heavy bombing. Now and then, the train stopped and we had to quickly run away from it into the fields to avoid getting hit and killed by the bombs being dropped by the Germans. I think we were heading for Warszawa and further to the east. Eating was very hectic since the only source of food was what we acquired from the nearby villages where the train stopped.

I remember some frightening bombing; we were all lying low in a field

---

26   The capture of civilians from the streets were called *'łapanki,'* (Polish) that is, 'round-ups'.

among some potato crops and, totally disregarding my own safety, I ran across the field to be near my mother. I just wanted us to die together! A few days later, as we were marching to some village along a road, we bumped into German soldiers who told us that all the territories were captured. We presumed we had lost the War already, after more or less 3½ weeks.

We started the painful journey back home to Poznań; Mother pleaded with farmers to give us a ride in a horse-driven cart. She had to pay a lot of money for these short rides. It really was madness to have left Poznań so quickly since we seemed to have traveled nowhere and, I think, we were very near the front lines of action most of the time. On many occasions we were sheltering in the fields and witnessed artillery shots going through the air above our heads. There seemed to be the continuous bombing of railway lines.

Figure 9. The Sobkiewicz family and their housekeeper, Częstochowa, Poland, 1940[27]

When we finally arrived back home, we were happy to see it all in one piece but deserted. We eventually found our two servants hiding in the neighbor's cellar. We also learned that our father had come to see us and regretted that we had left home since, apparently, our mother had promised that she would not do that. For a long time afterwards we had no news of him. Eventually we learned that he was a POW in Oflag II E, in Germany.

When the Germans occupied Poznań they had everything organized. All the schools were re-opened and all the teachers were German, teaching us in

---

27 Extract from her unpublished account: Sobkiewicz Łaskiewicz, A. (n.d.) *My Wartime Experiences 1939-45 and Beyond*, submitted for this book by her sister, Barbara Sobkiewicz Paleolog, England. In photo *(from left to right, front row)*. Barbara, Halina, Aleksandra and Blanka Sobkiewicz, with their housekeeper, Gosposia, and mother.

German. Our mother was also engaged to teach as she spoke German perfectly. Most Polish people living in the western part of Poland could speak German.

This situation lasted for several weeks. In the meantime decisions were taken that certain kinds of people would have to be evacuated as they would never be 'Germanized.' It seemed that all school teachers, university professors, priests, and lawyers were on this list.

I will never forget the night we were thrown out of our home. We were all in bed upstairs asleep when, suddenly, one of our servants, Gosposia, came to wake us and said that the German Gestapo would be taking us away somewhere. We were given half an hour to collect a few personal belongings. I remember that I was so frightened that my knees were shaking so that I could hardly walk. We all cried quietly, thinking that we may get hit if we make too much noise. Gosposia spread out a sheet on the floor in the bedroom and kept throwing in whatever she could manage from the chest of drawers and the wardrobes. She tied it all up together and asked us to go downstairs.

It was a very cold December night, some time before Christmas. They bundled us into a coach, together with some other people who were all sitting in silence. We were driven to some huge huts with big halls filled with make-shift bunk beds. We tried to wash ourselves outside but the pump was frozen. We stayed there for a few days. All these hundreds of people were moved to another part of Poland.

The train journey was unbearable since the train was either unheated or overheated, and people were dying from cold or from heat exhaustion. It took three days to reach Częstochowa. We stayed in some barracks and, finally, were allocated two rooms. We all slept on the floor, except for mother and Gosposia who had a bed each. The winter was very hard and we had to collect soup each day, walking across the town to get it. Mom had managed to find places in school for us. We had to walk to school barefoot on the cobbled stone roads during the cold autumn days.

Our mother also managed to place two of us in a children's orphanage for the winter so that we would get better schooling and be looked after by nuns. Somehow, none of us wanted to go there; we preferred to stay with our mother although the living conditions in the orphanage were superior to those at our home. Later, Mother found some work in a labor exchange. She had to walk right across Częstochowa to her office, and back, and was always tired because of it. All the better jobs were taken by the Germans, *Volksdeutsche*,[28] or by Poles who had agreed to work and be loyal to the Germans.

---

28 *Volksdeutsche* (German): 'Ethnic Germans', a term used to describe ethnic Germans living outside the Reich.

Once or twice, I escaped being rounded up in the street by the German Gestapo. When a German soldier was killed by Poles, they would drive into town and round up as many people as they could and shoot them publicly in retaliation. I just ran into some big gateway, ran upstairs and waited until it was all over.

Celina Kabala Wojciechowska
b. 1923, Warszawa
1944-45, Germany, Austria
1945-46, Italy
1946-present, England

On September 1, 1939, President Starzyński[29] announced on the radio that what was taking place was not a practice drill but that, this time, the attack was for real and that German planes were bombing our country. People were digging trenches in the roads to prevent German tanks from crossing. We were getting ready for war which is why we had a public address system and alarm drills. We didn't discuss this much among ourselves, though I'm sure the adults did. I was not too interested in all this. We had no drills in my neighborhood, but there was a fort in the area, Sadyba, where they had various drills and stored armaments. I remember the Germans coming from the west; first the German planes were bombing us, then came the tanks and, then, machine-guns and the army. There was shooting everywhere. One time, after they had occupied our neighborhood, my little brother ran out into the courtyard making a noise; a German soldier shot at him because he was disturbing him listening to his radio. Thankfully, he missed.

The Germans went from house to house, clearing out inhabitants by throwing grenades into the buildings. We hid in the cellars. We had a native German in our cellar who came out with his hands up before they threw a grenade and said that there were no soldiers or armaments there, only women, children and old people. He saved our lives.

The Germans forced us to leave the cellar. The women were separated from the men; my father, a seasoned soldier from World War I, later told me that he advised people to collect hay on forced marches so that they would have

---

29   Stefan Starzyński (1893-1943) was President of Warszawa before and during its siege in 1939. It is believed that he may have died in the concentration camp at Dachau.

something to sleep on. The men were locked in a church for three days and the younger men wanted to escape. My father told them not to as they would be shot. Indeed, when they left the church it was at gunpoint.

As a teenager I did not think about the War but, of course, things were different during the Uprising. The Germans used to capture Ukrainians and I remember how the women used to cry; they cried just like I did after the Uprising. Some Ukrainians collaborated with the Germans, but some had been deported from the Ukraine to Warszawa.

I remember being with my father in Łazienki Park on the second day of the occupation of Warszawa. They had removed all the human corpses from the Park but dead horses were still on the ground. The horses had had their meat removed for food and their saddles had been taken for use by shoemakers. Eventually I stopped going to school as the Germans had closed all but the elementary and vocational schools. My father was working as a builder so he was very busy; everyone was asking him for help. Eventually, he was taken east to build barracks for the German Army. My father was told by someone to escape because the place was going to be razed to the ground. So he returned, and had to register with the German authorities every week. He used to go to the local train station to collect sacks of bread and distribute them. My younger sister and I went to work in a factory where they manufactured items for the German Army. So, I was allowed to move about and worked there until the Uprising.

Figure 10. Celina Kabala Wojciechowska, Warszawa, Poland, 1942

CHAPTER 2

The Eastern Front

"Do not resist...we come to liberate you!"

Figure 11. *"Rescue Europe from the fetters of fascist enslavement!"* Irakly Toidze, 1941[30]

---

30   http://images.google.com/imgres?imgurl=http://www.graphicwitness.org, Irakly Toidze, (1902-85).

"The Polish-German war has revealed the internal bankruptcy of the Polish State. In the course of ten days of war, Poland has lost all its industrial regions and cultural centers. Warszawa has ceased to function as the capital of Poland. The Polish Government has disintegrated and shows no sign of life. Left alone, and without any leadership, Poland has become the convenient field of action for all those who could harm the Soviet Union. This means that the Polish state and its Government have ceased to exist... For this reason, (the Soviet Union) has so far maintained neutrality, (but) can no longer remain neutral in the face of these facts...

Keeping in mind this situation, the Soviet Government ordered the command of the Red Army to cross the border and take under their care the lives and people of Eastern Ukraine and Eastern Belarus. At the same time the Soviet Government plans to do its utmost to free the Polish Nation from the miserable war into which they have been pushed by the mad leadership and to allow it to live peacefully."

Walery Potomkin[31]

---

31   Walery Potomkin, Deputy Peoples' Commissar for Foreign Affairs of the USSR, to the Polish Ambassador in Moscow, Wacław Grzybowski, in a letter on the night of September 16, 1945, the eve of the Soviet invasion of Poland. Szcześniak, A. (1989) *Historia. Polska i świat naszego wieku od roku 1939. (History of Poland and the World in our Century from 1939)*, an eighth grade text book. Warszawa, Wydawnictwa Szkolne i Pedagogiczne (School and Pedagogical Publications).

Stalinists on the Eastern Front

Contextual Timeline[32]

- Poles had been subjected to colonialist deportations into northern Russia and Siberia ever since the first partition of Poland in 1772 (two more partitions followed in 1793 and 1795). The major waves of deportations came after the Kościuszko Insurrection of 1794, the two national uprisings of 1830-31 and 1863-64, and during the Russo-Polish War of 1919-20. Deportation was a way of eliminating economically strong and intellectually vigorous segments of Polish society, a stratagem designed to weaken the Polish population of the Russian-occupied part of the old Polish-Lithuanian Commonwealth.

- During 1936-38, 40% of the victims of the Stalinist purges aimed at national minorities were Poles living in the Soviet Union; 143,810 Poles were charged with a variety of offences as part of Stalin's war on national minorities; 111,091 were executed.

- On September 17, 1939, the Soviet Union invaded Poland, supposedly as a 'liberator', in the face of German aggression (the Polish-Soviet Non-Aggression Pact had been in place since 1921).

Adam Szymel

b. 1929, Berezowice
February 1940, deported to the Soviet Union
1942-46, Iran, Iraq, Palestine
1946-54, England
1954-present, USA

My parents with their four children lived in Berezowice, on an estate given to my father in recognition of his military service in the defense of Poland against the Bolsheviks in 1920.[33] My father was a legionnaire who he had served under

---

32 Piotrowski, T. Ed. (2004) *The Polish Deportees of World War II.* Jefferson, NC. McFarland & Company 2004. See also Hoffman, J. (2001) *Stalin's War of Extermination 1941-1945.* Alabama Thesis and Dissertation Press.

33 Land was given as reward to servicemen, often referred to as 'military settlers'.

Marshal Piłsudski, the 'Grandfather'.[34] My father had been wounded several times, sometimes seriously, and had spilt much blood but, above all, he loved his country and his Chief. I still remember the names of our neighbors: Adamscy, Błaszczak, Gołąb, Pajor, Bysiński, Dułemba, Czerkas, and Bauman.

Eventually, because my father did not have a farmer's calling, we moved to the town of Korelicze, about 5 miles from the estate. He had been planning to be a veterinarian when his studies were interrupted by World War I. However, due to the shortage of veterinarians after World War I, he received a special dispensation to practice. He was also very engaged socially and was eventually elected to be a town official; he was also the Commandant of the Reserve Army. I remember how, during the May 3 celebrations,[35] mounted on a beautiful horse, sword at his side, my father led his Division; I was very proud of him.

In 1936, when I was 7 years old, we moved to Nowogródek and established a meat shop. Several years passed without any worries or concerns. My parents worked very hard, and we were a loving, happy family, but this was about to end. On the horizon were gathering black clouds of war; the year was 1939. The front pages of the newspapers brought bad news about the unceasing territorial demands and threats of Germany towards Poland. We children had numerous meetings during which we created armaments for our 'army'. The Polish Army and, especially, the Cavalry were beautiful, and, in our minds, undefeatable.

It was September 1, 1939. From the early morning our two dogs were howling and nobody knew why. Soon we heard the news that Germany had attacked Poland. The first German plane appeared over our town, but it did us no harm. My father received an order to mobilize. Before he left the house, I knelt with him before the picture of the Mother of God and we prayed for her care over us. We said goodbye to him with tears and crying and I held onto his hand. Maybe he had a premonition but, during the previous Christmas, he took me on his knee and said that, if anything should happen to him, as I was the oldest boy, I had to look after my mother, my siblings, and the whole family.

During the first weeks of the War not much happened in our area. Father returned home the following week. Apparently the army had many officers younger than himself who were engaged in preparations for battle; my father was to wait at home for further instructions.

September 17 arrived and, while our army was bravely fighting the Germans, the Soviet Army crossed into eastern Poland. The next day they were

---

34   Józef Klemens Piłsudski, (1867-1935), First Marshal of Poland 1920-35, Prime Minister of Poland 1926-28 and 1930.

35   May 3, 1791, Poland received a Constitution, which was the first liberal constitution in Europe and, after the Constitution of the United States, second in the world.

in Nowogródek and some Belarusians and Jews welcomed them with flowers. We couldn't understand this as the Soviets were our common enemies. The Soviet Army looked pitiful in its unkempt uniforms, with the cavalry on scraggy horses. Yet our Polish Army was not there to stop them; the entire Polish war effort was directed towards fighting the Germans.

From the moment the Soviets invaded, there began a terror with the arrest of Polish policemen, army personnel, and government employees. The invaders wanted to wipe out all Polish leaders and intelligentsia so they could rule more easily. My father fell victim to this terror. On September 19, he was arrested but, after a few hours of interrogation, was allowed to return home. That evening I overheard my parents talking in hushed voices about the need to get Father to western Poland. He did not want to leave us. In fact, he never had to make the decision as, that night, one of the local Jews who had been elevated to a position of authority in the Communist Government, came with several Soviet soldiers with bayonets mounted on their rifles and arrested him. They handcuffed him and took him to prison. That was the last time we saw him. We were filled with great despair and a sense of helplessness.

My mother went to the prison every day in the hope of seeing Father, but she never saw him again. We were allowed to deliver parcels with food and clothing to the prison and foolishly believed that, as long as the guards accepted packages for our father, then he had to be alive. After a few weeks, the guards refused to accept packages for him, so we assumed that he had been deported to Russia. There was no trace of him and we could find out nothing about him, yet he was in this prison all the time; a family friend saw him a few months later, chained to other prisoners, being led to the railway station.

In Nowogródek life changed completely; the once lively town became grey and somber. Birds stopped singing and people stood in lines for everything. There were shortages of bread, salt, and other basic items; there was no point in even dreaming about sugar. We were forced to listen to Communist propaganda, even in schools. Yet, nobody was convinced by this propaganda. My mother fought bravely with the new administration which, first, took our shop and, then, wanted to take our house; they claimed that they needed it for the army. My mother, even though she knew they would eventually throw us out of our home, insisted that we would only move when provided with suitable alternative accommodation.

Józef Pankiewicz[36]

b. 1925, Lwów
February 1940, deported to the Soviet Union
1943-46, Iran, Palestine, Egypt, Italy
1946-present, England

1939 came and life changed, bit by bit; I was 14 years old and not too aware of what was happening, until September 17. The sirens sounded and we all looked at each other wondering if it was for real but, then, came a wave of German bombers. We fled into the cellar, joined by our tenants and some neighbors. We heard bombs dropping and we sat there petrified, wondering when one would hit the house. (The house was hit later by an artillery shell.) After a while it became quiet, so we went outside. There was smoke and destruction all around. The house was near a railway and the Germans had bombed it trying, I think, to destroy the bridge which, although damaged, was still there. Later that day, a unit of 12 Polish soldiers arrived and set up a machine-gun in our garden. They told us that they had only 12 rifle bullets each and four hand grenades between them. To make matters worse, they discovered that the machine-gun did not work, so two of them left to try to get a replacement. They never returned. More artillery shells started coming over so, once again, it was back to the cellar.

Eventually, a German soldier came down the steps to the cellar and ordered us out. It was dreadful; the entire Polish unit had been killed. They stood no chance but had fought bravely to the end. A neighbor arrived with a badly wounded Polish officer and asked the Germans to help. They said they would get him to hospital, but I doubt if they did as they set up a field hospital in our orchard later and I saw no Polish soldiers there. As the day wore on, it became increasingly distressing; dead and wounded everywhere, awful moaning and crying, and very little help available. One of the officers asked for a drink; Aunt Kazia gave him some milk but he insisted that she drank it first; I suppose he was frightened it was poisoned.

Next day, we were ordered to leave; the Germans said there would be a big battle. Grandma refused so Marian stayed with her. Mother and Aunt Kazia loaded up grandmother's pony and trap and we went to Konopnica, taking three Jewish girls with us; their mother remained.

We left the house and turned into the main road and could not believe the utter carnage that was before us; everywhere were bodies and smoking debris. One sight still haunts me; a gun pulled by four horses was standing near the

---

36   Józef Pankiewicz's written account submitted by his son-in-law, Keith Bannister, England.

bridge. Three of the horses were dead and the other poor creature stood there, shaking and unable to move. We could not help as guns were going off around us and the Germans were shouting at us to go. Luckily, the bridge was still passable and it was quiet closer to the village. Our house was approached by a drive about a quarter of a mile long. It was flanked on either side by large trees; now, it was full of trucks and soldiers. We were very nervous but they did not harm us. In fact, they called out and offered us food. The Jewish girls understood German but were too afraid to go near them.

A few days later the Russian Army arrived. At that time, the Germans and Russians were allies. The Russians were a sorry sight; badly dressed, ill-equipped, and full of lice. They had disinfectant chambers with them and a popular joke was one could smell them coming from 5 miles away; this was vastly different to the Germans who seemed to have everything.

We returned to Lwów. Now, it was very difficult to get food and we heard terrible stories about the German and Russian treatment of Jews. The rumors were that the Germans had killed all the patients in the Kulparków mental hospital[37] and the Russians had rounded up all the Polish Officers and executed them. One of my cousins, a young officer, disappeared and, to this day, we have found no trace of him.

> *"Russian atrocities toward both nationalities are on a scale which men, who have been prisoners in Germany for five years, had not imagined possible. It is an everyday occurrence for Russian soldiers to go into a house, shoot the children and rape the women — regardless of their nationality. It is almost unknown to see a sober Russian soldier, and officers are particularly bad, so that their main preoccupation is to loot and rape — producing a reign of terror — which affected all areas and took place at all times."*
>
> **British Junior NCOs and Privates (ex-POWs)**[38]

---

37   See: Jaroszewski, Z. ed. (1993). *Zagłada psychicznie chorych w Polsce 1939-1945.* (Extermination of Mentally Ill Patients in Poland 1939-1945). PWN: Warszawa. Publication of the *Polskie Towarzystwo Psychiatryczne* (Polish Psychiatry Society) and *Komisja Naukowa Historii Psychiatrii Polskiej* (Scientific Commission of Polish Psychiatry History). Jaroszewski estimates that 16,153 patients in psychiatric hospitals were killed by methods such as shooting and lethal injection, while another 10,000 died from deliberate starvation.

38   *Interrogation of British Junior NCOs and Privates (ex-POWs) evacuated through Russia and arriving in the UK, May 7, 1945.* Document stamped: 'Secret' HS4/21, M19/MS/BM/173/3, 1945. National Archives, England.

Maria Pawulska Rasiej
b. 1927, Lwów
April 1940, deported to the Soviet Union
1942-47, Iran, Iraq, India, Africa
1947-52, England
1952-present, USA

and

Kazimierz Rasiej
b. 1926, Przemyśl
April 1940, deported to the Soviet Union
1942-44, Iran, Iraq, Palestine
1944-52, England
1952-present, USA

Maria Pawulska Rasiej

In 1939, we were living in Lwów. My dad was a Captain in the Polish Army. My mother was a housewife; she looked after the three children of whom I was the oldest. When the War broke out my father was taken prisoner during the Battle for Lwów.[39] We were in Lwów during all the bombing. I had just come back from my summer vacation near Kraków but, on September 1, as I had a sinus infection, I had to go to the hospital which was near to my father's barracks. The plan was that we would go and see him so that I could say *"hello"* after the summer vacation. We hadn't yet reached our destination when we saw airplanes flying overhead. At first, we thought that these were some kind of maneuvers, but then we realized we were mistaken when we heard bombs exploding. The tram conductor told us to get off the tram and find shelter.

Those early days of the War were spent either at home, as school had not yet started or, if there was an air raid warning, in the cellar of our neighbor's house. Once the Germans entered Lwów, we spent days and nights in the cellar. Occasionally, someone would go upstairs into the house and cook something to eat and bring it down to us.

This is how it was until September 21, when it suddenly became very quiet. There was silence everywhere. We had heard rumors that the Germans were withdrawing and that the Russians had crossed the Polish border, but we didn't know what their plans were. Had they come to defend us or to conquer

---

39   Battle for Lwów: September 12-22, 1939, between the Polish Army and the invading German and Soviet Armies.

the Germans? On September 22, we realized that the Russian guns were not positioned to destroy Germans but, rather, to destroy Lwów. We also had no news of my father. Only later did we learn that my father, like all the other Polish leadership, had been told to report to the Russian command and ordered to lay down his weapons. My father was going to the meeting place as ordered but decided to stop at my uncle's home to let him know what was happening so he could inform us. My uncle gave my father an opportunity to escape as they were almost the same age, build and they looked alike. My uncle had a large dental office in a building with a front entrance on one street and back entrance on another, so my father could leave unseen. However, my father refused as he thought it was dishonorable for a Polish officer to save himself while his men had all gone to lay down their arms; he had his responsibilities towards his men.

We found out much later that they were taken somewhere on the outskirts of Lwów. This may be difficult to understand today, but we didn't know where to look for him; we knew nothing about his whereabouts and there was no information. Our home was not bombed. On the way home we saw a woman running and crying with a blood-stained pillow in her hands. She told us that her daughter had either been killed or seriously injured and she was running to find her in the hospital. This was our first contact with someone who had suffered a loss in the War.

After the Russians came, life became very hard. Instantly there were changes. The Polish currency, the *złoty*, was withdrawn from circulation so that even those people who had savings were not better off. The Russian currency, the *ruble*, fluctuated in value and I remember my mother worrying about how and where we would get supplies. What there was in the shops was immediately bought out by Russian soldiers. However, when there was a threat of war, people were advised to stock up on certain necessary articles such as flour, buckwheat, and sugar. My mother had done this and we now lived off these supplies.

The Russians also took everything and sent it to Russia. There was a joke that local famous watch stores were closed for the day because Stalin was coming to buy watches. Of course, all political criticisms were said as jokes, and rumors were passed around. I don't remember if we still had newspapers or if the radio functioned. My uncle, who was a radio director in Kraków, was instructed by the Polish authorities to move with all his equipment and staff to Romania from where he could broadcast. I do remember that, eventually, we had Russian announcements on the radio. My uncle made it to Romania where he stayed for a year.[40] After that, he had to go to Turkey, Palestine, and Cyprus. All this took months as the English authorities took control of these areas. We eventually met up with my uncle in Africa.

We received the first card from my father in November, from Starobielsk, where he was in a POW camp. There were different camps; one was for army personnel and another for doctors, lawyers, teachers, and police. My father wrote that many of our neighbors were together though he did not want to mention names. We now know there was an order to close these camps in March. We received a letter from my father telling us not to write as they were being moved and that he would send us his new address later. We never did see him again as he was murdered in the Katyń forest along with 25,000 Polish officers, teachers, lawyers, judges, police, doctors, and other intelligentsia.[41]

---

40   This was known as 'crossing the green border', escaping into Romania and then joining the Polish Armed Forces in exile. When World War II broke out, Romania declared neutrality, (September 6, 1939), but she supported Poland by facilitating the transit of the National Bank treasure and by granting asylum to the Polish President and Government as well as its troops.

41   "Some 250,000 Polish military personnel were seized and over 20,000 army, navy, air force, and frontier-guard officers were sent to three prison camps in the Soviet Union; Kozielsk, Starobielsk, and Ostashkov. Most of these officers were reservists: doctors, professors, school teachers, lawyers, judges, civil servants, priests, ministers, and rabbis. In March 1940 they were ordered to gather their belongings and were told they were being returned to Poland. Instead, they were taken deep into the Russian forests. There, each victim's hands were tied behind his back and, if he struggled, he was bayoneted and sawdust was thrust into his mouth to subdue him. His greatcoat was pulled over his head and a second cord was tied around his neck. The cord was passed down the back, looped around the bound hands, and tied again at the neck so that every move of resistance only tightened the noose. Then, one by one, each prisoner was murdered with a pistol shot to the back of the head.

The Germans discovered a grave in the Katyń Forest in 1943, with the bodies of prisoners from the Kozielsk prison camp, but the Soviets denied all involvement. It was not until the collapse of the Soviet Union in 1989, that the head of the Communist Party broadly admitted Soviet guilt.

In 1991, other mass graves containing the bodies of murdered officers from the Starobielsk and Ostashkov camps were uncovered near Kharkov and in Mednoye. In 1992, the Russian President released to Poland secret documents, including death sentences signed by Stalin and the head of the NKVD." *Text developed and written by the Signage Committee of The National Katyń Memorial Foundation - Richard P. Poremski, Chairman.* http://culture.polishsite.us/articles/art281fr.htm

Kazimierz Rasiej

My father was a Commandant in the police and was arrested on September 19, after the Soviets occupied Poland. After three months, all traces of him disappeared, except for a name on a list of those executed, which I recently acquired. Most probably he was executed near Kiev and buried in one of the mass graves, if you can call them 'graves,' though I suppose that is what they are. We are going there soon so I can lay some flowers on his grave. My mother, Helena, my older brother, Mieczysław, and I were deported to northern Kazakhstan on April 13, 1940. There was a train waiting in Brodów station to take away the inhabitants; some of my friends were deported with us. They took away everyone who posed a threat to Communist rule.

Kazimiera Miara Janota Bzowska

b. 1925, Tarnów

1942-46, Germany

1946-48, France

1948-present, England

Before the War, my father was the Headmaster of a school in Nowykorczyn. My mother did not work; she looked after her four children, of whom I was the oldest. We were quite well off. In August 1939 I was due to go away to school in Łuniniec, Polesie, where my grandmother lived. I had been in a private secondary school and, now, I would go to a public school. In 1938, there was talk of war and we had drills on how to respond to a gas attack, since the Germans had used gas warfare during World War I. We all had gas masks and were taught how to seal windows to prevent the gas from seeping in.

I said goodbye to my parents on August 27, and went to Polesie. My grandmother's tenants were very surprised that she had taken me as there was a war coming. The War broke out on September 1 and I wanted to return home, but my route was cut off. On September 16, everything was very quiet; there was no German action. On September 17, Polesie was taken over by the Bolsheviks and where my parents lived was occupied by the Germans. I still wanted to return home. Some of my friends wanted to escape to the German side where they thought they would be safer. In a way, I was really too young to understand or be frightened; my grandmother always tried to protect me and wouldn't let me listen to the radio or read about the War. My grandmother saw a spy in every person. She helped people escape to the German side and did not want me to know what she was doing in case I was captured and interrogated; at least this way I wouldn't know anything. When people talked about the Polish Army, it didn't make sense to me. Where was the Army? Where were the policemen? Why were children missing from my school? We'd heard that people were being deported. Some of the boys were conscripted into the Soviet Army. Out of 40 children who started in my class, only 15 were left at the end of the school year in 1940. I picked up a lot of news and gossip while standing in line for food.

**Figure 12. Kazimiera Miara Janota Bzowska,
Nowykorczyn, Poland, 1937**

My grandmother was arrested in March, 1940, and I was left, at the age of 14, completely alone.[42] I had to look after myself but I did not know how to cook. I did not have a ration card,[43] so I was always hungry. The only thing I knew how to cook were potatoes, and that's what I lived on, so I got a vitamin deficiency and developed sores that would not heal. My grandmother was eventually released but, by then, the Germans had taken over the area and I was constantly under threat of being arrested and deported to Germany for slave labor.

---

42 Kazimiera was not deported to Siberia because she did not appear on the list of residents in Łuniniec.

43 The Soviets issued ration cards to the local population for necessities such as bread but, not being a listed resident, Kazimiera did not receive one.

Tadeusz Król[44]

b. 1930, Mołodeczno
July 1940, deported to the Soviet Union
1942-58, England
1958-present, USA

In 1938, our parents bought a house in Mołodeczno and we planned to move there from Raków when our dad retired from the Army in which he had been for over 20 years. It was a large town, a sort of county seat, and it had a high school for us to attend when we were old enough (there was no high school in Raków).

By 1939, I recall hearing more and more about the possibility of war with Germany. Germany completed the dismemberment of Czechoslovakia and started to make claims on Poland. Things were heating up. Polish propaganda was taking a defensive stand. More troops were being conscripted and my uncle Frank was called up to serve in the Polish Army; he was about 19. Meanwhile, school at Raków progressed normally. I was involved in different youth activities, such as being an altar boy and a scout, marching and planting trees along roads. My Aunt Bronia, who was away in high school in Końskie, came back to Raków and tried to learn English because Grandma wanted her to go to America. Grandma hoped to have Bronia live and work in Rochester, New York, where Grandma's sister and family lived.

In early summer of 1939, more troops were mobilized. Dad was transferred to another post in a village but I do not remember its name. We had to move to Zalesie. I was not going back to school in Raków because there was a new school nearby, about three miles from the border post. The border post was rented from one of the farmers there. We lived in another farmer's house, about half a mile from the post. There were about 20 soldiers at the post, all older reservists, called up to the Army because the younger soldiers were transferred to regular army units and moved to face possible German attack. Dad was not transferred as he was almost 40 and they needed someone with border duty experience to stay behind.

Just as the new school year started, the Germans attacked Poland, on September 1. I knew that the War was not going well for Poland by the mood of my parents and from what I overheard when they talked. During the second week of the War we had hardly any news of what was going on. There were no newspapers, and the radio was no longer giving regular news. The only news from the

---

44   Król, T. (1996). *How Destiny and Fate Placed the Króls in America.* Rochester: unpublished.

border post regional headquarters, received by telephone, gave us an indication that the Germans were moving forward on Polish soil. No one expected that the troops on the eastern border could have any influence on what was happening.

School was still functioning normally, though Mom started making additional purchases of sugar, soup, and other products; everyone was trying to stock up on products in cities that were not under German control. We were not thinking about the Russians. We were glad that England and France had declared war on Germany and we were hoping that their military would soon force Germany to ease up on the Polish Front. But no major Allied push on the Western Front was materializing.

My father was spending a lot of time at the post, since the reservists there needed some discipline; they liked to take it easy. When they were sent to patrol the border they would often find a nice spot among the trees and rest or go to sleep. Dad had to go out at night to check if the soldiers were at their posts. At about 4 AM on September 17, Dad had just returned from checking the border post. I awoke because he was very mad and was talking loudly with Mom. He had again found soldiers sleeping under a tree, instead of patrolling the border. This time he was going to report them to the officer.

Not more than half an hour passed before Dad went to bed. I was trying to go back to sleep when we heard loud knocking at the window. Mom was not asleep. She put on a robe and opened the window curtain. A man in an excited but subdued voice started to tell her that the Russians had crossed the border, which was only a mile away and that they were already in the village. Moments later, shooting started all around us.

A soldier came to the door and banged on it, pleading to be let in. Dad dressed in a hurry and was going to return back to the post, but the soldier shouted that the Russians were all around the post and there was no way they could go back. The Russians surrounded the house and were already breaking in. I saw several Russian soldiers pointing rifles through windows and I remember one of the guns was aimed at my brother George. Mom grabbed George, although it could have provoked the soldier. Luckily the soldier did not fire.

Dad, the Polish soldier, and all of us had our hands up as the Russians took us into the kitchen. Dad and the soldier were led outside. Mom was crying and tried to say goodbye to Dad but they would not let her. The Russians went through the house searching for other people and guns. After 10 minutes they left with Dad and the soldier. About a dozen bullets flew through the house we lived in, but no one was hurt. We heard some more shooting in the distance, probably from other border posts that were putting up resistance. But that resistance was really useless; how could a dozen or two older reservists put up much of a fight against two companies or more of young soldiers? After about 3 hours, the Russians tied up all of the Polish soldiers, including Dad. They commandeered a farmer with a horse and cart to take the body of a dead Russian, (shot by friendly fire), and they left the village. It was not a very important post, not on a road to anywhere, so they did not bother to stay. However, they did appoint some local people who were Russian sympathizers to keep order in the area. Our village was mostly Belarusians so the Russians did not expect any problems from them. It was scary for Polish families in areas with a Belarusian majority. We heard that in some villages the local Belarus population murdered and robbed Polish families. They also went after Polish settlers, veterans of the war with Russia in 1919-20 who had been given land for their service to Poland.

With Dad gone to a POW camp somewhere in Russia, we were stranded in a village where we did not know anyone, and there was no way to get in touch with our family in Raków. We had to wait until the Russians introduced some way of communicating within the area they had now annexed to their Belarus Republic. There would be no more army pay. Fortunately, Mom had saved some money.

Being a child, the grief of Dad's forced departure did not prevent me from joining other kids in exploring what had happened at the border post. My curiosity was great and my mother had too many problems to keep track of me. We roamed around the perimeter of the border post, found a lot of ammunition, like unexploded grenades, lying around and we were so stupid that we even threw stones at the grenades hoping they would explode. Our border post had hundreds of bullet holes in it and all the windows and doors were broken. We saw the spot where the Russian soldier had been killed, about 200 feet from the post's wire fence. Some local Russian sympathizers had placed flowers on the spot. We roamed the soldiers' sleeping area, dining hall, Dad's office, and the emptied arms room. The Russians had looted anything of value, including the soldiers' private property, and the entire post was a mess.

About 10 days after the Russian invasion, some travel was allowed in the area and we went back to Raków. Mom got permission from a new local village leader, and rented four carts on which we loaded our possessions. Naturally, there was not enough money to pay for all of them so Mom had to sell some of her possessions in exchange for the farmers' services. The journey back to Raków took about two days. We rested during the night. A few times the Russians stopped us but, as Mom and the farmers spoke Russian, their explanation was somehow sufficient for them to allow us to continue to Raków.

Life was becoming harder, not only because there were shortages of everything, but also because people started to be afraid to talk to each other. The NKVD asked people to denounce elements unfriendly to the new order; even children were asked to tell tales about other children or adults.

Some of the activities we were involved in were dangerous. We used to play soldiers and made pistols from copper pipes which we would fill with gunpowder. Gunpowder was easily available because there was plenty of ammunition lying around. We would fire a projectile from the pistol and see how many layers of paper or wood board it would pass through. The projectile that we used was usually a piece of metal or a nail. It was dangerous as, sometimes, the pistol would explode in one's hands. When one of my friends lost most of his hand I stopped playing this game.

Soon, people started disappearing. There were fewer kids in school; later, I learned that they had been deported. We were lucky to escape not only the first, but also two more deportations initiated during 1940.[45] I was later told that many people perished from that first deportation because of the cold winter.

Romuald Lipiński

b. 1925, Brześć
June 1941, deported to the Soviet Union
1942-43, Iran, Iraq, Palestine, Egypt
1943-46, Italy, Lebanon
1946-53, England
1953-present, USA

Two weeks after the War started the Germans occupied Brześć and, then, the Russians came in around September 19. My father, a pharmacist, was immediately demoted from his position in the dispensary and replaced by a Russian physician. They moved us from our four-roomed apartment to one with only two rooms. My father used to put on his Red Cross arm band and go to

---

45   The Soviets began to implement a previously prepared plan for liquidating Poles as 'enemies of the people' such as civil servants, judges, the police, professional army officers, factory owners, landlords, political activists, and leaders of cultural, educational and religious organizations. Poland stood in the way of Soviet plans to expand Communism in Europe. Poles were moved to be imprisoned and to forced labor camps and to places of enforced settlements in the northern parts of European Russia and Central Asia where conditions would ensure their liquidation. Including the small percentage of Ukrainians, Jews (20%) and Belarusians, the total number of Polish citizens deported between 1939 and 1941 amounted to approximately 1,680,000 people, not including 250,000 POWs (Prisoners of War). By the middle of 1942, half of them were dead. Piotrowski, T, ed. Op. cit. pp. 4-5.

the army trains to help but this was, actually, an underground operation as my father used to leave the wagon door unlocked and tell the Polish soldiers where to find safe houses. This is how he saved the lives of many soldiers who would have otherwise died in Katyń. Before his dismissal, we had a room in our house for refugees and fed many people. We even had two Czech volunteers staying who had come to fight the Germans. Our house was like a hotel. My mother would cook huge pots of food and we'd all stand in line to receive it. Then there was a dispute between my father and a Russian doctor over coal, so my father was dismissed. We lived under Russian occupation for two years during which I did not go to school. Everyone was disorientated, but we were expecting a miracle that the French and English would come to help us. We thought this was a transitional period.

Figure 13. Romuald Lipiński, Brześć, Poland, 1939

On June 21, 1941, the Germans invaded Brześć. Just before the War, one of my brothers had been made a judge. He was taken as a POW by the Russians, but my father got him freed because he was so good to the Russian employees on the railway. Later this brother and his friend escaped through Hungary and Italy to France and then, after France fell, he was evacuated to Scotland to join the parachute brigade.[46] He was hurt in a jump, and the Scottish nurse who nursed him back to health did so well that they got married. Another brother was at the Polytechnic in Brześć. The Russians planted an agent provocateur in the college who pretended to be a Polish officer wanting to organize the Polish students against the Russians. Once they had a list of names they began to arrest the students. My father got my brother to confess to his activities and sent him

---

46   After the fall of France in June 1940, the Polish Government-in-Exile and Polish Armed Forces moved to Britain.

away to relatives before he could be arrested. I used to act as lookout for the group when they met in the dispensary, to warn them if anyone was coming down the street. I remember that, at one time, they took the crucifix off the wall and swore some kind of oath on it. I was considered too young to participate, but I did notice that my brother had many young people coming to visit. I knew that something was cooking. As Brześć was one of the exchange points between the Germans and Russians, my brother managed to cross into the German sector using false papers. However, he was later arrested by the Germans. One sister was in Warszawa, and the other in Milanówek. There were six of us altogether. We were not together again until we all came to London in 1948.

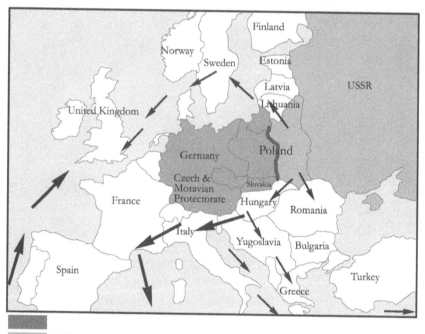

Poland under Nazi occupation
Poland under Stalinist occupation
Direction of evacuation: Hungary, Yugoslavia, Greece, Italy, France, United Kingdom, and Palestine.

Figure 14. Evacuation of Polish troops from Poland after the War of Defense, September 1 - October 1, 1939

RESISTANCE

CHAPTER 3

The Armed Forces

**Figure 15. Recruitment poster for the
Polish Army in France, 1940**[47]

The Polish Army

- After the capitulation of Warszawa the Polish Army started moving to eastern Poland.

- With the invasion of Poland by the Russians and the move of the Polish Government into exile, the Polish Armed Forces attempted to leave Poland to regroup outside the country in order to fight the enemy.

- After the fall of France in June, 1940, the Polish Government (which was domiciled there at the time), and the Polish Armed Forces, moved to England.

Kazimierz Bączyński

b. 1920, Bielsko Biała

1939-45, Hungary, Yugoslavia, France,

Morocco, Gibraltar, England, Scotland

1945-present, England

I was 19 years old in 1939, and had to fulfill my obligation to military service by going to Cadet School. We were sent to the Prussian border, to build fortifications at Nowogrodska. That's where the War found us, so the Regular Army arrived and the cadets withdrew. We could hear German artillery firing behind us. We went to Brześć-nad-Bógiem, where the Germans bombed our train and airport; thankfully I was not harmed. We were then moved to Wołyń, close to the Russian border. Just then, the Russians entered and surrounded us. I still remember a Russian Major standing on top of a tank and telling us, *"You Christian brothers, we will not allow you to fight, you go home."* But, of course, our homes were in the west[48] and they took us to the east. In Równo, at the station, there were a lot of trains and people. I said to my friend, *"Let's escape."* We were guarded but, when the guard was looking in the opposite direction, we hid un-

---

48   Says Kazimierz, "During this time I knew nothing about my family and only found our later, after the War, that my father had initially been allowed to stay in the Police Force but, then, he got word that the Gestapo was planning to arrest him. He took the family, which included five children, and fled into the mountains in southern Poland. My family lived in the mountains near Zakopane during the entire War and my father worked as a member of the *Armia Krajowa* (the Home Army) which was the Polish Resistance."

der the train and got lost in the crowd.

We started walking in the direction of Lwów, begging for food along the way. The poor people helped us out. One night we went to a house and slept in a barn. We did not realize that we were in the Wołyń area, where there were lots of Ukrainian Nationalists who were killing Poles. Fortunately an old lady took pity on us and came to warn us that the Ukrainians were planning to murder us and that we had better run. We had as our goal to reach Stanisławów where we had friends and hoped to stay with them while we decided what to do. Ultimately, we thought that we would cross into Hungary. We decided to separate and go in different directions to discover which way was clear for escape. I was not in uniform but was wearing my army coat because I was cold. Lots of people had these coats because the army had been dispersed and everyone was wondering where to go.

I was arrested in Wohorowcy and sent to a camp, but I had no intention of being held prisoner. (Our guard was a Jew, which was not unusual as the Jews co-operated with the Russians.) I don't remember precisely how, but I managed to escape and get back to Stanisławów. Despite the guards and checks, my friend and I managed to get on a train and, as the train slowed down to turn a corner, we jumped into the snow. We had no maps but we had visited this area on holiday so we had a gut feeling for where the Hungarian border was located. On the way we met a small group of Poles that included the French Consul from Stanisławów. We sent him back to Stanisławów as he was too old and frail to travel and we didn't think the Germans would harm him.

The conditions in which we traveled were terrible; there was snow and blizzards but, somehow, we made it to the border. We met more Poles in the mountains, a rather large group; it was a narrow mountain path so we walked in single file towards the forest. We also met some locals, *huculi*,[49] who said they would help us. I didn't trust them and said to my friend that we should be at the end of the line so that if there was an ambush, we had a chance of getting away. We were a group of 30 people so I didn't see how they could shoot all of us.

We had to get into the forest and climb up to the border which was on top of the mountain. Suddenly a Russian patrol came down from the mountain and started firing at us. I immediately jumped down into the forest below, but not my friend. I was left all alone. I ran up and up until the blood was pounding in my head. I found a tree and climbed up into it because I thought the dogs would

---

49   *huculi* (Polish): an ethno-cultural group of Ukrainian highlanders who, for centuries, have inhabited the Carpathian mountains, mainly in Ukraine, but also in the northern extremity of Romania (in the areas of Bukovina and Maramuse), as well as in Slovakia and Poland. There was suspicion of these highlanders as they lead a nomadic life and were considered by some to be outlaws.

find me on the ground and tear me to shreds. I hid in this tree until morning. I knew there was a Russian border patrol and observation towers and guards with guns, so I knew the crossing would be very dangerous. If I tried this in the dark any breaking of a branch would notify them of my presence so I went early in the morning, from tree to tree, until I reached the border. I hid in a ditch that had been dug during World War I. I saw that on the other side of the ditch there were trees so I dashed out of the ditch, across the border and into the shelter of the trees. From there I walked to a village where I found some very good people. I was very hungry and they gave me breakfast. We ate from a single wooden bowl with one spoon, some kind of *mamałyga*.[50] It tasted so good.

They told me where to go to meet Hungarian police who would help me. Many Poles did this. I met the police and they told me where to register. I was there for a few days, was interviewed and treated very well. More Poles turned up. We were sent by train to Eger, an officers' camp. I was there for nine months, working in the Chancellery. You could get a pass to move about but you had to sign a promissory note that you would not run away. The Hungarian officer asked me to stay and not to go to war but, of course, I was young and courageous and wanted to fight for my country. Despite the checks on the trains I managed to get to Budapest where there was a Polish Embassy and a camp with many, many Poles. A few days later I was sent to the Yugoslav border. They arrested Poles in Budapest and interned them; they had a saying that if you tied a Pole in a sack and put two guards next to him, in the morning you would find two guards tied up in the sack and no Pole. Poles knew how to escape.

There were many good Hungarians who helped Poles, but there were also Hitler supporters who captured Poles and put them into punishment camps. We went to the Yugoslav border where, at night, guides took people across the River Drawa into Yugoslavia. The group before me was caught so my group withdrew because it was considered too dangerous to attempt a crossing. We waited for a few days and tried again, this time successfully. We got to Zagreb where there was a Polish Consulate, got our documents and then were sent to the port of Sprit on the Adriatic. There, the transport was organized; the ship, *Patria*, was waiting to take us to Marseilles in France. There were a few thousand men, and no women, on the ship. We had used one of the two escape routes from Poland to the Polish Army under Allied Command; one led through Italy and the other through France.

We got to Marseilles with no incident and got to a camp in Brassiere where we received terrible, old Napoleonic-period uniforms. Then, we went by train to Brittany. The French soldiers were so dressed up and drunk, I thought, *"Oh*

---

50   *mamałyga* (Polish): cornmeal, a common food in the Huculi region.

my God, what a difference to the Polish Army." Initially, they treated us well but not so later. When I saw a transport of English soldiers, I thought, *"Oh yes, now this is a proper Army."* In Capestang, Languedoc, there was a Polish camp where they were organizing a division they had nicknamed 'The Battalion of Death'. I volunteered to join, and the Captain said, *"You pup, go back to your mom."* He was looking for professional soldiers and I was not yet a real soldier. Then, there was a German offensive and a group of us decided to escape towards Bordeaux. We met a different kind of Frenchman here; when we asked for water they refused to give us any. We reached the Spanish-French border. For me, this journey was just a matter of escaping, but there were those in our group who were Poles from France and knew where they were going. We reached Port Vendres on the Spanish border, waited a few days, and took a ship to the port of Oran in Morocco. The Germans were not yet in the area. From there we went by train to Casablanca.

In Casablanca we were housed in airport hangars. There were American Douglas planes in the airport as well as many Polish airmen. We hoped to fly to Britain, but this failed. The German influence in the area was already being felt. We went north of Casablanca to a port where there were two Polish ships, the *Wilia* and *Iskra*. We had no sailors as the entire Polish Navy had gone to England. The German Commission arrived and forbade us from going. As we had nothing to lose, we threatened to destroy everything around us; that got them worried and they let us leave. We really were ready to do anything.

We recruited a crew and reached Gibraltar where we were organized into a convoy and taken to England. We had a hard time keeping up with the British ships and were redirected to Portugal. We got a telegram from Britain saying that we would be interned in Portugal,[51] so we decided to follow the British convoy to Liverpool. We saw much wood floating in the ocean; the wooden Greek boats in the convoy that had been torpedoed. You were supposed to zigzag into the port to avoid the mines but our pilot went straight in; fortunately, we did not hit a mine. We were taken by train to Scotland, complete with all our armaments. The English and Scottish treated us very well. The Polish Army was being organized; I was in Ladybank, Fife, where I started my military education.

---

51   On September 1, 1939, Portugal proclaimed its neutrality, and was, therefore, obliged to intern members of the Polish Armed Forces as international law required that neutral countries had to intern alien military personnel.

Mieczysław Juny
b. 1913, Lwów
1939-45, Hungary, Yugoslavia, Greece, Lebanon,
Syria, Palestine, Egypt, Iraq, England,
South Africa, Sierra Leone, Scotland
1945-present, England

In the spring of 1939, I was an Army Commandant stationed in Kosów; then, just before the War, I was made Commandant of a company responsible for guarding the border with Hungary[52] replacing the corps that had been sent to the western front. This was done because there was an expectation that, as the Hungarians were German allies;[53] the Germans might attack over the Hungarian border. We were there for 17 days during which nothing happened; there was no sign that anyone was going to cross from Hungary into Poland. I received a telephone call on September 17 informing me that the Russians had crossed into Poland and were heading towards the central part of the country. We were told to cross into Hungary, which was not difficult because we were so close to the border.

We had a long journey and walked all night. In the morning we met my senior officer in Woronienki, then crossed into Hungary where there were two officers waiting to receive us. We were told to go about 3 kilometers to a clearing where we rested and were given food. We spent the night there and, the next morning, were taken by cars to Koszyce, (once a Czech town), then to Vitoszemedie where we were billeted in some empty army barracks. There were only a couple of chairs but, thankfully, there was running water. The Hungarians were very welcoming and brought us some food. After two weeks one of the Hungarian officers called me to follow him; would you believe it; my fiancée, Zosia, had turned up in the same town. We were married on March 3, 1940, in Hungary.

Shortly afterwards we boarded a train to Budapest from where we planned to escape to Yugoslavia.[54] The Hungarians knew what we were doing but ignored

---

52   In March 1939, Czechoslovakia was dissolved and Hungary occupied the rest of Carpathian Ruthenia. On March 23, 1939, disagreements with Slovakia over the new common eastern border led to an armed conflict between the two countries, as a result of which Hungary gained the easternmost strip of Slovakia. Poland, therefore, had a border with Hungary.

53   While the Hungarians were officially German allies, a long history of Hungarian-Polish association meant that many Hungarian officials and the general population provided assistance and a safe haven for the Polish military and civilians during the War, as opposed to interning them which was the official policy.

54   On September 5, 1939, Yugoslavia declared neutrality.

all these fleeing refugees. I had arranged for Zosia to go to a civilian camp near Budapest and had to be careful that nobody knew who I was. We spent four days in Budapest. We were woken in the night and directed to the River Drawa, which was on the Hungarian-Yugoslav border, where we crossed by rafts. There were people in Hungary who assisted us in our escape. We crossed the river, walked about 5 kilometers, and went to an abandoned building where other refugees were gathering. The next day some cars came for us and took us to the nearest railway station where we caught a train to Zagreb in Yugoslavia. We stayed in a small hotel in Zagreb for a few days after which we were moved again. My brother was in the same group as us. From Yugoslavia we were taken by train to Athens, Greece.

We waited in Athens for a couple of weeks until the Greek ship, *Constantine*, came; we thought we were going to France but the plans changed and we were taken, instead, to Beirut, Lebanon. Then we went to Syria where we were organized into the *Karpacka Brygada*[55] of about 3,000 soldiers, housed in wooden huts, dressed in French uniforms, and armed.

It was very hot; the buildings were not insulated and we woke up each morning under about 2 inches of red sand. Here, we trained and prepared for action until, one day, the French commander of the *Armée du Levant*, General Eugene Mittelhauser, ordered us to lay down our arms. The new Vichy Government of Philippe Petain had annulled all pacts made with Poland.[56] We refused and the French, who were on our side, rather than force us, gave us 30 cars so that we could go to Palestine which was under British command. On June 30, 1940, we left to join the British forces there. We made it to Latrun in Palestine, where we

---

55   The Polish Independent Carpathian Brigade, (*Samodzielna Brygada Strzelców Karpackich*), was a Polish military unit formed in 1940 in French Syria and comprised of Polish soldiers evacuated after the Invasion of Poland in 1939. It was commanded by General Stanisław Kopański, (1895-1976), and was originally part of the French *Armée du Levant*. After the fall of France, the Carpathian Brigade moved to Palestine which was under British rule. It was merged into the Second Polish Corps, the *Drugi Korpus Wojska Polskiego* under General Anders. The Second Polish Corps, 1943-47, was created from various units fighting alongside the Allies in all theatres of war and the deportees who escaped the Soviet Union after the 'Amnesty' of 1941. The Third Carpathian Division was formed in the Middle East from smaller Polish units fighting in Egypt and Tobruk, as well as from the Polish Army in the East that was evacuated from the USSR through the Persian Corridor.

56   Polish troops were originally under French command. Germany occupied only northern France and the southern part was ruled by the Vichy Government; it was not occupied by the Germans but the pro-German Vichy Government would not allow the formation of a Polish Army on its territory. The French Army lay down its arms in Syria and no longer fought the Germans.

stayed for four months, then, moved to a village outside Alexandria (El Amiriya). There was an airport nearby and the Italians began to bomb the area. However, rather than bomb the airport, they aimed at us, which was very unpleasant, and there were some fatalities. We were there three to four months. From Alexandria we were loaded onto a British destroyer and, in August 1941, set off for Tobruk. The *Karpacka Brygada* was constantly under bombardment in Tobruk; you never knew what would happen, and patrolling was very dangerous as the fields were mined. I remember, on one patrol, there was a flash dropped from a plane; it lit up the whole field so I fell on the ground to hide and felt some metal under my chin. I had landed on a mine but, fortunately, my weight was not enough to explode it. The only time there was quiet appeared to be around the time both sides were eating!

Jerzy Zubrzycki

b. 1920, Kraków
1940-41, Slovakia, Hungary, Yugoslavia, Italy, France
1941-55, Britain
1955-present, Australia

I finished high school in 1938 and was obliged to do my military service which I did at the Cavalry Reserve Officer School in Grudziądż. Upon graduation, in June, 1939, I was made a cadet officer stationed in Kraków and sent straight to the Front to fight the invading German Army. I was awarded a military cross for my service in the defense of Poland in the September Campaign in Częstochowa. In early October, I was taken as a POW but managed to escape. I was helped by a Jewish shopkeeper who hid me and gave me some civilian clothing. I had some of my army pay left and, with that, I bought myself a bicycle and, even though I was injured, cycled to my home in Kielce. I immediately joined the Polish Underground. At the beginning of 1940, because I spoke some English, my commanding officer said I should be trained as a courier in the west. I found myself crossing Czechoslovakia, Hungary, Yugoslavia, and northern Italy, and then reached the Polish Army in France.

After Dunkirk, in June, 1940,[57] I was evacuated with what was left of my regiment to Cornwall, England, then to a camp in Liverpool, after which I

---

57   The evacuation of Allied soldiers at Dunkirk, from May 26 to June 4, 1940.

moved to Scotland where I joined the elite First Polish Parachute Brigade.[58] I requested to join the Secret Service, which was training pilots for drops into Poland; they were the Polish Section of the Special Operations Executive (SOE),[59] under the command of General Sosnkowski. I was one of the first members and was trained in parachuting (I still have my parachute, number 12), and to conduct sabotage and intelligence work. I was due to be dropped into Poland in June 1941, but the order was revoked at the last minute. The decision was made that I was needed in Britain for further planning of major operations in Poland. I was assigned as a liaison officer to the Staff Operation Executive. I worked with the French, Dutch, and Danes, in planning special operations. The losses we suffered in the air were terrible. At the end of 1943, my operation was transferred to southern Italy because the flight from England to Poland took eleven-and-a-half hours while, from Italy, it was shorter. I was involved in the July 1944 operations, during which we landed in southern Poland and dropped off supplies as well as picked up agents, mail, and two eminent Polish leaders. For this, I received the Order of the British Empire. After the Warsaw Uprising[60] and all the other tragedies, my commander said to me, *"Lieutenant Zubrzycki, you are a bright boy; there is nothing more for you to do. Go to University."*

I knew by then that I could never return to Poland; my involvement in British Secret Operations and, especially, the SOE made it impossible. The new authorities in Poland would not look kindly on me so I went to The London School of Economics (LSE) in England. I was fortunate in that I applied before the main group of Poles arrived in England. I had my interview wearing my Polish uniform and they looked very kindly on me. The LSE had just moved back to London from its wartime location in Cambridge. I had no news about my family until December 1945. There was the usual 'invitation' from the British Government for all Poles to move to Poland, but I ignored that. During 1948-49, I studied for my Master's degree. I was married in wartime London in 1943 to a woman who had survived deportation to Siberia.

---

58   The First Polish Parachute Brigade was created in Scotland in September 1941. Their exclusive mission was to drop into occupied Poland in order to help liberate the country. They were under the command of the Polish Government-in-Exile until June 1944, when they were placed under British Command.

59   The Special Operations Executive, (SOE), the *Cichociemni*, (Polish: 'The Quiet and Dark Ones') was under command of Maj. Gen. Stanisław Sosnkowski, 1939-43, Deputy Commander-in-Chief of the Polish Armed Forces and, 1943-44, Commander-in-Chief of the Polish Armed Forces. This was a British World War II organization which conducted warfare by means other than direct military engagement. The SOE directly employed or controlled just over 13,000 people.

60   Warsaw Uprising: *Powstanie Warszawskie* (Polish), August 1 - October 5, 1944.

Kazimierz Szydło

b. 1922, Krosno

1940-46, Hungary, Lebanon, Palestine, Egypt, Iraq, Italy

1946-present, England

In 1939, I had just graduated from the Officer's Training School and was assigned to the 22nd Platoon which went to war. Unfortunately the War was a great disappointment to me. We had been told that we would reach Berlin within a very short period of time, instead of which we found ourselves having to retreat rapidly. Instead of using my equipment to defend Poland, we were told by the Polish Command to destroy everything as we were surrounded and we didn't want it to fall into the hands of the enemy. After this miserable campaign I returned home where I stayed until April 1940, waiting for an occasion to escape to the west and join the Polish Army. Our Government-in-Exile did well to support our spirits and there were many slogans, such as *"Nim słoneczko wyżej, nim Sikorski bliżej."*[61] The fact that we knew that there were the Polish Free Forces in France encouraged me, with my friend, to devise a way to escape through Hungary to join them. After crossing into Hungary, we were directed to Sprit in Yugoslavia, where we boarded a Polish ship, the *Warszawa*. There were already another five to six hundred volunteers there wanting to join the Polish Army in Marseilles, France. Unfortunately, the Polish ship which left for France on May 25, 1940, was redirected east to Beirut. The reason was the collapse of France and the establishment of the pro-Vichy Government which no longer permitted the formation of Polish troops on its territory. The French had been defeated. We hoped that the French forces would still offer some resistance to the Germans, which is why we were directed to Lebanon and Syria, both French Protectorates. The French Forces were told to dissolve all Polish forces.

In Lebanon those, like me, who had escaped from Poland, formed the independent *Karpatczycy*, a body of about 6,000 people. We thought that we would join the war effort and fight with the French. Unfortunately, the French Head of the Armed Forces, General Mitterrand, told our General Kopański that the French were done with fighting, that we should lay down our arms and go wherever we pleased. We told him that we would not lay down our arms and that we wanted to join the British Army in Palestine. The French agreed to our departure so, still dressed in French uniforms, we crossed into Palestine at the Golan Heights. Part of the *Brygada* went by truck, the other by train and, by the

---

61   *"Nim słoneczko wyżej, nim Sikorski bliżej"* (Polish): *"The higher the sun, the nearer is Sikorski"* Sikorski was the General of the Free Polish Armed Forces (1939-43) in France. In Polish, this slogan rhymes.

end of June, we found ourselves in Palestine. For the first night, my Division was in a camp on the shore of Lake Geneza, near Galilee. We knew only that Poland continued to be occupied by the Germans, and that people had lost their spirit because of the 'curse' in France, which was a shock to them as well as to us. The Maginot Line,[62] which was considered impregnable, was broken so quickly that we were all taken aback. We never expected France to collapse so quickly and morale was low. All we heard was that the Germans were having success. We did not know what we would be doing.

Figure 16. Kazimierz Szydło *(on the left)*, **Palestine, 1940**

However, once we joined the British in Palestine, our morale improved as we knew that the British would be resisting the Germans in a more effective manner than had the French. We knew nothing about the Soviet deportations; news did not spread quickly in those days. The Russians, of course, wanted to make sure that news of their behavior would not spread to the west. I had no contact with my family at this time; I once wrote from Hungary to Poland but heard nothing. It was only when we were in Palestine that I was able to re-establish contact. Once France had collapsed, the Italians decided to join the victorious Germans. Their forces crossed into Egypt, which was independent though it had an understanding with the British and had some initial successes, but the British stopped them. We were near Alexandria, building defenses for the city. The British started an offensive and took many Italians as POWs, as they offered little resistance. The German forces made a counter-offensive so the British had to withdraw to the west. The situation looked grave.

---

62 Constructed 1930-40, France's Maginot Line was a massive system of defenses built to defend the French from German attack. In theory, the defenses would hinder an invasion long enough for the French to fully mobilize their own army and act as a solid base from which to repel the attack. The Maginot Line failed to hold back the Germans in 1939.

This was the period of the desert battles in the west; it was a good thing that the battles were conducted there because civilians did not suffer. We were moved closer to Libya in September, 1941, where we played a supporting role. The Front was stabilized on the Egyptian-Libyan border. In September of 1941, we had to relieve the Australians who had been on the Front since the beginning of the War. On September 19, they left Tobruk by ship and our Brigade came from Alexandria to replace them. We were attacked by two planes that dropped torpedoes on us but missed. The shooting at these planes was intense; unfortunately, they were not hit. This incident has remained in my memory. We participated in the defense of Tobruk until December 9, 1941. Thank goodness this did not last long. We were mostly on patrol duty, anticipating an attack by Germans and Italians. In the meantime the British started

Figure 17. Passport belonging to Adjutant Jan Janota Bzowski, showing his movement through Romania (Roumania) and Hungary in September 1939

a new offensive and Tobruk was liberated. We joined the British Army, which followed the retreating German-Italian Army, until the end of January 1942.

In March, we returned to Palestine, where I first heard about the deportations from people who had arrived from Russia to join the newly-formed Polish Army. There were over 100,000 people from Russia while we were about 5,000. The freed deportees looked like beggars. They were skeletons, undernourished and dressed in rags. At this time, only the men capable of serving in the Army arrived; there were no women and children. In the end, they became the *Drugi Korpus* with over 160,000 people. From Palestine, we went to Iraq; we were told this was because the Allies were expecting the Germans to break through to the oil supplies in the Middle East so we had to protect the oil wells in Iraq. The second goal of our stay in Iraq was to give military training to those who had come from the Soviet Union, since the majority was untrained. There were no civilian women and children though there were women in the Army. Our goal was to train for fighting in mountainous terrain, to get us ready for battle in the Apennines, in Italy. We arrived in Italy at the end of December, 1943 and, in May 1944, fought at the Battle of Monte Cassino,[63] which was a turning point in the War. May 8, 1945, was the end of the War.

Wojsław Milan-Kamski

b. 1923, Lwów
1939-42, Romania, Iraq, Iran, Palestine
1942-45, Italy
1945-51, England
1951-present, USA

I was in the Cadet Corps just before the September Campaign of 1939. My family went on vacation to an estate in the Kresy region, as my father had recently been moved to Lwów to take up a command there. My sister and I were close to Czortków, near the Soviet border and, on September 17, the Soviets crossed into Poland. This was my first encounter with an occupying force. They marched towards Lwów as the Germans withdrew. We also moved to Lwów. My mother was dead and my father was appointed to lead the defense of the Romanian border against German attack. However, before he got to execute his task, the

---

63   Beginning of April, the Second Polish Corps was deployed to the front at Monte Cassino. The mountain was vital to the German defenses as it provided a fortified vantage point from which they could command the valley of the River Liri and the road to Rome. The offensive started one hour before midnight on May 11, 1944. In his Order of the Day, General Anders addressed his troops, *"Soldiers, the time to defeat our ancient enemy has come. With faith in God's justice, tonight at 11 o'clock, we are going into battle, beginning our last march to victory and on to our country, Poland."* Against all odds during the battle which lasted a week, the Poles beat the Germans and, on the morning of May 18, the Polish flag was hoisted over the ruins of the monastery. This was one of the most important battles of World War II.

Russians came, so my father and his men crossed into Romania[64] from where they planned to continue the fight against the Germans.

With Father in Romania and my sister and me in Lwów, I wanted to go into the Army; I felt that, as a cadet, I had sworn my loyalty to Poland and was ready. Many Poles were already in Romania; they had crossed the border in order to avoid being imprisoned by the Germans. On March 24, 1940, I crossed the 'green border', as it was known, into Romania. This was illegal but I found my father in an internment camp.

My sister remained in Lwów and was deported to Siberia. In the meantime, my father crossed into Turkey and got to Palestine where the Second Carpathian Brigade had formed after the fall of France. I was 16 at the time and was determined to join the Polish Army. My father said that, as long as I first completed my high school education, he would agree to this. I did, as an external student at the Polish High School Gymnasium in Tel Aviv. It was 1942. The Second Corps was being formed from the Poles who had been deported to the Soviet Union in 1940. The Polish officers had been murdered by the Soviets in the Katyń area in 1940, but many of the rank-and-file made it out of the Soviet Union. My sister had been deported at the age of 14. She survived all this by herself and was released under the so-called 'Amnesty'. Calling the permission we received to leave the Soviet Union an 'Amnesty,' added insult to injury. A 14-year-old girl had committed a criminal offence and was now receiving an 'Amnesty?' Nobody took notice of this nomenclature at the time. Civilians were sent south, to Kazakhstan, where thousands died as their most basic needs could not be met. My sister, fortunately, found the Polish Army; she was 16 at the time and was recognized by a family friend, Major (or Captain) Lewinski. It was a difficult situation but he took care of her.

I entered the Polish Army with my pilot's license as a volunteer in 1942, and asked to be allowed to join the Air Force or the Artillery. I was sent to the anti-aircraft artillery. The people from the Soviet Union were thin, starved, and ill. Young men volunteered to join the Polish Army and we had to get them back to health. The Second Corps was moved to Palestine while I was sent to the Officers' School. I wanted to repeat what my father had done; he had also been a volunteer and had attended the same school. I and the 40,000 men of the Second Corps fought at the Battle of Monte Cassino; 10% of them died; some Divisions fighting there lost as many as 30% of their men. Following my Commanding Officer's injury, I, the youngest in the Division, replaced him.

---

64   Hungary did not join the Axis until 1940 but, due to centuries of good relationships with the Poles, continued to provide a safe-haven for Polish troops. Romania declared its neutrality on September 1, and was therefore obligated to intern members of the Polish armed forces.

Józef Szkudłapski

b. 1925, Lwów

1940, deported to Russia

1942-43, Iran, Palestine, South Africa

1943-45, Scotland

1945-present, England

Figure 18. Józef Szkudłapski, England, c1945

We lived in Lwów. In 1939, when the War started, my father and I left to go west to join the Army. On the way, we heard that Russia had invaded Poland and, shortly after that, we were captured and taken to a POW camp in Staszków. We were forced to give up any arms we had and, also, my bicycle. At the end of October, they decided to release me because I was still a student; they also released some of the civilian women.

I reached Lwów; I remember eating cake in a café, but I don't remember how I paid for it. I went to a church to look for my friend. When I asked after him, people would not reply; this was not surprising as I looked terrible in a policeman's uniform, and I had pneumonia. I returned home and, as I was wearing my father's boots, my mother thought he was dead.

We were deported in 1940. My mother lost her head completely when they came for us. We got to the rail station at Jeworów and they took us to Russia. People called out, *"Look after yourselves!"* We arrived in a *sohoz*[65] and I worked on a combine-harvester; my younger brother tended cows while my mother and sister did not work. The winter was so bad; a woman who walked to get something from a neighbor did not return and her body was not found until the following spring.

---

65 In a *sohoz*, (Russian) workers were paid with money, not food, which was the case in a *kolkhoz* (Russian).

We got out after the Amnesty by bribing a train driver. My mother knew that we had to reach a large town in the south. In February 1942, I joined the Army. We slept in tents during the winter. We knew we were leaving and I wanted to go into communications which my older brother had joined in 1939; he had disappeared and I was hoping I could find out something about him. But, when I indicated my preference, I was told, *"You want to go into communications? I'm in the infantry and I'm still alive, so you are also going into the infantry."* My brother disappeared without trace. It was even difficult for a Polish soldier to cross the street as people would invite us into their homes. Yet there were many Germans and spies in the area who would try to find out where we were going and what plans the Polish Army had. We used to spread false rumor deliberately in order to confuse the Germans. We went to Krasnovodsk, then to Pahlevi,[66] in Persia. The conditions on the ship were terrible. Once we got there, we had to burn all our clothes. We slept on the beach. Many people died at this time from typhoid and starvation, and from eating food that they could not digest. Civilians were kept separate. Indians dug the toilets. We went to Palestine where I got malaria. I remember a man there who said, *"You and me, Catholic?"* and we conversed in Latin. The locals threw oranges at us when we arrived; oranges were cheaper than potatoes in Palestine. We had some contact with Polish civilians in Jerusalem whenever we went to the beach or shopping.

We were asked, *"Who wants to go to England?"* We all raised our hands. *"Who wants to steal horses?"* We all raised our hands. There were about 100 of us who were to be trained to parachute into Poland with supplies. My group left for England, via South Africa. We traveled on a Dutch ship on which the food was good. We were trained in South Africa and built up our health and strength.

2,000 of us sailed on the ship, *Queen Mary*, and reached Britain on a foggy day in April 1943. We went to Polmouth, near Stirling in Scotland. We continued the military education that had begun in Palestine. I was injured and could not join the First Polish Parachute Brigade. I was transferred to King's Langley, near London, where I worked as a telegraph operator, part of the so-called 'Sixth Division', making contact with Poland.[67] During the German occupation, we maintained contact with Poland; even during the Uprising, we facilitated communication between the participants as they had no means to manage it themselves.

---

66   Pahlevi/Pahlavi: known today as Bandar-e Anzali.

67   King's Langley was the headquarters of the Polish Resistance in England during the War, and was responsible for communications between the Government-in-Exile and the Resistance in Poland.

Henryk Franczak

b. 1918, Zagorzyce
1939-47, Scandinavia, Britain
1947-53, Pakistan
1953-2006, USA

When the War broke out I was a student at the Air Force Academy.[68] On the first day of the War, I woke to find bombs falling on our base. We were evacuated, and qualified pilots were moved to the east. When the Soviets invaded, about 70% of the personnel made their way, one way or another, to France. We got close to the Soviet border just as their army invaded. I got rid of my uniform; I was so darned lucky as, in one village, I was able to borrow clothes from the local peasants. I saw a truck with Soviet soldiers coming. It was after the harvest and the Soviet Army lived off the peasants. I could speak Russian so I asked one of the Soviet officers, *"Why did you do this to us?"* He said, *"We didn't invade you. We liberated you."* Apparently, I was very lucky because he could have had me shot straight away. He said, *"Don't worry about Germans. We will liberate Germany, France, and the whole world."*

After that, I had to decide what to do and I decided to go north to get to my home in Wilno. One day, there was a group of us from different services; from the Air Force, from the Army, even women, and the Russians surrounded us all and took us. They took all people of military age and loaded us on a train in cattle cars; we had no idea where we were being taken.

Figure 19. Henryk Franczak, England, 1940

---

68   Unpublished transcript of Helena Franczak Hayden interviewing her uncle, Henryk Franczak, January 2006, USA.

Figure 20. Polish pilots in England during World War II

After, maybe, 100 or 150 miles the train stopped and the guards opened up the doors. I looked around. I recognized the place as on a direct line from Wilno to Warszawa. We were to be transferred onto a different train as the Russian railway gauge was different to the rest of Europe. I looked young for my age and sneaked out. On the other part of the station was a regular passenger train which, I noticed, was about to move. I looked at my companion; he was a corporal and, when the guards weren't looking, we crept away. There were crowds of people on the platform and we just ran and jumped on the train. I had no idea where it was going but we were lucky not to have been caught by the Russian guards.

We sat down with the passengers. The conductor came in; of course, we had no tickets so we looked in our pockets for pieces of paper and gave them to the conductor. He was Polish, as was the rest of the train crew. He understood what we were doing and just clipped the pieces of paper and walked on.

Before they captured us, the Soviets were looking for watches; I was lucky because I had one so they bought it from me and I got some local currency. When we arrived in Wilno, we got on the bus and paid in *rubles* and went home. We rang the bell and our maid, Zosia, answered; she cooked us dinner. There was no one home except her as everybody was at work. My brother, Stasiek, and Dad were away. Apparently, they went to the estate that Dad was running for some wealthy man from Warszawa. That's where they were arrested, though they both managed to escape. They grew tobacco on the estate so, after their escape, they brought sacks of tobacco leaves home. We made money selling homemade cigarettes. The tobacco was raw and it was very strong. The Soviet soldiers loved it and would pay whatever price we asked.

My father was there in Wilno. Because the Soviets promised the Lithuanians they would look after their country, the Lithuanians voted 99.9% that they wanted to join the Soviet Union; but this was the result of rigged elections. Lithuania was a neutral country and there were many Poles there, yet international law required that neutral countries had to intern military personnel. The Lithuanian Army suspected we were military so my brother, Staś, and I contacted the British Embassy and told them that we wanted to join the Royal Air Force.

The officer at the Embassy knew that I was a cadet; he also knew Stasiek had a pilot's license. We wanted to take our third brother with us but he was not a pilot. Fortunately, the officer gave him documents that stated that he was also a pilot. However, there was a problem with the transport; a lot of our servicemen were crossing to Sweden, but Wilno was full of German spies. They warned that the next ship leaving would be sunk, so the transports stopped. Since they could not send us by sea, the British sent us by air; they engaged Scandinavian Airlines to transport us. On Christmas Eve, we landed in Stockholm, from where we went to London and then to France.

CHAPTER 4

The Warsaw Uprising
August 1 - October 5, 1944

Figure 21. Symbols of the Polish Underground[69]

The Uprising began at 5 PM on August 1, 1944 and was expected to last about a week.

- Warsaw's insurgents were an estimated 40,000 soldiers, including 4,000 women, and only enough weapons for 2,500 fighters. They were facing a German garrison 15,00 strong which grew to a force of 30,000 armed with tanks, planes and artillery.

- During the 63 days of the Uprising, an estimated 200,000 of Warsaw's inhabitants lost their lives. 80% of the buildings on the city's left bank were destroyed. After the suppression of the Uprising, all the city's civilians were rounded up and deported for slave labor in Germany and Austria. The Polish combatants were given military status and taken to POW camps in Germany.

---

69   *Left to right:* the symbol of the Polish Underground. The combined letters *'PW'* (Polish) for *Polska Walcząca:* Fighting Poland, *Wojsko Polskie:* Polish Army and *Powstanie Warszawskie:* Warsaw Uprising. The anchor is also a symbol of hope. The cartoon on the right symbolizes the death of the Nazis.

Lech Hałko

b. 1925, Warszawa
1944-45, Germany
1945-46, Czechoslovakia, Italy
1946-53, England
1953-present, Canada

Figure 22. Lech Hałko, Italy, 1945

In 1939, I was a 14-year-old boy living in Warszawa on a street that was then called 6ᵍᵒ Sierpnia; it no longer exists because the Communists changed its name to Nowowiejska.[70] Our house was bombed after the Uprising and never rebuilt. We had a large apartment with six rooms, but we also had a large family as some of those who lived with us had been expelled by the Germans from their homes in western Poland. My older brother was in the army and fought in Grodno but, after the surrender of Poland, he returned home. We were all involved in the Home Army, injured during the Uprising, sent to POW camps and, then, moved to North America. We could have escaped after the Uprising by pretending to be civilians; we decided not to do that as we were involved with the AK. We had to lay down our arms and walk to Ożarów where we were taken by train to Germany. As I lay down my arms, I saw out of the corner of my eyes that the Germans saluted. It was a very emotional and sad event.

On October 6, men and women were taken in separate trucks to Falling-bostel, Stalag XI-B, a POW camp. The women were separated by barbed wire from the men. *Wrześniowscy*[71] were also in this camp; they had been POWs since

---

70 *6ᵍᵒ Sierpnia* (Polish): 6ᵗʰ September, refers to the victory of the Poles against the Bolsheviks in the 1919-20 War, which the Soviet Union lost to Poland. *Nowowiejska* (Polish), literally translated, means 'new village'.

71 *Wrześniowcy* (Polish): Septemberians; soldiers who had been captured during the invasion of Poland in September 1939.

September, 1939, and had been supported by Red Cross parcels. When they saw our women, they went crazy, so we knew that ours would be well looked after. They had chocolates and cigarettes, all from the Swiss Red Cross.

In December 1944 my brother and I offered to go to work, because we wanted to escape. We worked in a mine in which the conditions were terrible. One of our friends was killed in a mine collapse and we decided it was time to escape. We first went by foot and then bought train tickets, though we only had money for less than 100 kilometers of travel. We had to keep changing trains, not knowing where we were going. Just before Christmas 1944, we were caught at the railway station in Brzeźno and imprisoned. My brother spoke some German and managed whereas I, because I could not find my German ID, was beaten unconscious since they thought I was a spy. They found my papers the next day and saw that we were POWs; after a couple of weeks we were taken to Muhlberg, Stalag IV-B. My brother, as an officer, had to serve his punishment for trying to escape whereas I, being rank-and-file, was not punished but sent to perform various types of manual work.

I decided to try to escape once more. Riding towards Poland I found myself in Germany and joined the Czech Partisans alongside whom I fought until the end of the War. I was in hospital, recovering from an injury when I heard from a nurse that the Russians had come into the area; I decided to escape again. With the cigarettes that I had been left by the Americans (General Patton had just liberated the area), I bought a motorbike and escaped to the west. Of course, I had adventures; when the Russians stopped me, they were willing to let me go on, but the Americans refused to allow me to cross into their zone. My brother was in Muhlberg and found himself in Paris after the War. He found out that the women from the Uprising were located in a camp on the Dutch border, and we both found our way to Oberlangen Stalag 6C.[72] From there we decided to go to Italy to join our uncle, Felix Konarski (who wrote the song '*Czerwone Maki na Monte Cassino*[73]), and General Anders' Army.

---

72   In October 1944 Oberlangen Strafflager VIC was struck off the POW camp register on account of its totally inadequate living conditions. Therefore the International Red Cross in Geneva was unaware of the fact that women POWs were later interned there.

73   During the Battle of Monte Cassino, the mountainous terrain was densely covered with red poppies at the peak of their bloom. These poppies became a main inspiration for Felix Konarski, the contemporary Polish poet, songwriter, and cabaret performer, to compose a combative, emotional song, *Czerwone Maki na Monte Cassino* (Polish): *Red Poppies at Monte Cassino*, which tells about red poppies that are deeper in color because they were nourished with Polish blood. Born January 9, 1907, in Kiev, he died August 9, 1991 in Chicago. He was due to visit a liberated Poland the next day.

> *"In the summer of 1944 the people welcomed Soviet victories and German re-treats, and expected a general rising to break out and, hence necessarily, Polish-Soviet collaboration. The tragedy of Warszawa and the perfidy of Russian policy radically changed these views and, by January 1945, the general view was that the Russo-German conflict was no business of the Poles. The rape of women and the looting of Polish property convinced people that it was only a change of occupation for the worse."*
>
> **Węgierski, (Ex-POW)**[74]

Hanka Piotrowska Orłowska

b. 1929, Warszawa

1944-45, Germany

1945-46, Italy

1946-present, England

In 1939, our house on ul. Sienna was bombed so we had to move to a small apartment elsewhere in Warszawa. The house had been beautiful, with seven rooms; it was left to me by my godparents, as they had no children, when they emigrated to the USA. We had a home help, Leonka, who was killed by the Germans. My brother was older and I didn't know much about what he was up to. My uncles, two of my mom's three brothers, were hanged two days after the Germans invaded; one was 31, and the other, 32 years old.

Three weeks before the Uprising, my brother made me swear that I would not tell anyone what he was about to tell me, that he was part of the Underground. He got me to get down on my knees and swear to the Virgin Mary that I would not tell anyone. He wanted me to join him in the Underground. He told me that three paramedics had been killed by the Germans and now they were short of paramedics. The hospital was on ul. Pańska. He taught me what to do with injuries. Someone took a picture of me which recently surfaced; an injured

---

74   Interrogation of British Junior NCOs and Privates (ex-POWs) evacuated through Russia and arriving in the UK, May 7, 1945. (1945). HS4/21, M19/MS/BM/173/3, National Archives, England.

soldier had buried photographs that were taken when the Germans captured us. On September 1, I was supposed to report at 4:30 PM on ul. Filtrowa. However, since the shooting had started earlier in some places, I couldn't get there and stayed in the hospital on ul. Żelazna as a paramedic and, then, at the hospital on ul. Pańska. I was with the wounded all the time. I also worked on ul. Sienna and ul. Grzybowska, always with the wounded.

After fighting for two months, we had to surrender to the Germans. I came out of the Uprising and had to go on foot to Ożarów,[75] and waited two days for a train. We slept on a concrete floor in an enormous hall. From Warszawa, we were taken to Germany. We were first at a camp in Lansdorf then, after three weeks, were taken to Muhlberg, then, to Saxony to work in a munitions factory. At the end, we were taken to the women's POW camp in Oberlangen.[76]

We were in camps for seven months. We were to be shot only if we tried to escape. I participated in the Uprising so I was classified as a POW. We were always hungry in Oberlangen. It was a very heavy camp as the work was hard and the food was terrible; coffee for breakfast, dirty water with something in it for lunch at noon and, then, a loaf of German bread for us 11 girls in the evening, and a spoon of margarine and sugar; that was our food for 24 hours. We'd put stale bread into water to make it edible. We were always terribly hungry. We received hot water once a day, in the morning, which we used to wash our hair.

We didn't know the War was coming to an end. It was amazing what happened; we were taken, as usual, to dig for potatoes. At noon we had our lunch break. All of a sudden one of the girls cried out, *"Those are not German tanks!"* The girls started calling out in all languages. Before the tanks reached the camp a man came on a motorbike and said, *"Oh rany, ile tu bab jest!"*[77] Then we realized this was a Polish man and that Polish troops were coming. I cannot describe the feeling we experienced. We kissed their feet. These were our Polish boys. While the Polish soldiers had been in Holland, a German woman told them that there was a very large Polish camp in this location. We cried so much. The soldiers were also very happy that these were Poles. They brought food and clothing for the children who had been born in the camp and, then, had to leave. About one-and-a-half hours after the arrival of the first Polish

---

75   The distance from central Warszawa to Ożarów was about 12.5 miles.

76   Lansdorf, Stalag VIII-B, later renamed Stalag 344; Muhlberg, Stalag IV-B; Oberlangen, Stalag VI-C, November 1944, 1,721 Polish women officers and soldiers from the Warsaw Rising arrived.

77   *"Oh rany, ile tu bab jest!"* (Polish): *"Oh Jesus, look how many women there are here!"*

soldiers, General Maczek[78] arrived. We stood to attention as the Germans were taken away. The camp consisted of 12 barracks and a small hospital. The Polish soldiers stayed in the barracks and we were moved into the local convent where they established a school for us. I remember my friend, Halina, was only 12 years old when she saved the lives of seven of our boys. Halina, (a.k.a. 'Tomek'),[79] was very small and could get into places where others couldn't. She was very brave and never cried, yet when she got a letter from her mother in Poland asking her to come home, she cried and cried, saying that she wanted to return. *"I want to return to my mommy,"* she said. We told her not be so stupid. She and another girl, foolishly wearing English Army uniforms, got on a ship bound for Poland; Halina was shot when she disembarked in Gdynia. She was 14 years old then; she was a child so, of course, she wanted to return home to her mom. Some girls managed to return to Poland, but not Tomek. She was such a great girl.

Figure 23. Halina, pseudonym 'Tomek', Germany, 1946

---

78   General Stanisław Maczek. After the fall of Poland in October 1939, General Maczek led the battered troops of his 10th Cavalry (Mechanized) Brigade to safety in Hungary and, then, to Romania. He then made his way to France and, before the fall of that country to the Germans, was evacuated to Britain. With scattered remnants of Polish units he formed the First Armored Division of the Polish Army-in-Exile in February, 1942, in Duns, Scotland. General Maczek was the commanding officer of all Polish forces in the United Kingdom, 1945-47.

79   Tomek: her pseudonym, used in the Resistance.

Most of us wanted to go to England. Some went to school in Italy, others to Belgium; some remained in Germany. Some of the girls married Polish servicemen. I had nobody left in Poland as my mother was killed by a bomb on September 11, 1944. She always went into the basement during a bombing but, this time, she stayed on the third floor. I don't know what got into her head. I had just come home to see what was going on because I knew that the bombing was close. The bomb had destroyed that part of the house where my mom was. I found her torn to shreds by the bomb. I buried her by the house at 2 PM. I wanted to tell my brother that our mother had died. I couldn't walk normally because I would be caught and shot, so I crawled on my stomach all the way to the Aleje Jerozolimskie. I met my brother's Commandant on the way and told him that I was going to see my brother. He told me that I had better go quickly because my brother had been seriously injured; he died that day. Many years later I was due to give birth to my daughter on September 11, instead of which she came one day later.

I started smoking cigarettes during the Uprising and have been smoking ever since. I met my husband shortly after I arrived in England and married him when I was 18. My husband could, also, not return to Poland as he had been in the Underground since 1939.

"The attitude of the people towards Russia was more favorable in 1944. The arrest of the Russian advance in the Warszawa sector during the Rising was regarded as a betrayal, and the persecution of the AK members who had materially facilitated the Russian advance, caused widespread indignation Finally, the behavior of the Soviet troops towards the Poles was worse than could be expected in a conquered enemy country. Red Army soldiers violate women, and do not hesitate to shoot in case of resistance. They enter Polish houses at all times of the day or night, and take whatever they want, whether women or property, at the muzzle of a Tommy gun. There are many houses in western Poland from which the Polish occupiers had been ejected by the Germans, and such houses were consistently destroyed by the Russians, although they were told they are Polish property."

Bieda, (AK member)[80]

---

80   Testimony of Węgierski & Bieda. *Warszawa Uprising, Polish Civil Population, Jawiszowice, Maydanek, Ravensbruck Concentration Camps.* HS4/21 File Number Special Operations Executive, Poland 101. Box number 6162, p.11. 1945. National Archives, England.

Andrzej Sławinski
b. 1929, Lodowa
1944-45, Germany
1945-46, Italy
1946-present, England

At the age of 13, I became involved in the Resistance as a member of the Scouts. At the age of 15, I graduated to level two, or 'Battle School,' which made me a full member of the Home Army. My father opened a shop and, like everyone else, we were involved in some black market dealings. I worked as a shop assistant for a while. It was a very busy time as, during the afternoons, I attended the secret grammar school and, in the evenings, went to the secret meetings of the Home Army.

My parents knew I was involved in something but I didn't want to tell them what this was. My father eventually found out on the very first day of the Uprising. As a member of the Home Army we were engaged in minor acts of sabotage, such as writing anti-Nazi slogans and hanging up posters. On the morning of the Uprising I was given white and red arms bands with the Polish Eagle, the number of our platoon and the letters 'WP', *Wojsko Polskie*, the Polish Army. I was supposed to go around Warszawa and deliver these arm bands to my section and tell them where we were meeting for the Uprising. Now I think about it, it was so stupid; why not distribute them when we met later? There were so many patrols and I could have easily been caught.

Before I left, my father came home and I thought I should tell him what I was doing and say "*goodbye*." He did not believe me at first as he said that I was too young to be involved. However, when I showed him what I had in my package he realized that I was telling the truth.

Bolesław Biega
b. 1922, Warszawa
1944-46, Germany
1946-50, England
1950-present, USA

During the Uprising itself, as very young soldiers, we could not be on the front lines but, instead, were at the barricades; eventually, we got weapons and I guarded a building with the small pistol I was given. During the Uprising, I managed to see my father and mother on a couple of occasions; I received a six-hour pass from the Unit, so I had a bath and changed my clothes, but a meeting was not possible because the Germans infiltrated my parents' district and they had to move, and I no longer knew where they were, or if they were dead or alive. They, too, did not know what had happened to me, and whether I was dead or alive. I found out, much later, that my father had been wounded and transported out of Warszawa and had gone to live in a small village outside of the city.

I was an Army Cadet when the War broke out. In the face of the advancing German Army we marched east but, with the invasion by the Russians in the east, we had to march back to the west. My family endured the siege of Warszawa without any serious injury; our apartment was only slightly damaged. We knew about the deportations to Germany. It was dangerous to go out on the street as you might get caught in a *łapanka*. Those of us who were in German-occupied Poland found out about the Soviet deportations when the first wave of refugees from eastern Poland reached the west. People were crossing the border between German-occupied and Soviet-occupied Poland because they believed it would be safer in the German-occupied zone. Of course, once they got there they found out that it was just as dangerous, but the perception at the time was that it was safer under German occupation than Soviet.

The Germanization of children was primarily taking place in western Poland, which had been incorporated into the German Reich. To those of us living in central Poland, these policies were not so obvious, though there was pressure on people with German names to declare themselves as *Volksdeutsche*. My wife Lili's family had a German name, Treutler, and a lot of pressure was put on them to declare themselves to be German. They refused.

Figure 24. The marriage of Bolesław Biega and Lili Treutler, Warszawa, Poland, 1944

Danuta Banaszek Szlachetko

b. 1929, Warszawa
1944-45, Germany
1945-46, Italy
1946-present, England.

In 1939, I was 10 years old and living in Warszawa at Nowy Świat, nr. 19. I remember the Germans bombing the city and destroying our homes and how we used to flee from building to building in search of safety. When we could no longer stay in Warszawa we moved to our house in Laski, where we lived for a year and I attended school with my sister. We returned to Warszawa in the spring of 1940 and, like everyone else, tried to build a life there. Because our building was bombed we moved to Nowy Świat nr. 57. Everything was badly bombed so the Germans allowed us to live wherever we wanted, and we renovated the apartment at our own expense.

**Figure 25. Danuta Banaszek Szlachetko,
pseudonym 'Wira,' Warszawa, Poland, 1944**

My parents were separated so I lived with my mother and sister. Women did not work in those days but my mom had to do what she could to earn money; she used to go out of town to get food and then sell it in Warszawa. Sometimes, the Germans caught her but she kept on trying. She even took me once so that I would see how it was done. It was terrible; I was so frightened. We had to travel by train at night to buy the goods in the villages outside Warszawa. On the return journey, the train stopped at every station and we were in constant fear of being caught by the Germans who searched us and would take away everything that we were carrying. The time I went with my mom we were not stopped. Also, there was a curfew so we had to be careful when we traveled; it was so hard for my mother.

My sister and I attended school in Warszawa: I was enrolled in a grammar school on ul. Bagatela, while my sister was at a technical school on ul. Królewska. In the summer of 1942, the Germans closed my school[81] and it was hard for me to find another school as each already had its quota of students. Fortunately, a priest helped me obtain admission to a private school where I could continue with a general education. However, as this school was full, I spent the first year being home-schooled with the help of an older student, Krysia Biernacka. She recruited me into the *Szare Szeregi*, the Scouts,[82] a patriotic organization whose existence was forbidden by the Germans. My sister continued going to her vocational school. My school was officially a fashion school; when the Germans came to visit we would pretend to be working on hats.

I had joined the Underground Movement two years prior to the Warsaw Uprising and was a dispatch courier. The couriers distributed various leaflets and information and pasted them to walls wherever they could. In this way, we kept the civilian population informed and made it clear to the Germans that there was a functioning Underground organization. This was, like other tasks, dangerous work as you sometimes had to travel by tram with a bag full of literature. Fortunately, the Germans always had the first coach to themselves and the rest of us were obliged to stand wherever we could find space. Sometimes there were traps to catch us but, usually, when we were forewarned, we got off the tram and fled.

The house in which we had lived was destroyed in 1939, so it was a good hiding place and I used it for my organization to hide our materials such as leaflets and books. This hiding place was discovered by the caretaker who told my mother. Normally a strict woman, she broke down and asked me, *"Dearest child, what are you doing?"* The day before the outbreak of the Warsaw Uprising, the city was very quiet. I went out on to the street with my sister who said, *"If you belong and want to go, then go, I will stay with Mom."* So I left the house, and my sister returned home. Even though I was missing, my mom took my sister to Laski, a village west of Warszawa, but returned the next day. My aunt came with her, having left her own children in Laski. Since I had run away to join the Uprising, my mother decided to return to Warszawa. Both she and my sister died during the Uprising, but I survived.

We all had our designated places to be at 5 PM on August 1, 1944. At

---

81   The Germans only allowed Polish children and youth to obtain vocational training in order to make them better workers for the future new German state.

82   *Szare Szeregi* (Polish): the Grey Ranks, the Polish Scouting Movement which had grey uniforms. It was part of the Polish Underground.

the beginning of the Uprising, I worked as a courier at the post office on ul. Świętokrzyska. After the attainment of the main post office on Plac Napoleona I was moved there as it became the center for the Uprising's mail. After that, I was transferred to the 'Bradla' Company. Then, I was sent to the Powiśle neighborhood. I had a special pass which enabled me to move about freely and have everyone assist me with my work. Then things went wrong because the house in which I was staying (there were 18 of us in the house; 16 boy soldiers and two female couriers), was hit by a bomb and several of the boys were killed. After this shock I lost my memory for a long time. Even now I can't remember much about this episode. However, I do remember that we were always very hungry and, after there was nothing left to eat, we caught dogs to cook as all the dead horses had been taken. We had to eat dog meat in order to survive so I remember how dog meat tastes. Then, when there were no more dogs, we ate cats and I remember, to this day, how horribly sweet cat meat tasted. Those were difficult times.

CAPTIVITY

CHAPTER 5

Nazi Oppression

Figure 26. *"Work will set you free"*
Entrances to *(from left to right)* **Sachsenhausen, Dachau,
Oświęcim, and Tereisenstadt concentration camps**

Germanization[83]

Halina Bartold Poślinska

b. 1934, Grodzisko

1944-51, Germany

1951-present, USA

Figure 27. Halina Bartold Poślinska's German identification card[84]

I wanted to go to summer camp in the Krynica area for two weeks and my mom let me go. It was 1944. On the journey home, the train detoured and took us to an unfamiliar town. That's where the Germans divided us, meaning that they picked out the children they wanted to re-educate, and those they didn't want. I don't know what happened to the ones they did not want; I doubt they were

---

83   An estimated 50,000 children were kidnapped in Poland, the majority taken from orphanages and foster homes in the annexed lands. Gumkowski, J. & Leszczynski, K., (1961), *Poland Under Nazi Occupation*. Warsaw, Polonia Publishing House, estimate the figure to have been as high as 92,000 children. Infants born to Polish women deported to Germany as farm and factory laborers were usually taken from their families and subjected to Germanization. If unions between forced laborers resulted in a pregnancy, and a 'racially valuable' child might not result, the mother was compelled to have an abortion.

84   The card states that she has *"blonde hair and grey-green eyes, a normal nose, a light complexion and an oval-shaped face".*

returned to their parents. I was still ten years old, (I didn't turn 11 until December), and was one of the oldest children. Some of the younger ones were crying and I tried to calm them on the train because we could see they weren't taking us home.

Here, everything was in German; the school was in German and we weren't allowed to speak Polish. We were taught in German; how to sit at the table, how to eat, and how to behave. There was nothing to discuss. They didn't tell us why we were there or what would happen to us, only that we were now to be Germans. I don't know what happened to the adults who were with us in the camp. I don't remember them being with us on the train.

I remember the sirens at night and having to hide in a shelter. During the War we were moved from camp to camp; it was only after the War that they gave us up for adoption. I remember one little boy died on the train; he had leukemia. After my departure, my mother and her brother (who was four years her junior) were taken to a labor camp. We were not allowed to write but, sometimes, I posted a letter in secret. I wrote home; my mother was not there, but she wrote to our neighbor just in case there was any word from me. That's how we kept contact, though we were all moved from camp to camp.

After the War, an older family wanted to adopt me; they didn't harm me but they weren't good either. I kept on writing to my mom. I was on the Russian side and my mom was on the British. She was in a DP camp and told the authorities where I was but nobody wanted to help her; they told her that there was no hope of getting me and that she should leave things alone. But my mom never gave up. There were Polish Missions whose job it was to persuade people to return to Poland. She went to one of these Missions and found a good man who agreed to help her. She knew roughly where I was and they found me; the Germans had to return me. I was told that my mom was in Warszawa and that I had to go there to her. The German woman was crying, *"Who will embroider my table-cloth?"* But the Missions also existed in various places in Germany. They kept on telling me that I was going to Warszawa to my mom.

I was in Berlin, waiting for a transport to Poland but, rather than getting to the station, they took me by car and told me that Mom was not in Poland but elsewhere, in a DP camp in Germany. They took me to the Russian Zone, though my mom was in the British Zone. On the border, the captain told me to say that I was his daughter. We got there very late. The captain's wife looked after me and gave me a bath. This was Saturday evening. The next day was sunny and they were going for a ride. It was the spring of 1946. We drove and drove and he said that we'd go and visit my mom. We got to the camp and the loudspeaker announced that my mom had to come to the office. They did not tell her why. I sat and waited for her, very frightened that she would be angry and that it had all been my fault, as I had wanted to go to this summer camp. The staff offered me chocolate but I didn't want anything. I was afraid of my mom. When she came in and saw me, she started hugging me and there was great joy.

All the younger children were given away to Germans; one of the girls was given to the baker, another child to the butcher. Not everybody found their children as they didn't know where to look because we were constantly moved from camp to camp. My mother was a widow and the men chased her; she did remarry but not from love. My dad was her cousin; he had already been engaged for five years but when he saw her at a family gathering he fell in love with her. He chased her; he drank a lot and she told him that she was scared of drunks. He promised to stop and didn't drink until the wedding day. Then he started drinking and didn't stop; he died from alcoholism at the age of 38. He told my mother that if she didn't marry him, he'd kill both himself and her. When she was still single, my mom used to say that her husband could beat her three times a day, as long as he was handsome. How she cried when she remembered these words while she was being beaten. The second husband was very helpful in the camp, but not good-looking and he turned out to be no better than my father; he wasn't a drunk but was still cruel. He used to chase me and I had to run from him. I couldn't tell my mom about this. I could never go to her to tell her anything. When they got to the USA, he found a mistress and they separated.

Eventually, I got work in a Siemens factory on a production line making telephones. I went to school but did not complete high school. As for the DP camps; I can't complain. UNRAA[85] tried hard to help the children and give them extra food. And then you could emigrate. We tried to go to Australia but were not accepted. My mom never thought of returning to Poland. The Polish Mission had told her to go to Poland and they would bring me there. She said that they should bring the child to her and then she'd go back to Poland. When the captain delivered me to her he whispered that she should not return. She had two sisters in Poland but did not know what had happened to them. We tracked down her sisters, just before 1970, when we were visiting Poland, and this was by accident; a friend had a visitor from Poland from my aunt's town and she said that she knew the family. The man was a baker, in Busków Zdrój. The second sister stayed in Germany.

I have never met anyone who was kidnapped for Germanization and was, eventually, reunited with their family.

---

85   UNRAA: The United Nations Relief and Rehabilitation Administration, 1943-47, was created to provide economic assistance to European nations after World War II and to repatriate and assist the refugees who came under Allied control. In 1947 it was replaced by the IRO, International Refugee Organization which, by 1948, was caring for 643,000 displaced persons.

"*My North American friends are constantly surprised when they learn that, not being a Jew, I was imprisoned in German Concentration Camps. One of my Canadian friends, having learned that I had been in a German Concentration Camp and knowing me as a Christian, thought that I must have been one of the guards there.*

Every time, then, when my North American friends express their surprise, I feel obliged to explain the enormously complex situation that prevailed in German-occupied Europe. I wish I did not have to do it, for when trying to clear up their minds, I have to be extremely careful lest my attempt at clarification detracts from the supreme suffering of the Jewish people of the Second World War. But in every Camp in which I was imprisoned, the Jewish prisoners constituted a fraction of the total number of inmates. To say that the Jews were the only race which suffered the German persecutions during the Second World War, to say that the Concentration Camps were created for the Jews alone, is a gross injustice to the millions of those who suffered and perished."

Stanisław Sagan[86]

86   Sagan, S., op. cit.

Captivity: *"Work will set you free"*

Nazi Concentration, POW, and Labor Camps

**Figure 28. Location of Concentration, POW, and Labor
Camps, and Slave Labor assignments**

"Criteria under the German Foundation Act

*The condition for payment in the slave labour category is that one must have
been detained in a concentration camp, a ghetto or other place of confinement
under the German Foundation Act. Alternatively, the conditions for payment
in the forced labour category are that one must have been deported into the
German Reich or a German occupied area across 1937 borders, subjected to
forced labour and held in prison-like or similar extremely harsh living conditions."* [87]

---

87   *'Notice of rejection of claim for slave or forced labour during the Nazi Regime'* from
the International Organization for Migration, (IOM), German Forced Labour Compensation Programme, to Joseph Wardzala. IOM Claim Number: 1101150, 20 December 2004, date of receipt of Claim: 07-06-2001.

Józef Wardzala
b. 1923, Śmigno
1941-50, Germany
1950-present, USA

Figure 29. Józef Wardzala, Warszawa, Poland, 1939

I was caught delivering food to a Jewish friend in April 1941. I had escaped arrest twice before but, this time, I was captured in Warszawa. I traveled for two days in a cattle wagon to a forced labor camp, Braunschweig, near Hanover, Germany, to build bunkers and air-raid shelters. We were housed in a camp behind barbed wire. Every day, they took us by trucks to work which was very hard; 12 to 14 hours a day with very meager food. On one occasion, I was suspended horizontally above the floor of my interrogation cell, with my hands tied behind my back; my hands were pulled one way while my legs were pulled in the opposite direction; the pain was overwhelming. We also suffered British and American bombing.

I was in this camp for four years, until liberation by the US 9th Army in 1945, when the forced labor camp was transformed into a Displaced Persons camp. The Americans did not allow us to leave the camp. I stayed there until I got a US visa in 1950. We were in the English Zone; the Americans had moved further south. It was hard to move outside this area.

In June 2001, I submitted a second claim to the International Organization for Migration, the German Forced Labour Compensation Programme, and requested compensation for my four years of suffering. My claim was rejected for a second time as, I suppose, it did not meet the criteria for eligibility.

Bożenna Urbanowicz Gilbride

b. 1933, Leonówka

1943-46, Germany

1946-present, USA

In 1943, everything we knew as our peaceful life changed to a life we were afraid of living. Parents[88] told us children nothing because it was dangerous for children to know very much. The Ukrainian Nationalist Organization, known by the initials UPA, was collaborating with the Germans in cleansing our area of Jews, Poles and Ukrainians who did not agree with their policies. The UPA burned and butchered most of the inhabitants of our village. Next morning, the Germans rounded up all the survivors of the UPA massacre and marched us to Równe railway station and we were all deported in cattle trucks to Germany for slave labor. We traveled for two or three days, often stopping and standing on the tracks for hours. The doors were never opened. Sanitary conditions were non-existent, so everyone did what nature demanded, right where we were. Most of us had little or no food, so hunger and thirst became our biggest problem. This was August, 1943, and I was 9 years old.

We finally arrived in Germany; the door of our truck was opened and we were ordered out. I glanced back and noticed some older people still asleep on the floor. Later, I heard that they had died. This scared me and I began to think a lot about what might be in store for us. We entered the stall shower; the parents huddled us around them as we waited in silence. I was scared. When the water came we stayed in a huddle until it stopped. It was very quick. Then, we had to stand in front of huge air ducts to be dried. Again, there was a terrible stillness among the adults; when the air was finally turned on, there was a gasp of relief as if they hadn't expected it. The children knew nothing. We simply observed in fear.

One day, after the bombing had torn down a fence, I saw a garbage dump and thought it could contain scraps of food. I sneaked in on all fours, hoping not to get caught. I found apple and potato peels. Being so hungry, I quickly ate the apple peels. I began to gather the potato peels into my skirt and, when I looked up, I saw a house high above the dump with a chandelier lit up. Then I saw a reflection of myself, digging for food in the garbage.

Sometime in 1947-48, after we had already come to the USA, we found out that our mother survived the concentration camps and was searching for us in

---

88   In 1941, under the Soviet occupation in eastern Poland, Bożenna's father had been arrested for hiding Jews on their farm.

Poland.[89] I began writing very emotional letters asking many questions. I sent pictures of us to show her how we had grown up since the last time she had seen us in 1944. My questions were always left unanswered and I imagined it was painful for her to write about her experiences in the camps and her current life in Communist Poland. Only in 1957, after we were reunited in America, did I learn she could not answer all my questions as it was very dangerous for her to complain about life as it was in Poland. She was hoping to, eventually, join us in the USA.

Figure 30. Bożenna Urbanowicz Gilbride *(second row, center),*
Labor Camp nr. Chemnitz, Germany, 1944

She had been sent to concentration camp at Ravensbruck where she was sterilized, then transferred to Gross-Rosen. She tried to escape from Poland to join us in America. She was captured and told that she could not leave the country because she had a prison record. When she finally arrived in America, we had not seen each other for 13 years.

Our maternal grandmother starved to death as a slave laborer to a German farmer and is buried in an unmarked grave in Germany. A baby boy was born to an aunt who went with us in 1943. It was her first child and the Germans took the baby from her and used it for blood transfusions for the Germany military. He, too, is in an unmarked grave.

In my American high school, my American teachers treated all the students who survived the War, be they Jew or Christian, with great compassion. I never knew that there was a difference between us. It was a wonderful feeling

---

89   Bożenna's mother had been moved to another camp.

knowing that I was not the only one that had such tragic experiences during the War. Yet, in May 2003, I delivered my resignation[90] to the National Polish American-Jewish American Council (NPAJAC), of which I had been a member for about seven years.

My Permanent Recurring Nightmare

"I am ten years old and alone, running away from the Nazis. They are gaining on me, but there is no place for me to hide. I try to dig a deep hole and hide in it. I dig with my fingers. I can almost feel the dirt under my fingernails. I dig faster and faster, but they are getting closer and closer. I finally bury myself, head first. I hear them above, looking for me by sticking their bayonets into the ground. Swoosh. Swoosh. I can hear them coming closer and closer. I then realize that my feet are sticking out above the ground and they will find me. And then I wake up. In a month or so, the dream will be back."

Bożenna Urbanowicz Gilbride

---

90   It stated: *"I can no longer serve as a member of an organization that excludes five million people as victims of the Holocaust."* On March 18, 2003, Urbanowicz Gilbride received a letter from the Council stating, *"That definition* [of the Holocaust], *in its specificity, recognizes the reality of the differences between the treatment of Jews and non-Jews under the Nazi occupation of Poland."* It adds, *"This definition is a critical and central part of the belief system of the Jewish community and the Council has always and still does accept it."* That letter was in response to a November 18, 2003, presentation *"Teaching the Holocaust in USA"* given by Urbanowicz Gilbride and referring to herself as a Polish Catholic Holocaust survivor and what she had learned in the past 13 years of teaching about the Holocaust in schools, temples, churches and universities in USA and abroad. Urbanowicz Gilbride says, *"The body of my presentation was dismissed as if, by saying that I am a Catholic Holocaust survivor, everything I said is invalid."* After reading her resignation at the Council meeting, Rev. John Pawlikowski, NPAJAC member of the U.S. Holocaust Memorial Museum (USHMM), responded to her *"... that the USHMM recognizes only the six million Jews as victims of the Holocaust. The five million others have a 'special place' in the Museum." CATHOLIC BREAKS WITH POLISH-JEWISH DIALOGUE GROUP* New York (PMN). http://www.sfpol.com/holocaust.html

Peter Tatrzyński Fleming

b. 1913, Łódź

1939-47, Germany

1947-present, England

At the age of 18, I volunteered to join the Artillery and moved to the town of Włodzimierz Wołyński. After one year, I was moved back to Łódź, to the *10 Półk Krajowskiej Artilerji Letkiej*,[91] first, as a cadet and, then, as an officer. When the War broke out I was mobilized and, on the fifth day of the War, was taken prisoner by the Germans near Sieradz, on the river Warta. I spent the remainder of the War in POW camps.

There were various camps where you were placed according to rank. The Germans were rather snobbish so, being an officer, I must say that I was treated well. Not many people know that. The first camp was Itsehore, in northern Germany, near the Danish border. It was then that I decided that I would never return to Poland but emigrate elsewhere as soon as I got the chance. We had access to books so I would look at maps and think of where I could go. I had contact with my family in Poland every 30 days, when there was a special POW post. My family was in Łódź. I had three sisters who, towards the end of the War, were forced to dig defenses against the Russians. I learned German in this camp; this proved to be very useful later. The man who taught me was a Polish officer who spoke German; it turned out that he was collaborating with the Germans and reporting to them everything that was being said in the camp. When I discovered this I stopped talking to him. Some of our Polish friends, the officers, decided to punish him for being an informer and beat him up very badly. Later, I was told that some of the Polish officers had killed him.

We were allowed to have German papers so were well-informed as to the progress of the War though, of course, the reporting was very biased. However, if you read between the lines you could tell that the Russians were making progress. I subscribed to the *Hamburg Daily*. We had a sense that the War was coming to an end; I learned German so I could read German manuals in order to learn Spanish to help me move to Chile after the War. By the end of the War I was fluent.

I was in Sandbostel, Lubeck, and Gross Born. Towards the end of the War, while I was in Lubeck, the Russians and Germans were fighting and one of the prisoners the Germans took was Stalin's son, Yakov. When they realized they had his son, they thought that they had an important prisoner and that they would try to exchange him for a German General. Stalin responded that he no longer regarded Yakov as his son because he should not have allowed himself to be taken

---

91   *10 Półk. Krajowskiej Artilerji Letkiej* (Polish): 10th Light Artillery Platoon.

as a prisoner-of-war, and that he should have committed suicide. The Germans realized he was of no value so they put him aside in Lubeck where I was; they really didn't know what to do with him. They couldn't put him in the Russian POW camp because the Russian soldiers would have murdered him; since Stalin had not signed the Geneva Convention,[92] the Germans treated the Russian prisoners terribly; they starved them. So Yakov finished up in Lubeck.

Yakov did not speak Polish and I did not speak Russian; however, there were 12 of us to a room and some of the Polish officers did speak Russian. We invited Yakov to our room for a cup of coffee to discuss things and I found myself in the position of discussing politics with Stalin's son. We discussed what would happen to Poland after the War, as the Russians were gaining the upper hand. I remember him telling me that, in his opinion, Poland should become a Russian republic. I didn't respond. He knew that his father did not want to trade him for a German POW in Russia. In fact, after the War, Stalin wanted to find out what happened to him, but Yakov had committed suicide because his father had rejected him. He threw himself at the barbed wire surrounding his camp, knowing that he would be shot.[93]

At the end of the War, we were marched from Gross Born westwards, as the Russians were advancing.[94] We started in the middle of January; 5000 of us walked for 90 days in very deep snow. When the snow melted, two months later, we had to march through mud and survive on two potatoes a day. Three months later, there were only 500 of us left. We were evacuated through the country roads, because the main roads were reserved for the army. We started

---

92 Under article 82 of the Geneva Convention (1929), signatory countries were supposed to give POWs of all signatory and non-signatory countries the rights assigned by the Convention. During the War, the International Committee of the Red Cross, (ICRC), failed to obtain an agreement with Nazi Germany about the treatment of detainees in concentration camps and it eventually abandoned applying pressure in order to avoid disrupting its work with POWs. The ICRC also failed to develop a response to reliable information about the extermination camps and the mass killing of European Jews. This is still considered the greatest failure of the ICRC in its history.

93 Yakov Iosifovich Dzhugashvili, (1907-1943), was captured by the Germans during the War. The Germans offered to exchange him for Friedrich Paulus, a German Field-Marshal, but Stalin refused. The Germans said that Yakov died by running into an electric fence in Sachsenhausen concentration camp; others said that he committed suicide at the camp or that he was murdered. The United States Defense Department was in possession of documents which indicated that Yakov was shot trying to escape. Official records do not mention that Yakov was in Lubeck but, as Lubeck was close to Sachsenhausen, it is very possible that he spent some time there.

94 This was one of the brutal 'death marches' undertaken by the Germans to move POWs away from the advancing Allied Forces.

in January 1945 and finished on May 1, 1945, when the War ended. So, I was back in Lubeck which was a port and where there were thousands of Red Cross packages which, for logistical reasons, the Germans could not deliver to the camps. Just before the War ended the Germans gave us all this food. I remember I was cooking something outside the barracks when I saw tanks approaching; we were still enclosed by barbed wire. Someone shouted, *"The British are coming."* I said, *"Leave me alone; I'm still cooking."*

"They (Polish POWs) spent about five days in this camp (Oflag II D at Gross Born, also spelt Grossbronne, Pomerania); on about January 20, the whole camp was evacuated westwards in view of the approaching Red Army. The Polish POWs were kept on the march for the next two months. Their route went through Stargards, Stetin, Neu Brandebur, Ludwigslust and Luneburg until about the April 8 and 9. They arrived in the vicinity of Bremen where they were admitted to Stalag XB in Sandbostel. Truszkowski described the shocking conditions during the long trek across Germany when the POWs were only given a ration of a liter of water a day and jacket potatoes. However, they were able to supplement their rations by barter with forced laborers, especially Poles, whom they met en route. In Sandbostel they found many other Polish soldiers from the Uprising. About ten days after their arrival the whole camp was evacuated to Oflag XC in Lubeck and it was here that they were liberated by the British on May 2, 1945."[95]

Second Lt. Adam Truszkowski

Andrzej Sławinski
b. 1929, Lodowa
1944-45, Germany
1945-46, Italy
1946-present, England

We capitulated, gave up our arms, and were taken to the town of Ożarów where all POWs were being collected; I was sent to Germany, to Lansdorf Camp, allegedly the biggest POW camp in the world. There were hundreds of thousands

---

95   Second Lt. Adam Truszkowski, ex-POW, *interrogation report to British authorities.* HS4/21, M19/MS/BM/173/3, No. 13, 5th June, 1945. Document stamped: 'Secret.' National Archives, England.

of Soviet prisoners living in dreadful conditions. We were better off as we lived in barracks; they lived in holes in the ground. Life in the POW camp was no Sunday School picnic. We were introduced to hunger, cold, and boredom. The most difficult part was sleeping. We were given bunks but no mattresses and no bedding such as pillows; we had to sleep very close together, with half a dozen upon a very wide bunk, to keep warm. Every so often one person would wake and all of us had to turn together because someone had cramp. In the second (Muhlberg) and third (labor) camp I got letters from Poland from my parents; I still have them. I remember my POW number to this day, in German, of course. Muhlberg had better conditions, as we were under the care of the Red Cross and the YMCA. There were 250 of us who had moved to Muhlberg. This camp had Poles and also British and French, and we received parcels.

We were waiting to be moved to a special camp for those under 18 years of age, so some people lied about their age in order to be sent to this 'special' camp. They sent us, instead, to a labor camp where we had to perform the hardest possible work available. We were in the grounds of a factory, all 40 of us. It was a porcelain factory but they were, in fact, making parts for weapons and they were deliberately starving us. We were told that we would receive two hot meals a day which we thought would be fantastic. Before, we had received a piece of bread, a plate of soup, and three potatoes once a day. Instead, we received a plate of thin porridge, which became thinner and thinner. Once every two weeks, we were taken to shower and we'd notice how each of us was getting thinner. This porridge had no calorific value whatsoever; it was potatoes with all the goodness removed, dried and, then, used for soup. We also got bread which is what kept us alive. So, they pretended to feed us and, yet, they were starving us.

By mid-April, 1945, we were told that we were being evacuated. The evacuation started on foot. For the next three weeks, we kept marching backwards and forwards, through Saxony and Turingen. If the artillery from the Russians in the east got louder they moved us to the west, and when the American artillery from the west got louder they moved us to the east. Our only food was three raw potatoes per person per day. When we stopped at night, we cooked these potatoes. On May 8, we were still being marched towards the Sudetenland when we were overrun by Soviet troops, or liberated, as they liked to portray it. There were signs of things breaking down but we were still being guarded; we knew that liberation was close. When the Soviet troops liberated us, the frontline soldiers were not bad; it was a fantastic sight to see them coming into town. But then they started looting the town, attacking the women, and drinking.

We now got food and drink, and celebrated our freedom; however, we didn't trust the Soviets. The second echelon of the troops, which included the NKVD, interrogated us and told us to stay put and wait to be transported to Poland.

We thought, *"Poland? How about Siberia?"* Half of the prisoners (20) decided to go back to Poland straight away; they stole a lorry and food from the Germans and returned. The other half of us decided to find the Americans, so we started marching west, which was very risky as we were dressed in US Army uniforms from First World War. We were very conspicuous and were stopped many times by Soviet soldiers and officers who asked us where we were going. We said, *"To Poland,"* and continued walking west. Not a single soldier or officer stopped us as they did not know where the west and east were! Three days later we reached the Americans.

Celina Kabala Wojciechowska

b. 1924, Warszawa

1944-45, Germany, Austria

1945-46, Italy

1946-present, England

At 5 PM on August 1, 1944, I was going home from work, but decided to visit my sister and play with my 18-month-old nephew. Then the shooting started. My brother-in-law and his friends went to the Uprising, but I could not return home. The next day the Germans announced that anybody wishing to leave the city could do so with a white flag and they would not shoot. So my sister, her baby, and husband, came to our home. My other brother-in-law, who later died in Oświęcim, helped them reach our home on ul. Bernadyńska. Our district collapsed on September 2; we buried our belongings in the garden but, still, people stole them.

On October 5, I went for water with which to wash my nephew. Next door to our home was a garden with a shelter, which is where my family was hiding. When the bombing started there wasn't time for me to return to it so I hid in another shelter and was taken away by the Germans to a fort in the area of Sadyba. Of course, we had nothing; just what we stood in. The Polish Army defending this area consisted of young Polish boys who were inexperienced, so they were killed. Some Polish soldiers asked civilians for their clothing, while others hid in rose bushes. The Germans shot the retreating boys one by one. Some jumped into the water to escape but they drowned. I don't know how many survived. When they collected the corpses and put them on wagons we, the young girls, threw flowers on their remains. One young captain had been shot in the kidney and asked for his wife to be informed. Another asked us to tell his sister that he had been shot, both of which we did. I don't know what they did with the wounded.

The Germans pointed guns at us and forced us to walk through the ruins of Warszawa. All you could hear was the sound of dogs barking or dying. The Germans set fire to the remaining buildings. They rounded us up throughout the day and all night, they chased us down to the lake and then to Nowogrodzka tram station from where they took us, by train, to Pruszków; this was a locomotive repair facility where we were segregated. Able-bodied men and women were sent for forced labor to Germany; the second group of people was deported to concentration camps, and the last group, consisting of old people and mothers with young children, were taken out of Warszawa to other places in Poland. I was in the group deported to Germany for forced labor. I remember that my shoes were very uncomfortable and that I was carrying a handbag. When you are in a state of such great fear you just don't think about anything.

Because I don't belong to the bravest of people, whenever they were organizing us into groups, I went first so that, being first in line, they would shoot me first and then I wouldn't have to see what happened to my friends. They grouped us in fives: my sister and her husband, my cousin and her husband and brother were in one group, and I was in the next group. My family was sent to Oświęcim from which my brother-in-law and my cousin did not return. I was in a group with strangers and was sent to Germany, as was my younger sister who was later sent to Ravensbruck concentration camp. My parents, considered too old for deportation, were left behind in Warszawa with my little brother who was aged seven or eight. My father's health was not good; he had always coughed since being subjected to gas warfare near Kowal in the Ukraine during the First World War.

We traveled by cattle trucks for two weeks, with 60 people to a wagon. I remember when we stopped in the sidings in Poznań people came and threw apples to us through the bars in the windows. I thought, just yesterday I was giving food to people and now they were giving food to me. Whenever we stopped, it was always at railway sidings, as we weren't allowed to get off the train. Eventually, the train came to the end of its journey; we saw that we were in Dachau concentration camp.

In Dachau there were two camps; one for men, and another for transients. Again, we were segregated. We stayed there for a few weeks and, every day, they took us to work at different locations. Sometimes we had to dig for vegetables or, at other times, we were sent to work in a paper mill, which was very heavy work. I remember that, one night, we lay in our bunks when somebody asked if anyone had a prayer book. I had mine, so we all started to pray. A German guard came in and shot a bullet into the ceiling light, ordering us to stop. He took my prayer book. That's what life was like in Dachau.

There was a further segregation. I was very worried about where I would be sent; I was afraid of horses and afraid of farm work; I was also afraid of factory work. They took us to Innsbruck, Austria, where 55 of us, single people and families, lived in a building between the commercial and passenger railways. The work at the station was very hard. We had to fill wagons with coal; these were sent to fill the locomotives. As soon as the wagons were empty, we had to fill them again. Apart from work, we lived in constant fear of possible bombardment, as the Allied Forces tried to paralyze the movement of the German forces and targeted railways. Fortunately, with God's providence, no one in our group was killed.

Danuta Banaszek Szlachetko
b. 1929, Warszawa
1944-45, Germany
1945-46, Italy
1946-present, England

When the Uprising ended we all walked out of Warszawa to Ożarów; we walked in groups of six for about 20 kilometers. The civilians in the suburbs and villages threw food to us, whatever they could, even though the Germans did not allow this. I was not wearing shoes but rubber boots which were long and stretched right up to my knees and rubbed my legs until they bled. My aunt heard that we were being taken to Ożarów and ran out to see if she could get a glimpse of me, which she did. We said our goodbyes at a distance.

In Ożarów we were sorted into hangars and stayed there for two days, sleeping on a concrete floor. On the third day, the Germans packed us into trains, so tightly that you could only stand, and took us out to Germany. During the journey, we had to stop during bombing raids but, fortunately, our train was never hit. At one point we were disinfected and some of us were sent to work in factories while I went to the international POW camp in Sandbostel. We had to walk about 25 kilometers from Bremmerhaven Station to Sandbostel Camp. The Poles who had been imprisoned in Sandbostel since 1939 looked after us; they shared their rations with us as, by then, they were receiving packages from the International Committee of the Red Cross. Sandbostel had Italian, Polish, and French POWs; the Russians were kept separate and were treated particularly badly.

From Sandbostel, I was taken to Oberlangen, a female-only camp with

1,728 inmates, where I was at the time of liberation by the Polish Army. Ober-langen had once been a concentration camp for Germans but was converted into a POW camp. The participants of the Uprising were recognized by the USA and Britain as army combatants, so we had to be treated according to the Geneva Convention's directives. Nevertheless, we were very hungry. We received one slice of bread daily, some margarine and some soup. The soup was made from kale and, occasionally, they added potato peelings. It was horrible but we had to eat it as we were so hungry. Sometimes, I would sit on my bunk and cry from hunger. The barracks were also very cold as there was no heating; all we had was a single wood-burning stove in the middle of the room. I remember seeing the lights shining in the watchtowers when we got up at 5 AM. We collected water from the well in the yard but it was so cold that you had to break the ice on it so that you could wash. We washed in this cold and, as a result, many of us developed illnesses such as rheumatism. The Germans also forced us to take tablets to prevent menstruation so they would not have to give us sanitary products. I was fortunate and was able to have children later in life, but some women never regained their menstrual cycles.

On April 12, 1945, we were liberated by General Maczek's soldiers. They knew there was a POW camp in this area but they did not know who the inmates were and never imagined that they would be Polish women. Also, we didn't have too much information; we knew the War was coming to an end as some of the Germans had left our camp and we no longer heard bombing. Then, there was silence. The Polish Army sent a few cars to check out the camp. They saw the camp and didn't know who was in it, and we didn't know that these were Polish soldiers. We were standing by the barbed wire calling out in different languages and they said *"Oh Jesus, look how many women there are here!"* Then they realized that these were women from the Uprising. There was great happiness. General Maczek, himself, arrived and even found some of his family members in the camp. They brought us food. We stayed in Oberlangen a while longer and then we were moved to Niederlanger Camp.

With the War ended, the Army had to do something with us women; some joined General Anders' Second Corps,[96] which is how I met my husband. Some women went to Italy through Murnau; the youngest stayed behind for a year and went to school in Germany. We talked about returning to Poland but we knew that this was not an option as people we knew who had returned had disappeared. I had some friends who returned and, to this day we have not heard a word about them. They were probably imprisoned or sent to Siberia by the Soviets.

---

96   The British officially did not allow this because that meant more food supplies had to be given to the Polish Army.

I knew that my family was dead as, out of curiosity, on the third day of the Uprising I went to see what was happening at home. The Germans were flying over Warszawa and shooting civilians on the streets with machine-guns. My aunt was at home and told me that, after I had left the house, my mother took my sister and left for Laski. However, she could not bear to leave me behind and so she, my aunt, and my sister returned to Warszawa. This was the morning of August 1. Skirmishes started at 3 PM though, officially, the Uprising started at 5 PM. They could not return to Laski at this time as the whole city was blocked. My mother and sister walked out onto the street. They were returning home when they were shot by the Germans. My mother was hit in the legs; my sister was running home and was shot in the arm. She managed to get home; my aunt could see her running towards the house, and saw her get shot through the heart. After a few hours, when the shooting stopped, she brought in her body and, then, went out and found my mom and buried both of them. After the Uprising she found someone to help her dig up the bodies and gave her and my sister a burial in the cemetery in Brudno. So, by the time I got home, they were already buried. When I found out that they were dead, my world collapsed. I was 15 years old and never imagined that I would lose my family. I spent one night at home with my aunt and then returned to my comrades. I don't remember what happened to me during the next few days as I was grieving so much.

My father died in a hospital in Wola where everything was bombed so that there was absolutely nothing left. My aunt moved back to Laski, to be with her own two children, which was also a terrible ordeal as the Front was there. Meanwhile, her mother-in-law had tried running away to safety with the children, and they eventually met up. So, I had nobody to return to in Poland. Therefore, I was at the mercy of the Polish Army and the Polish Government-in-Exile.

I went to Italy in the summer of 1945 and joined the school which had been set up by General Anders. This was at the time that the Polish Army was moving to England; soldiers were declaring us as their fiancées or family so that we could also go to England. They even took into the Polish Army Poles who had been conscripted into the German Army. The English were terrible at this time; they forced the Russian POWs to return to Russia knowing this was certain death for them.

A few years after the War, the Germans said that Oberlangen was a concentration camp and not a POW camp so that they would not be seen as in breach of the Geneva Convention. Some of the POWs who had been with us but who had returned to Poland agreed to this so that they could receive compensation from the German Government. Those of us who moved to England did not and continued to state that we had been POWs.

"In general, the Germans kept to the terms of their agreement and the treatment of the women members of the AK was correct. The accommodation in the various camps in which they were interned, as well as the rations, were bad, although not worse than other POW camps. The last camp in which Miss Douglas was interned was Oberlangen, which was liberated by the Polish Armoured Division on 12th April.

Following the liberation of the camp, the women reluctantly came to the conclusion that there was no immediate prospect of a free Poland. They have a fairly clear picture of what is happening in Poland, and very few, if any of them, would be prepared to return to Poland at present, even if a 'Government of National Unity' is patched up according to the Yalta formula. Distrust of the Russians is now so great that the women will not go back until they have definite news that the thing works, and that it is not likely to be overthrown by some outburst of popular indignation engineered from Moscow. The women feel certain anxiety regarding their future, and impatiently await some pronouncement as to their future status and place of residence."

Sgt. Joanna H. Douglas[97]

Józef Poślinski

b. 1927, nr. Kraków
1944-45, Austria
1945-49, Germany
1949-present, USA

In April 1943, I moved to Warszawa to work as a carpenter with my uncle. In 1942, one of my sisters had been taken to Germany as every family was obliged to send someone to work there. During the Uprising, captured Polish soldiers were shot on the spot, with no questions asked. When the Allies found out what was happening, they told the Germans that they would do the same to German prisoners. This made the Germans change their behavior. The civilians were not taken as POWs but we were seen as 'bandits', and sent to concentration camps; again, no questions were asked. I was captured after the Uprising and taken directly to Mauthausen concentration camp. My ID card stated that I was 15 whereas I was, in fact, 17.

---

97   Sgt. Joanna H. Douglas, interrogation report to British authorities. HS4/21, M19/MS/BM/173/3, No. 13, 5th June, 1945. Document stamped: 'Secret.' National Archives, England.

Figure 31. Józef Poślinski, Kraków, Poland, 1939

Figure 32. Józef Poślinski *(third from right)*,
Mauthausen concentration camp, Austria, 1944[98]

I remember the photograph (Figure 32) being taken; you see that they kept us naked during the day during the quarantine period of two or three weeks, and we only received blankets at night. We slept on a concrete floor covered with straw. This was September and, in the Austrian mountains, it was already cold. We were known by numbers and not names; mine was 95822.

I was in Mauthausen from September 1944 to May 5, 1945. By the time we were liberated I had varicose veins, fallen arches, and open wounds on my swollen legs, with water oozing out. This was due to lack of protein. After the War, I was put into a Polish Guard Company and, in 1947, was transferred to a DP camp where I completed my high school. When we heard that Poland was taken over by the Russians, we did not want to go back.

Our working day started very early. We had to milk the cows by hand in the

---

98   Józef chanced by this photograph in the New York Holocaust Museum.

stable; it was easy enough but it was an unpleasant job. It was very cold in the stable in winter and, as my milking was not perfect, I often squirted some milk on the sleeves of my old milking jacket; it became stiff and smelly. My brother, Czesiek, loaded milk churns onto a wagon and took them to the main road where they were picked up by the milk factory wagon. I cleaned stables, tossing the manure on a dung heap outside. In spring, we loaded it onto wagons, carted it to the fields and spread it there ready to plough in before the crop was planted. Later, we all worked with hand hoes around the young potatoes and beet, cutting weeds.

One of the supplements to our diet was rabbit. A Polish worker from another farm gave some to us so Czesiek and I started a breeding program in an empty stall in the piggery. We killed the first rabbit at Christmas and Mother roasted it; it was delicious. Frau Sprute, the farmer's wife, hinted that they would like to try it too, so we gave some of it to them. They liked it very much and talked about it for some time after. From that time on, we used to kill one rabbit for them and two for us. Although we had enough food for Christmas and, even the traditional *opłatek,*[99] to share which was sent to us by our relatives in Poland, these were sad celebrations of the season. Our thoughts were with our families in the home country.

Andrzej Zdanowicz
b. 1938, Białystok
1939-45, Warszawa
1945-50, Germany
1950-present, Canada

First, the Germans came into Białystok, but they were there for only a short time as they decided to divide Poland; soon, the Russians came in. My father and uncle were arrested and we never found out what happened to them. My father was a bookkeeper but his father was in the Army. My mother went to find out what had happened to him and was told not to ask otherwise *"she'd be next."* She was also told that she was young and would find someone else. After this, my mother was frightened and went into hiding while I stayed with

---

99   *Opłatek* (Polish): Unleavened, paper-thin, unconsecrated communion bread. The Polish tradition is to break this bread with everyone at the table and wish all the best.

my grandmother. My mother, grandmother, and brother-in-law tried to help us cross into the German-occupied area, across the Bug, but we were captured by the Russians. If we had tried crossing the frozen Bug we would be dead. We were released but, again, Mother went into hiding and got across the Bug by herself.

While there was stability between the Russians and Germans, I was able to join my mother in Warszawa and stayed in Sierab, a small town south-west of Łódź. I think it was 1941. My mother's family is partially German; they came from just south of the Prussian border. Maybe there was an exchange of people and that is how we were able to cross, but there was a lot of movement of people across the border.

My earliest memory is of Sierab where we had to draw the blinds and listen to the BBC[100] at night. We were on the main square and could see the marching soldiers; we left in 1945. My mother was scared of the Russians so, with some other women, she decided after the Warsaw Uprising (with the Russians in Warsaw by Feb 1945) to run to the west. We took a big wagon full of stuff; I remember being on top of it and it being a wonderful ride. When we got to the railway station it was full of people. My cousin told me that, at this time, we could see the German Army retreating from the advancing Russian Army. We went to Wrocław and then to Dresden, just before the bombing. Things were happening that had nothing to do with us.

My mother had a bad time in Warszawa but, when she joined her sister in Sierab, things were better for her. We got a ride from German soldiers in an armed truck in exchange for alcohol. My mother later found a job in Bilzingsleben, in eastern Germany. My mother spoke no German but my grandmother did, and my mother learned it quickly. My father was Catholic and Polish; she was German and Lutheran. In Poland, before the War, this was not a good combination. People were suspicious so, as a kid you learned to keep your mouth shut. They had lived in Poland for a number of generations, just south of the Prussian border, but moved in 1914 as this area was right in the middle of the potential conflict of the First World War. My grandfather, a miller, sold his business and moved to Russia (there was no Poland at the time). People in Poland thought we were *Volksdeutch*.

---

100   BBC: British Broadcasting Corporation.

Wacław J. Jędrzejczak
b. 1927, Toruń
1942-50, Germany
1950-present, Australia

I was going to be 15 in November, 1942, and that meant that the employment exchange, the *Arbeitsamt*, would send me to work for local German farmers who were notorious for treating such workers badly. My brother, Czesiek, was still too young to work, but Mother expected to also be given such employment but, most probably, at a different farm. Under these circumstances, the idea arose that we should try to join Father in Germany and all work at a farm there. At least our family would be reunited.

Father made inquiries locally and found a farmer by the name of Wilhelm Sprute at No. 29 in the same village of Schöhagen, who was willing to take all four of us. After several approaches to the *Arbeitsamts* in the towns of Detmold and Lage in March, the authorities finally agreed, on April 10, to our coming to Germany. Mother and the two of us then reported to the Gniezno *Arbeitsamt* and documents were made for us to travel on May 1, 1942.

**Figure 33. The Jędrzejczak family, slave laborers,
Germany, 1942** *(Wacław is the first on the left).*
Note the letter 'P' pinned to their jackets.

Gniezno railway station was busy and, while waiting for our train, we watched the arrival of long hospital trains with wounded German soldiers traveling home from the eastern front in Russia. Aunt Stanisława also came to the station with gifts of gingerbread cake and bacon for the road. After tearful farewells, we boarded a packed passenger train and, towards evening, passed through the main station of my home town of Toruń, bypassing the city station and, therefore, not being able to see much of the town. There were no vacant seats on the train; my brother and I traveled standing in the passageway. After a few hours, the train moved through Berlin along a raised track. The city was blacked out and we could just make out the outlines of some of the buildings below. At five in the afternoon of the next day we reached our destination; it was the railway station of the little town of Bösingfeld, where yet another wartime existence unfolded.

Figure 34. The letter 'P' worn by all Polish slave laborers

It had been arranged that Father would meet us at Bösingfeld station, but he was not there when we arrived in that strange town and country. The stationmaster sent a telephone message to the Schönhagen *Bürgermeister*,[101] who informed my father of our arrival. It was another two hours, though, before Father could come because his farmer insisted that he complete his work before leaving. It was a very emotional moment to see Father again and, after this long separation, he seemed a little strange to me. It was not until October 2, 1942, that Father could join us at the farm where we were working, because of his farmer's unwillingness to let him go.

The first part of the village name, '*Schön*', means 'beautiful' and Sprute's farm with its surroundings was, indeed, a beautiful place. Approaching from the township of Bösingfeld, the road ran through a plain and then descended into a little valley with the farmhouse at the bottom of it. A creek ran through the valley with wild cherry trees and hazelnut bushes on its banks and meadows and fields on both sides of it. The slopes of the valley were wooded; oak trees, beech trees and mostly young pine trees with their undergrowth provided a habitat for local wildlife such as hares, roe deer and foxes. Unfortunately for us, the beauty of this place was marred by the fact that we were far from home in what was a foreign, enemy country. Officially, we were considered people of a lower class, almost slaves, obliged to wear a large, identifying, yellow, diamond-shaped badge with a purple 'P' on it; it stood for *Polen*.[102] At least we were now together, the family was reunited.

---

101   *Bürgermeister* (German): Mayor.

102   *Polen* (German): Pole.

Cattle Train to Magdeburg

She still remembers

The long train to Magdeburg
the box cars
bleached gray
by Baltic winters

The rivers and the cities
she had never seen before
and would never see again:
the sacred Vistula
the smoke-haunted ruins of Warszawa
the Warta, where horse flesh
met steel and fell.

The leather fists
of pale boys
boys her own age
perhaps seventeen
perhaps nineteen
but different convinced
of their godhood
by the cross they wore
different from the one
she knew in Lvov.

The long twilight journey
to Magdeburg
four days that became six years
six years that became forty

and always a train of box cars
bleached to Baltic gray

© **John Guzłowski, 1999**[103]

---

103   Previously published in Fishman, C. ed. (2007) *Blood to Remember: American Poets on the Holocaust.* MI, Time Being Books, Guzłowski, J., (2007), *Language of Mules.* Steel Toe Books.

Lilka Trzcinska Croydon
b. 1925, Warszawa
1943-46, Germany
1946-48, England
1948-present, Canada

Figure 35. Lilka Trzcinska Croydon, Warszawa, Poland, 1940

In preparation for the Uprising, I was training to become a military nurse, while my brother, Tytus, was preparing in the Underground Cadet School. We were very, very involved in the Polish Resistance. My brother participated in an armed rescue of the now-national hero of Poland, Jan 'Rudy' Bytnar.[104] We were arrested on the night of the rescue. That night the Gestapo came to our apartment in Warszawa and arrested all of us; my father, my mother, my two sisters, and me.

My brother was not sleeping at home that night because he had participated in the armed action and we all felt, in case they come looking for him, that he shouldn't be there. He spent the night with our cousins a few streets away. Their son was already in Oświęcim for involvement in the Home Army. Anyway, they came to arrest us; they left my grandmother behind, and my blind aunt who lived with us, and the maid. They took all of us to the Gestapo headquarters where we were interrogated several times. They were probably looking for a slip in our responses, so they repeated the questions over and over, and we repeated the same story, as we had prepared it that night, during dinner.

We spent the night at the Gestapo headquarters, and my father was beaten while we were just questioned. However, they left the door open so we would hear how they were beating him. Then, in the morning, the trucks took us to

---

104   Jan Bytnar's codenames: Rudy, Czarny, Janek, Krokodyl, Jan Rudy. He was a Polish Scoutmaster, resistance activist, and Second Lieutenant of the Home Army. He was arrested by the Germans on March 23, 1943 and, despite being rescued by the Scouts three days later, died on March 30, at the age of 22, from injuries sustained during interrogations by the Gestapo.

Pawiak, the political prison in Warszawa. We were not put together in one cell. My youngest sister, who was just 14, was with my mother. My sister, Maryna, and I were in different cells, and my father was in the male section of the prison. Then, a couple of weeks later, I was looking out of the prison window, looking out at the yard, and I saw my brother carrying garbage out, so I told my mother during the washroom breaks that he was there too. He had been arrested at a meeting; he walked in and the Gestapo was already there. In his hand, he had a briefcase full of guns. He dropped it behind the door and they did not notice, but he was arrested with the people who lived in the apartment. My whole family was in Pawiak prison. Six weeks later, we were told to prepare for a transport and, on May 13, were lined up, ready for a trip into the unknown. To tell you the truth, I was very naïve; since my boyfriend was already in Oświęcim, I thought, *"If they're going to send us to a concentration camp, maybe it's a good thing if it's Oświęcim because, then, I would be close to him."* I think this is the way a 17-year-old, who is in love, thinks.

We were transported from Pawiak prison to Oświęcim. My father and brother were in the main camp, in Oświęcim I,[105] while my sisters, my mother and I were in Birkenau. We only had one dress each, which also served as a night-gown. It was a very rainy time, and we had to dry those dresses on our bodies. One day we got very wet working in the fields and my mother developed pneumonia. Because we were new in the camp and were in the quarantine block, she had to be transferred to the camp hospital. We were not allowed to visit her. My brother, who had joined a unit of carpenters, visited her every day. I would come out to the side of the road where I knew I would catch a glimpse of him, and he would report to me how she was. One day I saw him walking and crying like a little boy. He told me that he went to visit her and she was gone; she had died during the night. So there we were, walking on different sides of the road, crying like two little children. That was one of the worst moments of my internment, because of the horrible sense of helplessness and loss.

In January 1945, we were sent to the concentration camp at Bergen-Belsen. There was no bread in Germany and there was no bread in Bergen-Belsen, so we were really very hungry. And, of course, we had no parcels; nothing. My sister, Maryna, who had been studying architecture in Poland, was asked to join a unit making signs for the captain. She had to move to that part of the camp where the people who worked lived. We were just left there to die, really, because we were not working; therefore we had no hope. She said she would be happy to move to that block as long as her two sisters could come with her;

---

105   Oświęcim (Polish): Auschwitz, had many sub-camps. Birkenau, or Oświęcim II, was the largest.

they agreed, so the three of us were moved. At night, she would bring bits and pieces of food for us and, this way, we somehow managed to survive.

When there was an announcement that they needed help in the kitchen, my younger sister, Zosia, and I volunteered. The work started at five in the morning so we had to get up very early, and went to the kitchen to work. Most of the day, we carried kettles with either some hot herb tea or some soup; I can't remember why but it was terribly exhausting work. By the end of the day, we were given a bowl of hot soup with meat and whatever. When I looked at that soup, my stomach turned and I wanted to vomit. I couldn't swallow it. The same was with Zosia; we both decided this work was not for us. We couldn't even enjoy that soup at the end. So this was my last effort at work.

Then, my little sister started to run a high fever. We didn't want her to go to the hospital which was overcrowded anyway, and there were about 40,000 prisoners with typhoid. We didn't want her to get typhoid because we knew she would not live. I had a job, sorting out clothes from one pile to another. These were civilian clothes from the last prisoners who had arrived. I hid my little sister under a pile of clothes so she could sleep there.

We were without hope in this Bergen-Belsen death camp. One of the first things that I noticed was a mound, a small hill in the middle if the yard that was surrounded by prisoners' blocks; it was snowing. All the male prisoners were walking around that mound. Once in a while they would sit down to rest. When a thaw came and the snow started to melt, it turned out that the hill was made of human corpses. That was the most horrible sight. They had a crematorium in Bergen-Belsen but I think it was so crowded, they ran out of room to burn the bodies, so they left them piled up, and they froze, and the snow covered them.

Then, as I say, the end was close for us. It was the end of March and we could hear the Front getting closer; we heard the shooting, the bombing, and the fighting. When the War ended, my sisters, Zosia and Maryna, were with me in Bergen-Belsen. It was a terrible three-day death march from Oświęcim to Breslau, because the railway tracks were bombed and we had to walk. We slept one night in a barn with animals, with cows, and calves, and so on. Another night, we slept in another barn. There was hay, so we made ourselves beds in it. Then, we arrived in Breslau, were loaded onto cattle trains and stopped in Ravensbruck for a few days. They put up a huge tent outside the camp. There were triple bunk beds in the tent. They didn't want us in the camp. I think the commander of Ravensbruck was afraid of us because we were carrying lice that were infected with typhoid.

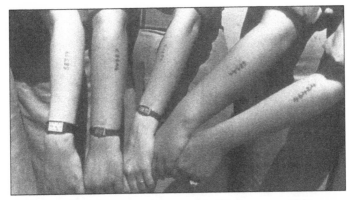

Figure 36. Lilka Trzcinska Croydon,[106] **Germany, 1945**

Ravensbruck was a more civilized camp in the way that there were mainly political prisoners. But, by then, my little sister was already in Ravensbruck but we didn't know that. In the morning, we walked outside that tent, just looking who was on the other side of the road, because the Ravensbruck prisoners came out too and, suddenly, we hear our names being called. We recognized the face but it was on one of the tallest girls in the group of prisoners. Zosia was the youngest one and had been the smallest when were arrested. In a year, she had grown to be the tallest in the family. And, she said later, she was looking for two tall sisters and we didn't seem to be so tall anymore. We talked and, then, she went to talk to her *kapo*,[107] who was a very strict German woman. Zosia was working in a sewing group. She said that her two sisters were in the transport from Oświęcim and asked if they could join her in the sewing unit. The woman agreed. I remember, I woke up the next morning and I thought I had died and gone to heaven because I was in a clean bed wearing a rough, but clean, night-gown. Next to me, was my sister, Maryna, smiling at me mysteriously. I said, *"What's happened? Where are we?"* and she said, *"Well, Zosia managed to convince the kapo to take us into her sewing unit."* But before we could move we had to be deloused, bathed, and put in the hospital for a few days to gain some strength because we were so exhausted. We joined Zosia in that sewing group in Ravens-bruck, but only for two or three weeks because, then, all young women prisoners were moved. So we embarked on another cattle train into an unknown destiny. But the comfort was that, this time, the three of us were together.

While I was working, (it was, by then, April 1945), I suddenly heard a

---

106   Lilka is No. 44787; Zosia, her sister, is No. 44789.

107   *kapo* (German): a prisoner who had an administrative and/or supervisory role in the camp.

strange sound on the camp road, so I went out to see what was making that sound, and I saw a tank rolling towards us the road. In front of the tank was a jeep driven by a soldier. He stopped the jeep, the tank stopped, and the soldier ran up to me. All I noticed is that he had three stripes and that he was a sergeant. He was a British soldier.

We never found out what happened to my boyfriend, Jerzy. It's hard; it's very hard because all those years, each time I went to Poland, I thought, maybe his family heard something about him, but they hadn't. He lived through two-and-a-half years of Oświęcim and yet nobody saw him after we were liberated. Perhaps he was killed by the Germans during the disorder that occurred after liberation.

15 December 1996
For Jerzy's 75th Birthday

Kampinos Forest
Heather meadow
Cricket's song
Cobalt-blue skies of autumn

Our world pervaded by fear
The enemy waited in the streets
Lightless nights full of phantoms
The murderers' song entering our dreams
Its sharp edge slashing our hopes

We escaped into this forest
That held secrets of buried guns
We escaped into the shade of ancient trees
We escaped with our newborn love
And held it firmly in our hearts

Your face your hands
A quickened heartbeat
In my sixteen-year-old breast
Enclosed in a love circle forever
For love like eternity is one

Figure 37. Jerzy Masiukiewicz, Warszawa, Poland, 1942

We've guarded it through those years
By the banks of the Acheron
Through war and fear and hunger
I brought it to the other shore of an ocean
Where I've pitied the sun the moon the stars
That shone on the world without you
And I mourned the tiny buds of heather
Since then turned into ash

I unpetal stars for you
They know your mystery
Where and when it was
And under what skies

You felt your last heartbeat
As you whispered
I love you I love you I love you
These words breathed life into me

Soon we shall wander together
Among the stars that glow in the sky
Like those tiny white daises
On the meadows in our country

Years tumble around me
All the Nativities and all the Resurrections
Always you always our love
Always the heather meadow
Always the cobalt-blue skies of autumn

© **Lilka Trzcinska Croydon, 1996**

CHAPTER 6

Stalinist Oppression

"Comrade, come join the kolkhoz!" [108]

Figure 38. Russian propaganda poster, 1930[109]

---

108   *kolkhoz*: (Russian): a Soviet collective farm where workers were compensated with food.

109   http://en.wikipedia.org/wiki/kolkhoz

Deportations to the Soviet Union

Poles had been subjected to deportations into northern Russia and Siberia ever since the first partition of Poland in 1772 (two more partitions followed in 1793 and 1795). Deportation was a way of eliminating the social and economic core of Polish society as a means of weakening the Polish population under Russian control. During 1936-38, 40% of the victims of the Stalinist purges were Poles living in the Soviet Union. 111,091 were executed.

Between February 1940 and June 1941, there were four mass-deportations of about 1.5 million Polish citizens:

1. **February 10th 1940:** 250,000 men, women and children deported to northern Russia and Siberia on 110 cattle trains. From towns: civil servants and local government officials, judges, police force, and Army families. From the country: forest workers, settlers, Polish, Ukrainian and White-Ruthenian small farmers and several entire villages.

2. **April 13th 1940:** 330,000 mostly women and children, were taken by 160 cattle trains to Asiatic Russia: Kazakhstan and further eastwards to the Altai Kraj; families of those previously arrested, families of persons escaped abroad, tradesmen (mostly Jews), farm laborers from liquidated estates, and another group of small farmers of the three nationalities.

3. **June and July 1940:** 250,000 Poles, mainly refugees from central and western Poland were moved to the north USSR around Archangel, Sverdlovsk and Novosibirsk. Practically all refugees from central and western Poland, small merchants, doctors, engineers, lawyers, journalists, university professors, teachers. All belonging to categories enumerated above who had so far evaded deportation, children from summer camps and orphanages.

4. **June 1941:** totaling around 200,000, mostly from the Wilno area of Poland, scattered widely across the USSR.[110]

Independently of the four mass-deportations, small batches of a dozen or several score persons were continually banished to the interior of the USSR. The deportation plan was not carried out in full on account of the outbreak of the Russo-German War.

Including the small percentage of Ukrainians, Jews and Belarusians, the

---

110   Piotrowski, T. ed. (2004). *The Polish Deportees of World War II*. North Carolina, McFarland & Company Inc., p. 219

total number of Polish citizens deported between 1939 and 1941 amounted to approximately 1,680,000 people, not including 250,000 POWs.

By the middle of 1942, half of them were dead.

Timeline: the fate of the deportees:

- June 22, 1941, German forces crossed the Molotov-Ribbentrop line.

- Stalin sought help from the Western Allies.

- August 1941, Poles who had been deported were granted an 'Amnesty' and were free to join the new Polish Army that was forming in the south under General Anders.

- It took some deportees a year to leave the Soviet Union. Some did not reach the Polish Army before Stalin closed the border at the end of 1942.

- Little, if any, assistance was given to the Poles to help them leave; rations in the newly-forming Polish camps in Kazakhstan were deliberately kept short of what was required.

- Approximately 120,000 men, women and children reached Iran.

- In 1957, 780,000, or 78% of the deported Poles were still unaccounted for.

- In 1943, the Germans discovered mass graves in the Katyń Forest; 22,000 Polish officers, border guards and police had their hands bound and were shot in the back of the head and buried in mass graves. The 'Katyń massacre' refers to the massacre at Katyń Forest, near the village of Katyń, of Polish military officers from the Kozelsk prisoner-of-war camp, executions of POWs from geographically distant Starobelsk and Ostashkov camps, and the executions of political prisoners from West Belarus and West Ukraine. All were shot on Stalin's orders at Katyń Forest, at the NKVD headquarters in Smolensk, at a Smolensk slaughterhouse, and at prisons in Kalin (Tver), Kharkiv, Moscow, and other Soviet cities. The Soviet authorities denied their role in this massacre until 1990.

He was just walking,
enjoying
a balmy June evening
near Nowa Wola;
everything seemed safe enough.
But this was 1940.
The Russian soldiers were quick
to take him,
a young man
of twenty-two.

They actually stopped by the house
to let him pack something.
He made sure
to take
the dark woolen coat
he'd sewn himself.
He knew
he'd be gone
far, and long.
The family wept.
A quick embrace,
a mother's blessing
against peril,
no time for more.

In Murmansk,
guarded closely
by the soldiers,
he was forced to labor
outdoors
in all weather
with little to fuel him.
But his coat served him well.

His group knew they were lucky;
sometimes, there were edible things
in the watery soup,
a potato now and then.
Sometimes,
a piece of herring!
Still,
he was hungry.
And he ached for his family.
Suddenly, a package from home!
How could it be?
What could it be?

The pre-opened wrapping
revealed
a tin
of
lard.
Precious,
life-sustaining
lard
carefully melted
and poured
to fill the tin
completely.

He stabbed his spoon into it,
quickly unloaded the lard onto the table.
He'd heard talk about this kind of thing,
long ago.
His was not the first
generation
to be taken
to this dismal, frozen place.

A false bottom
revealed a wad of *rubles*,
painstakingly collected,
lovingly rolled
rubles
that would save him
several times
before this would be over.

Today,
he keeps things
just in case.
Things
painstakingly collected,
lovingly hidden,
in hopes that someday
the need for them will be over.

© **Anon (2), 2007**

Emilia Kot Chojnacka
b. 1931, Berteszów
February 1940, deported to Soviet Union
1942-50, India, Africa
1950-present, England

There were three children in my family; my sister, my brother, and I. When the Soviet Union invaded Poland, the local Ukrainians felt empowered to abuse us. My father was an estate manager and they wanted to kill him but, luckily, he was protected by a Ukrainian woman who hid him and said, *"What, you want to kill this man who used to give you work and bread?"* She saved his life. My father and another man escaped from our village to the village of Miejsce Piastowe, about 10 kilometers away; the three of us were left with our mom. We were frightened of the Ukrainians; we left the village and went to live in our aunt's village until

February 10, 1940, when we were all deported to Russia.

It was early morning on a Saturday, February 10, 1940, when we heard a knock on the door. We opened it and there stood a Russian soldier pointing his gun at us, ordering us to pack. He was accompanied by a local Polish Jew, which was very fortunate for us. My mom started to pack porcelain; this Jewish man told her to take things like clothing and bedding instead. My aunt had just put some bread into the oven, and asked if they could at least wait until the bread was ready and then she'd also give them some. We took all day to pack, which is how we got to be the last ones on the transport.

Figure 39. Emilia Kot Chojnacka
(back row, center) **with her family, Siberia, 1941**

We were in transit for three weeks. We traveled in Polish, then, Russian cattle trucks. They gave us some water and bread. In the trucks we cut a hole in the floor to serve as a toilet and hung some cloth around it for privacy. My father and older sister, who had not been deported, did not know what had happened to us until we wrote to them from Siberia.

In Siberia, the healthy adults worked at cutting down trees. My mom had heart problems, yet, was told to work. She was sent to the doctor who confirmed that she had a heart condition. Nevertheless, they still wanted her to work. In the summer of 1940 we were thrown out of the barracks because of the bed bugs. They had to be fumigated while we waited in the forest. I heard someone say that my mommy had been arrested so I ran to the camp and watched to see what had happened. They brought out my mom and I threw myself at her, put my arms around her waist and clung to her. They told me to let go and that I would see my mommy again in two weeks. I clung to her all the way to the railway station. I saw her from the train window looking at me. They arrested her because she refused to work; they said that she was spoilt, that she had been wealthy in Poland but, in Russia, a wealthy person was an enemy.

Figure 40. Letter written by Emilia and her brother Zbigniew from Siberia to her sister and father in Poland, Christmas, 1940[111]

My grandfather, grandmother, and a number of aunts, uncles, and a cousin had all been deported, and we all lived together in the same barrack. There were two stoves and some wooden bunks in each barrack. On Christmas Eve, for the Polish *Wigilia*,[112] instead of the usual feast we had potatoes and mushroom sauce. This was it, but it was fantastic, as our regular diet consisted of very heavy, dark bread. This dark bread apparently helped adults with gastric problems, but children under the age of two, and the elderly, did not get the nutrients they needed and died. We used to pick blueberries in the summer and sell them to the locals. There were no mushrooms or animals for us to eat. The big treat was to get a potato under your pillow as a present on St. Nicholas'

---

111 *".. dream about Daddy and Uncle (a priest). Darling sister Bronia, how did you spend Christmas, happily or sadly? Write to me how things are with Daddy. Is he healthy and strong? I send you my sincerest wishes for a happy New Year from far away Siberia."* Courtesy of Emilia Kot Chojnacka.

112 *Wigilia* (Polish): literary, the 'vigil'; a meal eaten by Polish Catholics on Christmas Eve. Traditionally, it consists of 12 food courses, one for each month of the year, and the sharing of *opłatek*.

Day.[113] Then, we had something to eat. The only meat we had was from horses that had died from exhaustion. We were hungry and particularly needed flour so we gave what we had in exchange for it with the locals. We had milk and our family in western Poland sent us seeds in the summer which we planted so that we'd have some fruit and vegetables.

Henryk Jopek (Jopeck)
b. 1928, Wołyń
February 1940, deported to the Soviet Union
1942-47, Iran, Palestine
1947-52, England
1952-present, USA

Figure 41. Henryk Jopek, Palestine, 1943

I am the son of a Polish settler who received his estate in Piłsuczyzna, Wołyń, from the Polish Government for participating in the battle against the Soviets in the 1919-20 War. He received 30 hectares of bare land and told to do with it as he wanted. Those with families built their homes first and then brought the children. They all helped one another; there were forests nearby so we had wood for building. There were three children in my family: myself, an older sister and a younger brother, born in 1933. At first, there was no school at our *osada,*[114] so we walked 3 to 4 kilometers to a village called Hipolitówka. It was hard to walk this in the winter. Two or three years before the War we got a

---

113   St. Nicholas' Day: December 6th, traditionally, the night when he (Santa Claus) pauses on his way to prepare for the coming Season by placing little gifts under bed pillows.

114   *osada* (Polish): settlement.

school in our own settlement.

We received news between September 1 and 17 of the German attack and saw planes flying overhead. The larger towns were bombed; we just saw some shooting from the air as we dug potatoes in the fields. When the Russians were present, the Ukrainians continued to behave; they had not yet been given any autonomy. Both the Ukrainians and Jews made red arm bands for themselves and formed a militia. Only later, after we had been deported to Siberia, did the Ukrainians take control and start murdering Poles. If we hadn't been deported we would have been murdered; over 85,000 Poles were murdered during the War by Ukrainians in the most bestial manner. Larger towns, like Lwów, could better protect themselves; smaller, more isolated places could not. Bands of Ukrainians wandered around murdering people.

As Army families, we were in the first wave of deportations on February 10, 1940. Our entire family was deported. We traveled for about three weeks, to the Archangel area. Kotlas was the largest and nearest town where there was a railway station. I was old enough to understand what was going on and remember the journey very clearly. After the train journey we traveled by horse and sleigh for three days to the settlement. At the settlement, 90% of the adults worked in the forests, and they formed a 'boy's brigade' of us younger ones. We would go into the forest to work but without an axe and saw; we would cut down the smaller branches and clear the snow from around the trees. We had to clear enough space around the trees so that two adults could work with a manual saw. Once a tree was cut down we would pick up the smaller branches and use them for firewood and keep the fires going so the elders could warm themselves. My mother looked after pigs which often died from the cold as it was -40 °C. The Polish veterinarian wrote that they had died *"from a heart attack"* so that my mother would not be punished.

We had a school in our settlement but, then, we moved to another location where there was no school. The women were not used to working in the forests. There were 40-50 families in the second settlement. My sister was 15 years old so she had no job.

Kawałek Chleba[115]

Breaking into the warmth of a piece of Christmas bread
I can't help but remember the words that my father said
"Kawałek chleba in a soul destroying camp with bitter cold
If taken away, becomes more valuable than riches or gold

To steal bread could become one's death by punishment
To not steal could be death from starvation and torment
It was knowingly unforgiveable to steal another man's bread
And to hear "Nie ma chleba"[116] were words of dread.

Most times the badly baked bread was heavy and wet
This bricklike, tasteless necessity of life is hard to forget
When you got the heel of the loaf you felt lucky that day
They were driest of the black slices that were given away

Behind barbed wire, a package came to Archangelska camp
A sugar sack parcel from my brother covered in Polish stamps
Inside were summer onions tucked in amongst garlic cloves
But the best by far were those dried, bread loaves.

It never mattered from which part of the loaf came my next bite
The memory of home was in every slice golden and light
A crust of bread and a warm bed to sleep in were always dreams
Tho' well remembered, it was such a long time ago it seems

The tasty loaves of bread from home never lasted very long
But I enjoyed the last crumb and tried to keep my spirit strong
A few crusts were tucked in my pockets to soak up watery soup
Sadly, not enough to share with joy in our hungry group

Kawałek chleba you could trade for a smoke or a wool sock
Or munch it with a rare onion dipped in boiling kipiatok
It's hard to imagine any bread that really has a better taste
Than the one received in the depth of hunger by God's grace."

---

115 *Kawałek Chleba* (Polish): A Piece of Bread.
116 *"Nie ma chleba."* (Polish): "There is no bread."

So I share my kawałek chleba with the spirits that knew hunger
And I share this with memories for the survivors when younger
Break a piece of bread and share your family's story today
And most of all, my blessings to all, for a Merry Christmas Day.

© **Hania Kaczanowska, 2008**

Stefan Mączka
b. 1922, Równe
February 1940, deported to the Soviet Union
1942-46, Iran, Palestine, Iraq, Egypt, Italy
1946-present, England

and

Danuta Mączka Gradosielska
b. 1925, Równe
February 1940, deported to the Soviet Union
1942-46, Iran, Palestine, Iraq, Egypt, Italy
1946-present, England

Stefan: In the morning of September 17, I heard on the radio, a broadcast in Polish from the Soviet Union announcing that their forces had crossed Polish borders. *"We are coming to help Poland fight Germans. Do not offer resistance; we are coming as your friends."* Noticing the Red Army marching, I walked to the roadside. Our military settlement was about 26 miles from the Soviet border. The column had stopped for a rest, and I was astonished to see this many soldiers equipped and dressed so poorly. A number of them carried old rifles tied with string over their shoulders and they had no proper boots or uniforms.

Danuta: On September 17, 1939, the Soviet Army entered the eastern borderlands of Poland. I remember Russian tanks passing though our settlement. There were immediate arrests of prominent soldiers by the NKVD and, during the following days, Polish soldiers and, even, whole regiments were transported by train to labor camps in Siberia and other parts of the Soviet Union. Our county of Wołyń was joined to the Ukrainian Republic of the USSR. Within a short time a governing committee of Ukrainians was formed. One of their first actions was the ousting of military settlers from their properties. From this moment, my happy childhood on the Krechowiecka Settlement ended.

Stefan: Our newly-built house was about 100 yards from the road, its new zinc roof shining in the sun, the driveway lined with cherry trees. The Russian officer leading the column asked, *"Whose is this house? It must be a kulak's."*[117] I replied, *"It is my father's house but he is not a kulak."* Without further comment, the soldiers resumed their march. I found leaflets dropped by Soviet planes, stating, *"During the last few days the Polish Army has been destroyed. Over 60,000 soldiers have voluntarily come over to our side from the following towns: Tarnopol, Galicz, Równe, and Dubno. Soldiers, what is left for you? Why are you risking your life? Your resistance is futile. Officers are pushing you to senseless slaughter. They hate you and your families. It is they who have shot the delegates you sent to us to propose surrender. Don't believe your officers. Officers and generals are your enemies; they want you dead. Believe us! Only the Red Army is your friend. Signed by S. Timoszenko, Commander of the Red Army, Ukrainian Front."*

**Figure 42. Stefan, Zosia and Danuta Mączka
with their step-mother and father, Poland, 1932**

In the evening, one of our neighbors, *Pan*[118] Podhorski, came to see my father. He was carrying a long parcel wrapped in material covered with tar. Father called me to fetch a spade and to go with him and *Pan* Podhorski to bury the parcel at the cemetery, near the church, about 300 yards from our house. It was getting dark when we went to the grave of Kakol, a pilot who had died in a plane

---

117   *kulak* (Russian): A rich peasant or farmer.
118   *Pan* (Polish): title of Mister.

crash. I dug a hole under the slab at the foot of the grave, about 18 inches deep by 3 feet long. I buried the parcel containing a duplicate standard of the First Krechowiecki Lancers Regiment which had been donated by the Regiment to our settlement and had been hanging by the altar in the church. On our return home, Father decided to bury his rifle, hunting gun, revolver and ammunition, as well as the silver cutlery which had been my step-mother's dowry. We buried the parcels under the large pine tree next to six beehives, located about 300 feet from our house.

The next day the NKVD officials arrived in our area to introduce the new Soviet administration, and requested that we all surrender our arms. On October 22, the Soviets held local elections and disenfranchised most of the Polish population because everyone who owned over five hectares of land was automatically disqualified. Communist candidates, most of who were not known to the local residents, were selected by the NKVD. The next step in Sovietization was the decision by the Soviets to declare all people resident on land occupied by Soviets on Nov 1, 1939, to be Soviet citizens.

I returned to Równe to continue my education but found that my place had been taken by the son of a local Communist official. My family was evicted from their farm and allowed to take only a few personal possessions. Father found accommodation for us in Tuczyń, about 3 miles away.

Danuta: Our settlement was gripped by great fear. We did not know what to do. We felt deserted by the Polish officials since we did not know, at first, that some of them had been arrested. The Soviet officials were reassuring us that they would not throw us off our farms. However, in October 1939, the Ukrainian Committee announced that about 12 families would have to move out, and without any show of resistance as *"resistance could cost lives."* Among the farms chosen was ours, maybe because it had a big brick house with good, fertile land. We were instructed to leave our home within 24 hours; we were allowed to take a few personal possessions, food, some furniture, and our two dogs, but no farm livestock. I was 14 and felt all that was happening very deeply; this was the end of my carefree childhood. The War came to destroy our quiet life in eastern Poland. Our fate of being homeless was just beginning.[119]

Stefan: Father and our neighbor, Wincenty Cala, decided to explore the conditions in German-occupied Poland. They were heading for Starachowice, my father's home town, when they were captured by German border guards and

---

119   In addition to the interview conducted by Bogusia Wojciechowska, see also: www.kresy.co.uk/memories.html

handed over to the Soviets. However, on their second attempt to reach the town they were successful, and Father wrote that it would be better for us to live under the Germans than the Soviets and that he would come for us soon. On February 9, 1940 we were reunited as a family in Tuczyń.

However, on February 10, 1940, we were awoken by a loud banging on our door. A NKVD official in civilian clothing, and two Ukrainian militiamen armed with rifles, stood at our door, and read out a deportation order, giving us two hours to pack. Fortunately they told us to take warm clothes and tools such as axes and saws. My father asked if we were being deported to Siberia: we were told that, indeed, we were. Most people who were being deported did not know where they were going. While our stories are similar, there were differences in our experiences because so much depended on individual circumstances. We were one of the 'lucky' families who were told we were going to Siberia and advised on what we should take with us. We took a barrel of flour, salted pork and other meat, and honey. A lot of people were deported with just the clothes they stood in. So this is an account of what happened to us, and not necessarily what happened to other people.

After two hours, the NKVD officer returned; the sleighs were waiting for us. Father explained that his mother was not capable of travel due to a weak heart; she was allowed to stay behind. Our family was loaded onto a sleigh, with our luggage on another sleigh behind us. We were lucky that we were allowed to take quite a lot of food with us; it was a very cold winter, -30 °C, with snow two feet deep. We were herded into cattle wagons and spent the next two days at Lubomirka Station, during which time the NKVD collected more people from our area.

Danuta: On hearing that we were being deported, my grandmother had a heart attack. After some discussion with Father, the NKVD man agreed to leave grandmother behind. We were given two hours to pack. Father instructed me to sell the chickens to the owner of our house who bought them. I did not bother counting the money for I knew him to be an honest man; anyway, in his position, he didn't have to give me anything at all. As we set off on the sleigh, my sister Zosia and I cried. We felt great sorrow at leaving behind everything we loved and knew so well. Our sheepdog, Lulus, followed behind the sleighs but, in the end, the deep snow proved too much for his little legs and my heart filled with grief as he was left behind.

Along the way, we met other settlers' families; they were all going in the same direction as us, to Lubomirka. I did not realize that this was a huge deportation of Polish settlers from the entire eastern borderlands.[120] In our wagon were

---

120   Eastern borderlands; known as *Kresy*.

42 people. The train moved out of Lubomirka towards Równe. I could not sleep even though it was night. Others could not sleep either and we spoke to each other in whispers, wondering what would happen to us.

I remember that we were all crying in the train wagons when we were being deported, yet my brother Stefan remembers none of this; he remembers us singing, not from joy, but from defiance.

Stefan: The next day, at about 6:30 AM, we arrived at Równe station where more deportees were loaded onto our train. Later on, two people per wagon were allowed off the train to collect water and coal for the two stoves we had in each wagon.

There were 72 people in each cattle wagon, including my friends from school with their parents. Each wagon had two sliding doors on each side; at each end there were two levels of wooden planks, allowing 10 people to sleep like sardines on each level. In the middle of the wagon, between the two doors, was a hole in the floor which served as the toilet. The people in our wagon hung a blanket around this hole to provide some privacy. Personal luggage was placed below the bottom layer of wooden planks. Each wagon had two iron stoves for heating and cooking. At some stations we were lucky to receive bread and a bucket of soup to be shared with everybody in our wagon. The frost outside was -35 to -40 °C. My sister, Danuta, who slept on the top bunk next to the wall, remembers that her hair froze to the wall. The traveling conditions in these locked cattle trains, crammed with people without room to move, no privacy, and with no washing and toilet facilities, were absolutely awful. However, I later learned that other deportees were treated far worse than we.

After traveling for 17 days we arrived, on February 27, at Kotlas in the Archangel region. During this time we still did not know precisely where we were going and how long it would take to get there. The entire train was unloaded at a school opposite this station. We had to sleep there on the floor among our belongings; it was crowded and I remember children crying. The next morning the sleighs arrived and we were taken to a narrow gauge railway on which we traveled deep into the forest. We arrived in the evening at a small settlement called Kotovalsk, which consisted of four wooden barracks, a small shop and a communal kitchen, all constructed from logs. We were crammed into one of the larger barracks together with other families.

On the morning of March 6, the Camp Commandant ordered all men to go to work in the forest. They were issued with axes and saws and promised pay for their work, though there was nothing to buy in the settlement shop. The work in the forest, felling trees in snow two feet deep with temperatures at -30 °C, was very hard. My father and I worked in the forest cutting trees. The pay was extremely low, well below the subsistence level. When there was no more snow to clear, Danuta was given the task of gathering branches from the felled trees and stacking them up in piles which were then set on fire. Forest regulations required workers to burn all the branches on the ground during the winter in order to reduce the danger of forest fires during the dry summer. Later, we were moved to a larger settlement where we were employed in a saw-mill.

Local Russians, comprised mostly of deportees sent to Siberia during Tsarist rule, were warned by the NKVD that we had been deported because we were kulaks, and that they should not believe our stories that life in Poland was better than here. My sister, Zofia, and my step-brother Ted, along with other Polish children, attended a local school. We heard how, one day, the teacher asked the children if they believed in God; only the Polish children raised their hands. Next the teacher asked them to pray for bread. After a short wait, the teacher said, *"No bread, no God."* She then asked, *"Who believes in Stalin?"* The Russian children raised their hands. The teacher asked them to pray to Stalin for bread. Immediately a woman entered the classroom carrying a tray with slices of bread which was distributed only to the children praying to Stalin. Bread and food were rationed; dry rye bread was more valuable to a Russian than a cake to a child in the west. During my time in the Soviet Union I never saw white bread, cakes or butter. According to the school books, all discoveries in science and medicine were made by Russians.

The first snow fell in September 1940, when the nights were getting very much longer. On October 1, I and two others were sent to a settlement called Sieviernoje, about 22 miles away, to work in the forest. The three of us shared a log barrack with eight Russian men; each of us had a wooden bed. In the middle of the barrack was a wooden barrel with drinking water and, at each end of the barrack was a stove.

Shortly afterwards, a large group of single young Russian men and women arrived to work in this settlement. They were placed in two adjoining barracks, with men separated from women. Each of us was allocated to work with Russian gangs of four people, cutting trees. In the morning we had to walk briskly in order to keep warm, for about a half a mile over open deforested land to our place of work in the forest. The snow was knee deep. After a while we would point out to each other, *"Your nose is white,"* and we would pick up snow in our gloved hands and rub our nose. Very quickly, circulation was restored. We were dressed in quilted jackets with sweaters and vests, and quilted trousers with long-johns; fur-lined hats covered our necks, ears and cheeks, with flaps fastened under the chin, only our nose was exposed to the elements. We wore knee-length boots made from felt; the soles were about an inch thick, with three-quarters of an inch of felt covering the foot, and the rest, up to the knee, was about three-eighths of an inch thick. The boots needed to be one or two sizes bigger to allow room for wrapping the feet well while still allowing space inside the boot. We also wore fur-lined gloves. We were only excused from work in the forest when temperatures dropped below -50 °C.

At lunchtime, soup was delivered in a wooden barrel, on a horse-drawn sleigh driven by a Russian woman. She sold the soup with a piece of bread. Often, I had no money to pay for this food as our pay was below subsistence level. The lunch break lasted only 15 - 20 minutes, since it was too cold to stand still.

In April 1941 I was sent back to Monastyrok to rejoin my family. To my great sorrow I found out that my youngest sister, Zofia, had died of meningitis on December 24, 1940. My step-brother, Ted, had broken his leg in October 1940 and was still in Kotlas hospital. Fortunately, my grandmother had sent us a parcel containing communion bread, honey, sugar, biscuits, and vegetable seeds. My step-mother was going to plant the seeds in the little garden by our barrack so that the vegetables would supply us with the badly-needed vitamins.

Danuta: It was Christmas Eve but, as the family was apart, I was far from happy. For the last two weeks, Zosia had been ill in the hospital in Priwodnia. I was going with my father to visit her in order to share the *opłatak* with her. It was 3:30 PM. My friends, Wanda and Lodzia, were working in the hospital. When Lodzia saw us she came up and said, *"Zosia is already covered."* I had no idea what she meant, but my father started crying. I had never seen him like this before, with huge tears rolling down his cheeks. I wondered what was wrong with Zosia. When Lodzia lifted the sheet I saw Zosia's pale face and I realized what had happened and, then, I also started to cry. My father brought her home with us and made a coffin for her. On December 26, we gave Zosia a very simple funeral. My step-mother, father and I prayed, walking behind the sleigh, and escorted her to the grave. My father, with tears in his eyes, buried her in the fir forest outside Priwodnia. So, day by day, life went by with us all working hard; some in the saw-mill, Stefan far away from us in the forest, and my father in construction.

Stefan: People in the camp were desperately short of food; I was given permission from the Camp Commandant to take a group of women to pick mushrooms in the nearby forest. As an experienced mushroom-picker in Poland, I hoped that I would find some here. The forest was like a jungle; dense with trees and undergrowth and with no footpaths. We managed to locate mushrooms and I led my party safely out of the forest. Danuta also made several successful mushroom trips.

Stanisława Robaszewska Woźniak

b. 1927, Kobylnik
April 1940, deported to the Soviet Union
1942-46, Iran, Africa, India
1946-present, England

My daddy was arrested during the night of April 9; I remember my father standing with his arms raised. My mother was told that she could visit and bring him some clothing, as he had left with very little. My mom left on April 11 to tell the rest of the family what had happened. They came for us on April 13 during the night while she was still away. My younger brothers and I had been left alone with my grandmother who became hysterical and could not help me pack. They sent a cart to collect our mom, and said that they would wait until 9 AM to see if she returned; if she did not, then they'd take us without her. My granny started screaming, *"This is the end, this is the end."*

We had no suitcases, but I had to get us packed. Despite the fact that I was normally a shy and unenergetic girl, I somehow managed to get everything organized and packed a lot of things. They told one of the sharecroppers[121] working on the farm to help me pack, but she wanted us to take as little as possible so that there would be more left for her. My youngest brother started crying and vomiting because he did not understand what was happening. We knew about the February deportations to Archangel so I asked what I should pack; whether clothing for warm or for cold weather. They told me to pack for the cold so we started getting dressed, with my brother vomiting, and my granny crying. Nevertheless I packed a lot, even a sewing machine and a samovar.

Just as they were ordering us to leave, my mom arrived. She asked whether or not I had packed the meat that was hanging in the attic. I hadn't, so she went to get it. Half of it was already missing. We had no bread. My mom was in shock seeing her children being forced out of their home. I remember that, as we were driving away from the house, I turned around to look at my home as if sensing that this might be the last time that I would ever see it. As we drove, I saw carts coming from every direction. We went through one village where the women came out to look at us; my mother asked one of them for some bread. She gave us a large loaf.

We traveled for about another 20 kilometers to the railway station where a train was waiting for us. Each wagon housed 20 people, five families, and we were lucky that we got the top bunks and so could look out of the window.

---

121   Sharecroppers: farm laborers who worked the land in exchange for giving some of the produce to their landowner.

There was no toilet in the wagon so the men cut a hole in the floor, but we had no toilet paper, not even newspapers. I just don't know how we managed; how did the women cope with menstruation? I just don't know, but somehow, for the two weeks that we were being transported, we managed. They only allowed us off the train once, when we were in the steppes where there were no forests, so there was nowhere to hide. They allowed us to walk around for one hour. My cousin started singing the Polish national anthem; they quickly took her away to a separate wagon.

Jadwiga Krzysztoporska Piasecka
b. 1935, Warszawa
June 1940, deported to the Soviet Union
1942-44, Iran
1944-68, England, Scotland
1968-present, USA

Figure 43. Jadwiga Krzysztoporska, Tehran, Iran, 1942

Jadwiga Krzysztoporska Piasecka: We were originally from Warszawa, but my father was a lawyer and worked as a customs and duty inspector in the free port of Gdańsk. When things started getting 'complicated' in Gdańsk during 1939, he was transferred to Lwów and the family followed him so, when the War broke out, we were in Lwów. I was only four years old but I remember standing on the balcony of our house and seeing the Soviet Army marching by. I also remember there being blackout curtains on the windows and that we sometimes had to hide in the cellar of the house.

On June 28, 1940, the Russians came to our house in the night; I was gathering books to take with me and some sandwiches made with dried bread. We were taken by sleigh to the railway station where we sat in the wagon for two days before the train moved. The children were on the upper bunk in the wagon where there was a small window, and we all tried to get next to it so we could see what kind of places we were passing through. They used to wake us in the night and give us some kind of tea, or *kipiatok*.

Maria Krzysztoporska:[122] *"On the evening of June 28, 1940, we were warned of an air raid. The city was completely in darkness. I was attaching black paper to the windows, the children were asleep, and my husband was getting ready for air raid patrol. Only the sounds of car horns and street patrols broke the silence. Midnight was approaching when the sudden ringing of the door bell echoed in our hearts. This time they had come for us; officials from the NKVD, policemen, three soldiers with their guns, in the company of the frightened caretaker. We were given two hours to pack and get ready for the journey. At about three o'clock in the morning we were put in a truck along with our belongings. Our poor, frightened children showered us with questions as to where we were going and why. The journey resembled a funeral procession; every few feet we encountered more sleighs and carts carrying luggage, followed by groups of frightened, crying people; 90% of them were the Jewish poor.*

Along with 30 other people we were piled into a cattle wagon that was dark and dirty. We occupied one of the top bunks and, having placed our luggage, we started to look around us. Our companions were all Jews. Near our bunk was an old man who had once been an office worker. His sheepskin coat was infested with flees, which soon infested us. In this packed wagon we stood at the station the whole day. People came looking for their friends and families in the hope of passing something to them for the journey. I was able to pass some notes out to them. The children were restless; Wojtuś got a fever and Anna lost her first milk tooth."

Jadwiga Krzysztoporska Piasecka: I was a rather passive child and remember just sitting on my belongings in the wagon and not doing much; maybe my mind shut down to protect me, I don't know. I was the middle child; my elder sister, Anna, was considered the good child who always looked after our baby brother, Wojtuś, and I was always considered the naughty child. Maybe that's why I wasn't too curious; I just isolated myself. The journey was rather long. I remember sitting and looking out of the window as we passed through forest after forest after forest. My mother kept a diary during the journey and recorded our experiences during the War.

---

122   Excerpts from the diary of Maria Krzysztoporska, Jadwiga's mother. Krzysztoporska M. (1981). *Pamiętnik Matki: 1940-1942. (Mother's Diary: 1940-1942)*. London, Veritas Publishers.

We changed trains many times and, finally, got to a settlement in the Urals with lots of small cabins. We shared ours with another family (we divided the cabin with our suitcases), and I know they were Jewish because the grandfather used to place his yarmulke by his bed. I used to play with their little boy. The adults went to work in the forest. I remember the hunger and 'coffee' that was made from burnt bread. My mother did not have to work at first but, because two of our servants had opted to be deported with us, they looked after us and, eventually, my mom went to work. She was away all day and used to come home with frozen milk for my baby brother who was about a year old at this time (my sister was seven). We did not go to school, but our mommy taught us. My sister was beginning to read but I did not learn until we had left Russia in 1942. I don't think there even was a school in our settlement.

Maria Krzysztoporska: *"The Commandant wanted to place us in a 22-person barrack with no windows or doors, a stove and a large hole in the ceiling and floor. I became hysterical and, this time, it helped. We were allocated a barrack to share with a family of eight Jewish traders from Kraków. Barrack #39 was surrounded by uninhabitable barracks, so we are guaranteed 'splendid isolation.' There are holes in the roof, there is also no stove, but the floor has been repaired, the windows are intact and there is a chamber that could serve as a bathroom. As there are no internal walls to create two rooms, we agreed on a demarcation line with the other family and made a 'non-aggression' pact; this was made easier by the fact that there were two entrances to the barrack. Our eight-person family had 16 square meters of living space (144 square feet) which was our kitchen, bedroom, workroom, children's room and 'salon.' In the winter it was also our laundry room and bathroom. There was a communal toilet outside though, eventually, they built a bathroom for each barrack."*

Jadwiga Krzysztoporska Piasecka: Our family in Poland knew where we were and we received some parcels from them; I remember we got sugar. Our family did not know we had been deported but, at first, thought that we had moved to a luxurious Jewish settlement in Azerbaijan. Christians were in the minority in our camp; it was overwhelmingly Jewish.

Maria Krzysztoporska: *"Those who had families in Soviet-occupied Poland or in Russia, received packages with food and money, so their diet was much more varied. A terrible fate was suffered by the poor Jewish population who had no contacts in Poland and who could not earn enough to buy food. In a short space of time people turned into shadows and skeletons and sometimes suffered badly from scurvy. People started dying from hunger; first the elderly who had no material help and who could not work to earn money. Actually, our whole settlement was a graveyard. There were* *many graves of Cossacks who had died in their thousands, years before. When digging our garden we would sometimes find human bones."*

Jadwiga Krzysztoporska Piasecka: I remember we received the news that we could leave; my father was in prison, and my mother looked for him but did not find him. People were spinning tops to decide where to go; nobody knew in which direction to go. We left without my father. My mom went out and sold as much as possible so that we would have food and money to buy train tickets. At first she didn't know which direction to go in either but, eventually, found out where the Polish Army was forming in Buzluk, Azerbaijan.

Maria Krzysztoporska: *"My husband was arrested exactly one year after our deportation from Poland, on June 28, 1941. He packed his backpack, a portion of boiled nettles for dinner, and said his goodbyes. God gives strength in such situations and there was no moaning or tears. It was difficult for my husband to leave the children, especially little Wojtuś; he loved to sit him on his knee and sing soldiers' songs to him. Maybe he knew that we were seeing him for the last time. I was left alone with 15 rubles in my pocket, with the great responsibility for the fate and the raising of the children. The news of the Amnesty reached us. What am I to do all alone, almost without money, with small children? Where I am to go in these unknown, boundless spaces? A premonition of a terrible fate waiting for us shook me to the core. Staying in the settlement was out of the question, as the only thing waiting for us was death from starvation. After much debate a group of us decided to head towards Orsk.[123] I waited for my husband to return and, eventually, went in search of him. I left a message with the NKVD in Perm that I was going to Orsk."*

Jadwiga Krzysztoporska Piasecka: The place we eventually reached, Buzluk, had lots of civilians; there was an outbreak of measles, so my mom wanted to get out of there as quickly as possible. Unfortunately, we all got measles; I was the first to get sick but I got well. Then, Wojtuś got ill and died before we reached Tashkent, Uzbekistan. The doctor could not reach him to help but who knows if it would have made a difference? He was two years old, undernourished, half-starved, and had pneumonia. I remember well how some locals came and took away his body. You couldn't keep a corpse in the wagon because the days were already getting warm.

---

123   Orsk, Russia, was to the south of their settlement.

Figure 44.   Anna and Wojtuś Krzysztoporscy, Poland, 1939

Maria Krzysztoporska: *"I was very worried. On the second day after we left Buzluk, Dzigunia (Jadwiga), got sick with measles. The measles was the least fatal of childhood diseases in Europe, at least if you kept the patient warm and in an even temperature. Here in Asia, however, it is one of the deadliest of childhood illnesses with a 90% chance of the patient developing pneumonia. On the train, the cold nights competed with the heat from the stove, while the days got hotter as we headed further south. Dzigunia was very ill but slowly started to recover. After her, Wojtuś fell ill and then Anna. All three of them sat still for hours on the bunk with a glassy stare gazing at some undefined point and, only occasionally asking for a drink.*

Why am I so frightened? After all, his temperature is 38.5 °C, and the doctor is just trying to reassure me. The caffeine injection has not helped; I monitor his fast pulse. The nurse comes to place cold compresses on him; we turn him over, he whimpers pathetically. Suddenly Wojtus stops squeaking and lies still, helpless. We turn him onto his back; his bluish face turns towards us with sightless eyes. I try to find his pulse, hearing the rapid beating of my own heart. The doctor gives him another caffeine injection, this time straight into the heart, but in vain. My son lies alone on the upper bunk, dressed in his best clothing. He lies still, peacefully. In his hands he holds a picture of the Black Madonna of Chęstochowa; on his breast he has a plain, black cross, the cross of Polish deportees; under his head he has a bag of Polish soil.

He remained alone, somewhere in Uzbekistan; nobody will pray at his grave. The youngest Polish soldier has followed in the footsteps of his uncle, who died in 1920 somewhere in the Ukraine."

Jadwiga Krzysztoporska Piasecka: My sister, Anna, also got tuberculosis when we got to Kagan, Uzbekistan. She was taken to hospital where she was neglected terribly. We lived in the local park for several weeks. I remember that I was not allowed to get up as I still had a fever. My mother made contact with Jan Piłsudski, the brother of Marshal Piłsudski, whom she had met on the maiden voyage of the *Batory*.[124] He invited us to live in his quarters. The doctors said that there was no hope for my sister and that she was completely spent. She was brought back to our room and lived with us for the last two weeks of her life. As a child, you don't fully understand what is happening. Anna couldn't sleep at night and one night she woke up and asked Mother for some chicken soup, thinking that would give our mother pleasure. I remember thinking, *"Don't be ridiculous, just die and don't bother Mother."*

She died shortly after that and for a long time I imagined that I was in some way responsible. So my mother lost two children in 2 months. Shortly after this there was an outbreak of typhoid, and the doctors thought I would die as I was so malnourished. Fortunately, Jan Piłsudski, coming from the family that he did, had some privileges and this helped my recovery. He saved my life, as my mother was in hospital with typhoid, so he looked after me. He would sit and talk to me which was good for my spirit. So many people were dying at this time that you could forgive any family that did not make this effort. We left Russia on the last transport and arrived in Iran on March 4, 1942.

Maria Krzysztoporska: *"Anna was taken to hospital where I would visit every day and read her temperature on the notice that was pinned to the gate. We were only allowed to see our children through a window. And, one day, I saw again a high temperature next to Anna's name and that she was in a serious condition. This time I went and offered her blood for another transfusion and, under this pretext, I was able to enter the hospital. Anna was in a very weak state. She had a sick stomach, infected ears and, because of her painful lungs, could not speak loudly and ask for water or a bed pan. The food I brought her every day lay untouched next to her bed as she did not have the energy to reach for it; instead, she was infested with cockroaches. Some food items were returned to me, others disappeared into the stomachs of the so-called*

---

124   The merchant ship *Batory* was a large (14,287 BRT) ocean liner of the Polish merchant fleet, named after Stefan Batory, 16th century king of Poland. Dubbed the *'Lucky Ship'* for her military career during World War II.

nurses. The ill were never washed so her growing hair was infested with fleas. The bedpans were never washed. None of the hospital personnel cared about the lives of the sick. That was the reality of life in a country where, apparently, children are greatly loved. Under my care Anna started to eat, and her temperature fell.

On December 2, I went to the gate as usual and was met by the doctor who told me that, while Anna's temperature was almost normal, there was no hope of recovery for her as she had tuberculosis. I managed to get permission to bring her home. Anna lay unconscious looking around the room while, in the corner sat her miserable but healthy sister, watching the end of her sister with fear. The child, surrounded by love and care, even started to talk and was interested in everything around her. She asked me about Wojtuś and told me how much she missed him. She was worried about her daddy's fate and would not let me sell his coat "in case he came back from prison, then what would he wear?"

She was saying goodbye to everything and everyone; her light was being extinguished. Despite plenty of nourishment, she was getting thinner and thinner; her weakened heart stopped responding to the medicines and her feet swelled. But she longed to live; with great patience she accepted all the medicines and injections, counting to 10 during an injection. Her breathing became more and more labored; she had more and more attacks of inability to breathe, during which the usually independent Anna only asked that we hold her hand. On the morning of December 15, she fell asleep for ever. She left us quietly, peacefully, saying goodbye to me by calling out, "Mother, Mother." She left, not having seen her father. At least she was no longer missing Wojtuś."

A White Wave of Goodbye

Kochaneczko mój,
My little precious one,
Gwiazdeczko moja,
My little star,

all I have to give you now,
Aniołeczku mój,
my little angel,
is this little white gown.

I made it
with my own hands,
cut from my wedding dress.
I did not know
on that day of
love and happiness
when I first wore it
that my dress
would go with us so far,
to Siberian snows
where we were forced
to labour and starve.

This dress,
sacrificed
one
piece
at
a
time,
bought us life.

One day,
a piece
made your baby brother's
burial gown.

I made one for you, too,
Iskiereczko moja,
my little light,
hoping against hope
it would not be for this.

What I wore in love and hope for the future
Now wraps your body in love and hope for your soul,
żebyś nie został sam,
that you would not be left alone,
żebyś został z aniołami
that you would be left with angels.

Kochaneczko mój,
my little loved one,
życie moje,
my life,
I must leave you now.
Your little white gown
must not lie in the mud.

I wait,
for the bodies to be piled.
I place yours,
only just three,
tenderly
at
the
top.
The breeze
gently ripples your gown.
My heart
explodes in my throat.

The train
pulls away,
struggling to cross the border
in time
and I
hang,
as far out of the window
as humanly possible,
as long as possible,
so my eyes can engrave
this last view
of you
upon my soul.

Your little white gown,
from high
atop the pile,
waves in the breeze
a gentle good-bye
up, down, up, down, up, down, up, down.

Mamusia moja,
my dear Mummy,
Your love enfolds me,
I am freed of strife.

Duszo moja,
my soul,
this last piece of veil
I will keep all my life.

© **Anon (2), 2007**

Anita Paschwa-Kozicka

b. 1929, Rokitno
April 1940, deported to the Soviet Union
1942-43, Iran, India
1943-46, Mexico
1946-present, USA

My father died of lip cancer when I was three-and-a-half years old. My mother took his death badly and died a year later. I remember going into her room and shaking her, screaming, *"Mommy, don't play games with me! I'm hungry!"* There were six children in my family, seven years apart (my father had been away at war for seven years with Piłsudski). In 1939, when the Russians entered our town, home to a Polish Army battalion, my sister, who lived close by in Tamszgród, took me in to live with her husband and their little girl.

In 1939, my brother-in-law, Walter, drove his employer, the Duke, to Warszawa, a fact that had been conveyed by jealous neighbors to the Russian authorities. On his return he realized that he would be arrested, so we planned to escape to Warszawa. We got only as far as Włodzimierz; by this time, the Russian-German border was closed for good and there was no way to get to Warszawa, no matter how much money one had. Walter found a farmer who was willing to hide us in his barn full of hay and cows, where we lived from the middle of February, 1940. The farmer promised that my niece and I could sleep in the house during very cold days; before the sun rose we would have to go back to the barn.

One day in March, the NKVD began to question the neighbors, saying that someone had told them there were wanted people hiding somewhere in the neighbors' house. We were not the only people who had escaped deportation to Siberia. The farmer's wife wanted us out immediately. We hid in the attic of a synagogue along with seven other families. I didn't know why it was closed; I was too young to know such things. The first transport left for Siberia. We lived in the attic and climbed up by means of a wall ladder which was nailed permanently in place. The adults had to go out at night to go to the bathroom, while the children used chamber pots. Food was purchased by one person who would leave the attic early in the morning while the townspeople were still asleep and come back at night when it was dark.

Then, one night in April 1940, our worst fears were realized. Six Russian soldiers with guns and rifles climbed up into the attic and began to read our names one by one. They told us to get ready within half an hour. We were ready anyway, but not for Siberia. We had hoped to get to Warszawa to the house of the nobleman whom Walter had helped escape. My sister began to cry and begged one of the soldiers saying that I was not her family and that I had been an orphan since the age of four-and-a-half but he just pushed her aside and continued reading, name after name. He said that everyone from this hiding place had to go to the train.

After a few days waiting in a boxcar at the train station, we moved towards the Russian border via my birthplace, Rokitno. My sister begged the soldiers to let me go, but they refused. In each boxcar were between 50 and 70 people. Each car had double benches for sleeping; there was straw on these benches as mattresses. The children's toilet was the hole in the middle of the car, but the older people waited until the guards let them out once a day to go into the fields or bushes. It took us two weeks to reach Novosibirsk but, at least, we were not as cold as those who were deported in February. People who were taken from their homes were lucky. At least they could take clothes and food; we had nothing. All the better clothes, silver spoons, knives and forks were exchanged for food at the city market in Włodzimierz. We each had one piece of bread and a cup of water. People knew they were being deported; train wagons everywhere were being fitted with bunks. On April 13, they finally took us.

Fortunately, it was warmer by the time we arrived in Zalomnaya, Siberia. As I was too young to be sent to work in the forest (you had to be 14), I looked after the small children while the adults worked; we were in Novosibirsk. My two friends were already there; they had been deported in February. Our whole settlement consisted of deportees. The winter lasted 10 months and we used snow and ice as water for drinking, cooking and washing. To wash two pillowcases, I had to spend two hours thawing the snow. There was no electricity, no radio or newspaper. We didn't know what was going on in the world. We had a small wood stove for cooking, for warming the barrack, and for lighting the cabin which had no wall at the top so we could hear the family next door and they could hear us; we had no secrets at all.

In Siberia, people were dying like flies, especially the oldest and the youngest. I was almost twelve-and-a-half years old, and determined to survive, no matter what. There were many pine trees, so I tried to eat pine buds and sucked on the branches; this seemed to satisfy my hunger. Hunger is the most terrible thing. First your stomach growls, then you get a headache and feel very tired and weak, then you just lie down and don't care about the world around you. These were my symptoms in Siberia. My sister always begged me not to give up or we would all die of starvation. You see, while the adults were at work for 10 hours each day, the children and very old people stood in line outside the Russian kitchen for a cup of watery soup for each person and a piece of bread. I had to wait in line to get this food, in weather that was 50 or 60 below zero. This soup was made of fish bones and potatoes (if there were any), and it was our meal for the day. The older people who tried to push me out of line always told me that I was young and I could survive this cold weather better, but they would freeze to death if they had to stand in line for 10 minutes longer. I just couldn't understand why our own people were so cruel to children. On top of it all, I was a babysitter for my seven-year-old niece.

Once, my brother-in-law arranged with a loyal Russian to exchange our embroidered pillowcases from Poland for a kilo of grain. I was observed by a NKVD man. He caught up with me, grabbed my hat, pulled my hair and kicked me with his heavy leather boots, yelling, *"Now if you want to live, tell me the name of this man or I will kill you!"* At that moment he pressed his gun against my head and kicked me again. I was so scared I urinated on the floor and his shoes got wet from it. Then he jammed the gun into his pocket, pulled my hair again and pushed me with all his might into the urine. He stuffed a dirty rag into my hand and told me to wipe it or lick it, but the floor had to be clean. At this moment another NKVD man walked in and when he saw my red face and messed up hair, and my clothes all wet, he asked what had happened to me. I told him that I had paid for the grain with two pillowcases. My sister was severely punished for giving me the pillowcases by having to work one hour later every day for about two months. It was a crime for us to associate with local Russian people.

We had nothing from Poland; no parcels, no news. Then, one day, the settlement supervisor came and told us that we were free to go, but that we had to make our own way to the Polish Army. We knew nothing about what was happening in the world, we didn't even know that the Soviet Union was at war with Germany. Many people were left behind. My brother-in-law was clever and immediately got us to leave. There were no trains or roads where we lived. The only way out was by horse and sleigh, but this was August and there was no snow on the ground. We had no money, just a few *rubles* in our possession. There was no way out for us but to wait until snow covered the ground. Besides, we had no money to pay for a horse and sleigh even if there had been snow.

My brother-in-law had an idea that we could build a raft. We didn't even have rope to create rafts to get across the river, and we had no oars. He knew that this river, the Chulym, went into the River Odra and that we'd be heading south. The NKVD came to tell us, *"Poles, you are free, the Polish Army is forming; Sikorski and Stalin have agreed to let you go."* Men could leave for Tashkent where others were gathering. I don't know what happened to the other families from the settlement, as we were the first to leave; we just let the river take us wherever it chose, as long as we got out of the camp. We knew that the Chulym eventually entered the River Ob, close to Asino where there was a train station. We just wanted to reach the station.

It took us a week to reach Asino and, when we got to Tomsk, we had to wait in line again to go to Novosibirsk. Here, we waited almost a week to catch a freight train to Tashkent where it was so hot that many of the older people began to faint from exhaustion and starvation. My niece and I went to the locals in the village, begging for food, but they were very poor and didn't have much for themselves. In addition, they were afraid of us because of the typhus, dysentery and malaria which afflicted the Poles during their imprisonment; they had brought the illnesses with them. Their dogs chased us so that we couldn't get close to their houses, but any stray dog that we found on the street became our feast that day. Many people died in the streets, with no one to pick up the body and bury it. The Russians were letting the Poles die of starvation, one after the other. We just waited and waited, sleeping on the sidewalks of the town. Once a day we received one piece of bread for which we had to stand in line for two or three hours in the hot, burning sun. Also, the water was polluted but at least we had something to fill our empty stomachs.

We were taken to Nukus, in Uzbekistan, where we worked on collective cotton farms for 2 months. This is where Nina became very ill. She suffered from dysentery, passing blood, and could barely walk. I tried to help her by going to the city from early morning to late afternoon and begging for food. The local people who couldn't speak Russian were very mean to us; they chased us out of there with whips but I never gave up. From time to time, they threw me a fish skeleton with the head untouched so I would run back to the clay hut were we lived and give it to Nina, but she just sucked on it; she was so weak that she couldn't chew it.

We were moved again, this time by barge, and my precious niece, Nina, was near death as she drank dirty, polluted river water to quench her thirst. It caused her dysentery to come back and every few minutes she had to go to the bathroom; her stomach was empty with no food, and blood was pouring out, along with about five inches of her intestine. She was pushing it out, thinking that her stomach would stop hurting. My sister, Maria, had to push the intestine back each time after Nina relieved herself. She used to say, *"Mommy, if I only I had a piece of bread then I wouldn't be ill."* Soon our Nina got stomach typhoid. When we reached Kerkichi, Uzbekistan, she was taken to a hospital where they gave her morphine. Maria was told to leave the hospital but, with no place to go, she fell asleep leaning against the wall of the hospital where Nina was dying. When she awoke she noticed Nina's little hospital blanket hanging on the line with many others. She was told that Nina had died along with five other children and had been buried at 5 AM. The nurse told my sister that, every day, they bury children early in the morning so that parents will not see their corpses; it would be much better if they remembered their children as they were alive. That was the hospital's policy and no one could change Russian law. How that hurt; she was my little girl.

My brother-in-law joined the Polish Army; my sister joined the Polish Women's Army, and I was really alone. My sister placed me in the Polish orphanage from where I was sent to Iran; later, my sister searched for me and found out where I had been sent.

Stella (Stanisława) Synowiec-Tobis
b. 1928, Brantowce
February 1940, deported to the Soviet Union
1942-43, India
1943-46, Mexico
1946-present, USA

In 1939 my father, Wawrzyniec, was 42; my mommy, Zofia Baklarzec, was 41; my brother, Stanisław, was 15; my sister, Irena, was nine; my baby brother, Jerzy, was 2 months old, and I was 11 years old. We lived in the settlement of Brantowce, Białystok. This was a military settlement; my father had been a legionnaire with Piłsudski and was given this land by the Government. In

1939 he was retired and looked after our estate. We were comfortably off. As a child, I used to tell people that my dad did nothing, and I thought that he should be working (which, of course, he was). I was told that he needed time for thinking. Our life was very good.

When the War broke out we were not very affected, as all that was happening in the west. Of course, we saw the occasional plane and we knew these were German. We had no radio and no Polish newspapers, so we didn't know what was happening in the west. But Daddy always managed to find out some news. When the Russians entered Poland, my father was immediately arrested. He was in prison for several days but my mommy got his farm workers to sign a petition claiming that she needed help on the farm as she could not cope by herself, especially as she had a baby. Consequently, he was released. Then I really got to see how heavily he worked. January, 1940, was a terrible winter and we stayed at home. On January 5, a neighbor's car came and we saw several people get out, including our neighbor, Pan Dziekojski's, young chauffeur; he was a Belarusian. Our father was frightened by these soldiers and this Belarusian. They came to the house and ordered my daddy to show his photographs. Daddy had, in the past, worked in a prison and had plenty of photographs; I'm not quite sure what he did, whether or not he was in charge, but he had many photographs; they took everything away in his attaché case, along with his military documents and medals.

They also took my father away, promising that he would return the next day. He was taken from the small local prison to a larger regional one where he had once been in charge. Then, we no longer had any contact with him; we could no longer go and see him. The prison was 35 kilometers away and it was impossible to get there through the heavy snow. One of my mom's friends went with my older brother with fresh clothing for Dad. Unfortunately, they were not able to see Dad, so I don't know whether or not he received the clothing. While my father was alive I never asked him whether or not he had received our parcel. This was a very painful chapter in our lives which, even after we found him, we could not talk about.

My brother did not return to school after Christmas. He was 15, but stayed at home so that my mom would have some help, and I also tried to help by feeding the animals. Unfortunately, the animals were not ours. On February 10, 1940, we were deported. At 4 AM, we heard knocking on the door and loud shouting, *"Get up, because we are moving you to another state,"* in other words, to Siberia. First, they deported the government officials like my dad, and the police, teachers, and doctors. Many of the fathers in the settlement, like my dad, had already been arrested but many others were still with their families. They had a list of everyone. By the time we were deported, many fathers such as teachers, doctors, government officials, and army personnel, were already missing from our settlement. Without my dad, my mom was deported with four young children. She was, at the time, suffering from a hernia. I don't know if her hernia got worse but when they put us into the train boxcars, she fainted. Maybe she had picked up something. When we were being deported, she cried terribly as did the baby. She knew what was happening and was beside herself. She knew what the Russians were capable of doing, as she had lived through the 1919-20 War. She saw her whole future before her and knew what awaited us all. When we were in Siberia, she could not work because of the terrible pain she had in her side, but she didn't talk to us about it because she didn't want us children to know about her suffering.

The man who oversaw our departure was very good; he helped us pack. He took blankets, laid them on the floor, and placed blankets, comforters, and furs on them and tied them up. Everything was loaded on the sleigh. We had a trunk full of towels and sheets; he put that on the sleigh also. Even our little sleighs that we used for play came in useful in Siberia. They knew what we would need. They told us to get packed, but we didn't know what to include; I took some books and a prayer book. They helped us get dressed. I had my own clothes and my father's coat over me. It was terribly cold. We would have died immediately if we had depended on my mom, because she was so ill.

It took almost a month to get to Siberia and, once we got off the train, another week on a sleigh to get to our destination. We slept at night in the homes of deported Ukrainians who gave us hot *kipiatok*. We didn't take tea when we were deported, but bread. We were put into one-roomed barracks for two families; the five of us, and five from another family. The next day, the manager of the *kolkhoz* said that unless someone worked, we'd have no food. My mother couldn't because she had a small baby, so my 15-year-old brother had to go and live in the forest in which he worked. We didn't see him for a long time but he sent us some money so we could buy bread. The manager would bring the money home to us after each weekend. I think he was honest; he was a Ukrainian who had been deported 20 years earlier during the Russian Revolution. There were about 1,000 people in the camp. The Ukrainians moved to the lakeside and we were put in their old barracks. We came with some clothing and bed linen, which they did not have, and they wanted to exchange these goods with us for potatoes which grew very quickly in this area.

The Ukrainians had small houses which were easier to heat with wood than our barracks. In the winter we cut down small trees into smaller pieces and burned them in the clay fire on which we cooked. In the summer we cut down the dry trees for summer cooking. My sister and I, aged nine and 11, were very pleased that we could help Mom. She had our baby brother who needed her all the time. When we had enough wood, we also cut wood for the manager, for which we were paid; we were glad to be helping the family.

In the camp there were families; most included fathers and husbands. Maybe the ones who were arrested were due to be sentenced to hard labor. I don't know; as a child I was not interested in their history. I was only interested in getting my 40 deko of bread which is what I received as I did not work. Those who did not work received less than those who did. We got 40 as opposed to 60 and you had to buy it; it was not free. 40 deko was only two slices of bread that wasn't thoroughly baked and was very heavy and not suitable for children. Maybe they had no yeast. The children who got bloody diarrhea all died. My little brother died in the first summer there, aged 13 months. He had such terrible diarrhea that his insides came out of him. Breast-feeding mothers had no milk as they had no food for themselves, so their children also died. My mother tried to breast feed until her milk dried out. The day my brother died, a little girl also died and they were buried in the same grave. The coffins were made from pine trees; all we did was put them in the soil and cover them with earth. All the children died.

There were some families with no one to work for food. In the Nowak family, the father died from an infectious disease so the whole family was moved to a separate building. They had between four and six children and when the mother died, they were taken to a Russian orphanage. They wanted to take us too; they told my mother that she would be better off with us in the orphanage. They probably wanted to finish her off as she wasn't working.

One day they took all the older people away and they never reappeared; we don't know what happened to them. Rather than sell them bread, they got rid of them. I had an uncle in Moscow, Mom's brother who, in 1913, was arrested and taken into the Tsarist Army. This was before our freedom in 1920. We didn't know where our uncle was; only later did we find out that he was alive in Moscow. This uncle saved our lives and made it possible for us to leave. He supplied the money, about 40 rubles,[125] for our train tickets and transportation to the railway station. If you didn't have money for your ticket, you were left behind. Many went on foot and froze to death on the journey.

The Amnesty occurred in August; we only found out about it in November.

---

125   The average monthly wage for a manual worker in the Soviet Union in 1940 was 32.3 *rubles*. Lane, D. (1970). *Politics and Society in the USSR*. London. Weidenfeld & Nicolson, first edition, p. 204.

Our manager must have received the information; then, the workers were let go from their jobs in the forests; they had the choice to work or not. My brother returned home and we were given travel permits and IDs. You needed this ID card in order to buy bread; they sold us as much as they were allowed to. My mother was left behind with the documents and money; a small purse we had disappeared and I think that it was stolen while we slept. No reporters were allowed in to Russia so our knowledge of what was happening in the War was almost non-existent. We just knew that we had to go south to where the Polish Army was forming.

You would travel during the day and then ask for refuge for the night in a local's home; they were very helpful. Those who had no money stayed behind; sometimes the father went and said he would come back for the family but never did. I walked the 100 kilometers to the railway station because we did not have enough money to buy me a seat on the sleigh. We sold everything we had, such as bedding and towels, which is what the locals wanted. We had 100 *rubles* from my uncle and we raised more money for the journey. My mother gave my brother nearly everything she had so he could go and join the Polish Army. I remember running after my brother calling for him to stop so I could give him the extra money, but the wind was taking my breath away. Finally, my brother stopped and I caught up with him.

After we left, some 1,000 kilometers later, my mommy went to buy bread and the train left without her. My sister and I were left alone. I was 13 and she was 10. One other person, who returned later to Poland and was in the same truck as us, also left the train to get bread. His son jumped off the train to find him and my mom in order to bring them back to the train. This son returned to Poland seven years later and happened to have contact with someone from our wagon. He said that my mommy and their father were on the station and they did not know in which direction our train had gone, whether to Moscow or the Urals. Only on the next day they learned of the direction; I found out that my mother had caught a train for the Urals trying to catch up with us. Near the Urals, we went to a Polish collection point; we don't know if my mom ever found this out. If they were trying to catch up with us they probably did not stop at any Polish offices. I don't know what happened to our mom; I tried in various ways to find her but I had no luck. No one heard anything about her. We left Siberia on January 17, 1942; my brother had left the settlement in November and joined the Polish Army on December 24, 1941. He was only 17 years old but lied, saying he was 18 years old.

"My Dearest Mother,

For 55 years, I carried you in my heart. For 55 years, I searched for the site of your grave, where, exhausted and heartbroken from the loss of your two little girls, you died. For 55 years, my sister and I shed tears on all the continents of the world for you. For 55 years, I could not place flowers on your grave.

Now, at the time when I am concluding this book, I am placing a bouquet of wild Polish flowers on your grave, wherever it might be; the same wild flowers which I picked for you during the summer of 1939. The same flowers which you took with a smile and placed on our family's small altar in the corner of our dining room, that summer when we were all happy, free and in our beloved HOMELAND, Poland."

Stella Synowiec-Tobis[126]

Stanisław Milewski

b. 1930, Bagrów
February 1940, deported to the Soviet Union
1942-47, Iran, Palestine
1947-59, England
1959-present, USA

In 1933, during the economic crisis, my father moved from the Poznań area to Polesie where he was given an *osada*, Staniewicz, near Ibaczewicz. In 1936, he was a member of the *Sejm*.[127] In 1939, he was recalled to the Polish Army as a Major but captured in Lithuania.

When War broke out, German planes flew overhead, shooting at civilians. There were also occasions when the Ukrainians encircled our house demanding my father. Fortunately he was not at home, as they would have killed him. After the beginning of the War, food was in short supply. The Russians took away our guns so we couldn't hunt for wild pigs. When the Russians entered, malnourished and with half-starved horses, they looked a sorry sight. They raided all the shops. Our house was later taken apart and moved to another location.

On February 10, 1940, at about 5 AM, we were awoken by Communists,

---

126   Synowiec-Tobis, S., op. cit., p 237.
127   *Sejm* (Polish): During the Second Polish Republic (1918-39), the term *'Sejm'* referred to the Lower House of Parliament, the Upper House being called the *'Senat'*.

Russians, Ukrainians, and Jews, who encircled our house and lined us up against a wall. We thought that they were going to shoot us all; instead, they told us that we had an hour to pack. We were told that we were being deported to Russia, but not where. A family staying with us then was told to go upstairs as they were not on the list. My sister was also not on the list so was not taken. She cried and begged to be allowed to join us and, a day later they brought her to our wagon.

We were loaded onto cattle trucks and, here, began the tragedy. We stood for three days in Wasowicze before heading towards Moscow. Some young people managed to wedge the door open, and then jumped off the train. This was not an option for families with children. I understood we were being deported to Russia and that there was great hunger there. The train would stop between stations; we would jump out and collect snow for water. It was terribly cold; I remember two old ladies froze to death.

We were taken to Archangel. Each day people were taken away, heaven knows where to. After four days we, too, were taken away. It was very cold. Due to a shortage of space on the sleigh, my brother and I often had to run alongside it. At night we stopped at various *posioleks.*[128] There were no roads so we traveled on frozen rivers all the way to Kokoris. They kept us waiting outside for an hour in temperatures of -30 °C. We were taken to an old Tartar and Ukrainian settlement whose inhabitants had been deported by Stalin in 1933. There was nothing there at that time; they were just dumped into the forest and most of them had died. Those who remained tried to help us as best they could. It was an agricultural settlement and they had to be self-sufficient. The rich soil was good for growing fruit and vegetables in the short summer months.

My brother was sent to be a lumberjack, my mother and sister worked in the *kolkhoz*; I went to school. I already knew Belarusian and learned to speak Russian quickly so I didn't have too much of a break from school. I worked in the summer, grazing horses and cows; this helped the family a lot. We received letters and parcels from those who had not been deported from our Polish settlement. Also, one of our aunts in Warszawa sent us life-saving packages. In Kokoris, we had our own allotment where we grew potatoes and beetroot, but we all had scurvy since we had no vitamins. In 1941, there was an epidemic of typhoid and half our settlement, both Poles and Tartars, died. We had no medicine and my sister almost died; I remember how we sat with her, cooling her forehead. She was dying and yet, suddenly, she recovered. We were subsequently moved to yet another *kolkhoz* where the conditions were terrible. There was hardly any food.

---

128 *Posiolek* (Russian): workcamp.

Witold Mazur

b. 1936, Kołodno
February 1940, deported to the Soviet Union
1942-48, Iran, Iraq, India, Africa
1948-58, England
1958-present, Canada

My parents, Jan Mazur and Janina Kulesza, lived near Wiśniowiec Castle. My father was a farmer and I was an only child. On February 10, 1940, we were collected at three o'clock in the morning. That afternoon, one of our neighbors had killed our dog which, in retrospect, saved my father's life because had the dog barked when the Russians came for us, my father would probably have gone out with his gun to see what was wrong and would have been shot.

The Russians told us, *"Come as you are."* The Ukrainian accompanying the soldiers asked them to give us time to pack because I was a small child, so we were able to take our sheepskin coats and other clothing. When they walked in they looked all around. One of the soldiers, I don't know what his rank was, but I remember he had a red star on his arm and it came off. I remember his face, and the fact that he had an upturned nose. He asked if we had weapons, and I said *"yes."* My father went white, because just a few weeks earlier he had made a secret compartment in the house where he hid his weapons and documents. He knew that I knew where the rifle was. The soldier asked me to show him, and I walked over to my little corner and pulled out a toy gun with a string and cork at the end of it. The soldier started laughing and didn't bother looking anywhere else in the house. We'd heard from other people that they would generally bang on the walls or pull them apart, looking for weapons.

They loaded us onto a sleigh to take us to the railway station of Bozurka, which was between 10 and 15 kilometers from our village. The Ukrainian fellow with the soldiers gave my father a sack of dry bread and three metal cups. This probably saved our lives as we needed something in which to collect the hot water to drink in Russia. My mother hid silver and jewelry in her underpants. There was a Jewish fellow in a buggy, checking off names as people were taken. Not everyone was taken in the first transport, so it was obvious that he had denounced us. Anybody related to the Army was taken in the first round.

I have memories of the camp near Guzara, of the fleas and lice. To this day I shake violently when I smell scotch, as it reminds me of the fleas.[129] I was a little fellow and I remember being in a kindergarten and we were being taught to read and write in Russian. One day, a well-dressed woman came in to see us; she had

---

129   Alcohol was used to kill fleas and lice.

a star on her epaulet. There were 30 children in the class. She asked: *"Do you believe in God?"* We all replied, *"Of course!"* She brought a nice statue of the Virgin Mary and told us to pray, and then he said, *"Look, your God does not respond to you. But, if you pray to Uncle Stalin,"* and she brought out a bust of Stalin, about the same size as the statue, *"he will listen to you."* And suddenly sandwiches were brought in, with bread with a gray fluid which was supposed to be milk. In the class there was a girl, aged 14, who was much older than us but she was very small, and we referred to her as our guide. So when we were told to pray to Stalin we looked to her and she said *"Yes."* When I got home I told my father about this and he said, *"Son, but do you know the difference between the Virgin Mary and Stalin?"* I said, *"Yes."* *"Good,"* he responded, *"that's all I need to hear."*

God, How I Hate the Cold

As the piercing frost of winter begins to take its hold
I can't help but think *"God, how I hate the cold!"*
As I wrap my clothing closer to keep out the chill
My thoughts instantly dash back to a time past and still.
Of valiant suffering and strength and a story rarely told,
Of a journey remembered by those who are now old.
On February 10th, 1940, a mass deportation took place
In God's silence, masses of Polish people were to be erased.
Ripped from their homes and herded like lambs to slaughter,
Barely surviving on bits of frozen bread and boiled water.
In bondage and deprived by brothers of kindness and humanity
Clinging to each other like wounded sparrows in a boundless eternity
Because of one man's evil soul and murderous hand
A nation of people were sent to an inhuman land.
The life they'd once known disappeared as tho' it had never been
And was replaced by images that should've never been seen.
Mothers huddled their children as they drew their last breaths
As the wicked Siberian winters drew them to their deaths.
Fathers lost their sons and sons lost their fathers.
No one was spared this wrath as it awaited all the others.
Their cries of pain must have reached Heaven's gates
As they prayed to be released from this insufferable fate.
Every day they worked the frozen forests with each step patrolled

And all must have silently whispered *"God, how I hate the cold!"*
Gnawing pains of hunger replaced joyous memories once shared
As children of Poland faced each day confused and scared.
Weakened by sickness, thousands of broken spirits soared to the sky
And were guided by waiting white eagle's wings in order to fly.
There would be no more hunger and no more cold
Except for those who remained on earth and dared to grow old.
And they, like the spirits of their pasts, fly by guided eagle's wings
As they remind us of their youth and teach us many valuable things.
The blood of our ancestors flows directly within our earthly veins
That is why we remember the cold, their sorrows and their pains.
I think many of Poland's children can truthfully say
They all recognize this chill I speak of, on a frost-laden day.
For in that moment, spirits of past within you entwine
So you won't forget their passage of time.
And with guided angel wings and white eagles leading the way
The trail of their history is brought to your life everyday.
Learn from their stories of the journey to hell
Make note of their struggles and remember them well
And when the frost of winter fleetingly bites at your face
Embrace it as you exhale its pain with dignity and grace.
For you are now the voice silenced many years ago
And the cold just makes you remember what the world must know.

© **Hania Kaczanowska, 2005**

Franciszek Herzog

b. 1931, Lubaczów
April 1940, deported to the Soviet Union
1942-47, India
1947-52, England
1952-present, USA

My father was a professional officer in the Polish Army; he was in charge of a garrison in Lubaczów, 100 miles west of Lwów. My mother was from the Wilno district and my father was from Kraków. I was the youngest of three brothers;

Wacław was born in 1924, Tadeusz in 1926, and I was the 'after-thought', born in 1931. My father was captured in Lwów and taken as a POW by the Russians to the Ukraine and executed in Kharkov, in eastern Ukraine, in the Katyń Massacre. All the prisoners were executed. We knew that some people, those that had been given land after the war of 1919-20, had been deported. People suspected that something was going to happen because there were trains at the station with chimneys in the wagons. My mother planned to go back to Wilno,[130] thinking we'd be safer there.

We were deported to a village in Lugavoj, where we arrived at the end of May. We received a postcard from our father in June; the postmark shows that the card was mailed with our address in Lugavoj even before we were deported. Clearly, the deportation lists had been prepared well in advance. In June 1941, Germany attacked Russia and an amnesty was declared for all Poles who had been deported to Russia. Together with my brother, Wacek, we volunteered for the Polish Army. Our second winter in Siberia was approaching. We had no news of our father's whereabouts but we had some financial help from Uncle Strumiło who had come to Russia from London with the Polish Embassy.

1942 arrived and the Polish people in our village, especially the weaker ones, began to die. Deep down inside we were all worried about Mother. Unfortunately, she did not survive the winter. She died around midnight on January 17, 1942. She was sick for no more than a week. Mother was not physically worn out; if we had been able to get medical help we would certainly have saved her. True, the food was not too good, nor abundant, but Mother did not work hard physically. It is only today, however, that I understand her lack of appetite; when we returned from work and the four of us would sit down to a meager supper, tears would often fill her eyes and, to our unthinking appeals for more, (as *"work takes it all out of us"*), she would answer that, unfortunately, there was no more.

A few days into her illness, we began to realize that things were going badly. At times her memory would lapse; she would forget where she was and drift into a delirium. Then, there would be times of apparent well-being and Mother would return to the living. She would try to eat and to converse. Once, we were reading aloud from the Russian newspaper and happened upon a reference to the fact that India had agreed to accept 250 Polish orphans. *"You see, boys,"* said Mother, *"When I die, Tadzik and Niusiek can go to India, and Wacek will join the*

---

130   Wilno is the capital of Lithuania. Before the War, at least 50% of its population comprised ethnic Poles. During World War II, Lithuania was occupied by the Soviet Union (1940-41), Nazis (1941-44), and the Soviet Union, again, in 1944. Lithuania was, as a neutral country, officially supposed to intern members of the Polish Armed Forces. However, the country was generally very sympathetic to Poles so many soldiers and pilots found their way to the west via Lithuania.

Polish Army." We felt most awkward, knowing she was serious. We tried to dissuade her, as one does in these situations, but I suppose that, by then, Mother had found the courage to look truth in the eye.

After this, things grew steadily worse. It was futile to call the doctor as he resided some 28 kilometers away; the roads were banked with high snow and we had nothing on which to ride. The answer always came, *"Wait. In February, the doctor is due to make the rounds of your area, then he will see what ails you mother."* Wait? Wait for what? Death?

Death came ever closer to claiming Mother. We would gather what we could; some medicines and prayers, prayers ardent to the point of tears; this was all we had at our disposal in the battle against death. Mother got to recognize us rarely. Her mind wandered back to Wilno, to the days of her youth. From what we could understand of her delirious mutterings, she spoke with her great-grandparents. We could only look on in bewilderment. Eventually, Mother lost consciousness completely, only starting convulsively when some attack of the heart seized her. Then, we would run for Valerian drops which we had been able to obtain from some 'good people.'

On the evening of January 17, 1942, we lay on the floor, and Niusiek, as usual, lay asleep, next to Mother on the bed. We kept watch by the light of a small oil lamp made from a bottle with a piece of wick. We lay, half-sleep and half-watchful. Every rustle woke us. I remember holding my breath to ascertain better whether Mother was still breathing. We feared that she would leave us, though we never spoke of it. Suddenly Mother moved and let out a kind of moan or whimper. We rushed to her side, immediately pressing a spoonful of Valerian to her lips. We clumsy, dim, boys found in those moments the most tender phrases springing unashamedly from us. We knew or, rather, felt that a great moment had arrived. Our state of nervous tension, intensified through so many sleepless nights, came to a peak upon hearing the liquid we poured down Mother's throat, flow down as into an empty well, from the top to the bottom. Her lips never closed. We understood. Mother lived no more, yet our minds couldn't fathom what we were seeing and, in our hearts there was no room for the feeling.

I grabbed the night lamp and brought it closer. On Mother's forehead, white as alabaster, sweat shone like a light frost. I cried, *"No, it can't be!"* I put my ear to her breast and heard a clear and loud beating of a heart; boom, boom, boom! I felt a wave of joy wash over me, a hundred times greater than the fear and uncertainty which had previously held me in its grip. I had often, in the past, laid my ear against her chest to hear the faint beating of her heart, like the fluttering of a caged bird. All these thoughts crossed my mind like lightning, but it was my own heart which I heard. Then, I had no more illusions.

Wacek wept. I knelt beside the bed and felt a desire fill my heart; a desire for revenge that grew stronger and stronger. The desire to run somewhere, to tear someone apart and to snatch Mother back from death. I did not cry, but the pain ripped me apart, as did the consciousness of the unfathomable wrong which had been done to Mother and to us. Niusiek had woken earlier but seemed not to understand what was happening. We told him, *"Mommy died."* How strange the words sounded in our mouths, spoken for the first time, and how terrible. I cried only at the funeral.

For me, Mother's death was something unreal; it was a few years later that I realized what had happened. I did not follow Mother's casket, a wooden box made from rough boards, to the cemetery as I did not have any shoes.

Katyń

There were no Great Walls there,
No towers leaning or not leaning
Declaring some king's success
Or mocking another's failure,
No gleaming cathedrals where you can
Pray for forgiveness or watch
The cycle of shadows play
Through the coolness of the day,

And soon not even the names
Of those who died will be remembered
(Names like Skrzypinski, Chmura,
Or Anthony Milczarek)
Their harsh voices and tearing courage
Are already lost in the wind,

But their true moments
Will always be there, in the dust
And the gray ashes and the mounds
Settling over the bodies over which
No prayers were ever whispered,
No tears shed by a grieving mother
Or trembling sister.

© **John Guzłowski, 2008**

Maria Pawulska Rasiej

b. 1927, Lwów
April 1940, deported to the Soviet Union
1942-47, Iran, India, Africa
1947-52, England
1952-present, USA

When the train left us at a station in Kazakhstan we had to wait for trucks to take us to various *kolkhozes*. Since there were no trucks left, we were placed into carts pulled by bulls. We traveled even further east for seven days and seven nights. There were no towns or villages as these were the steppes; just sometimes, we came across a *kolkhoz*. The old lady who had been traveling with us, her cart broke and she and all her belongings fell into the fast-flowing river. It was not deep, and her maid managed to save her. We got to a *kolkhoz* in Kalim where they made a place for us to stay (I think there were about 10 families there). They shared their blankets with us, and we lay on the floor. We had no idea where we were going; the people leading the bulls were Kazakh-stanis who spoke no Russian.

We were placed in a *kolkhoz* where there was arable and dairy farming. The inhabitants had, first of all, to send a certain amount of produce to Moscow; then, they kept the rest for themselves. We also made bricks from straw, cow dung and mud. They had to walk in a circle to tread this, place it in moulds, dry it, and make it into bricks. Cow dung was also mixed with water and straw to make fuel for burning. There were some trees but this area consisted mainly of thousands of miles of tall grass. We used to collect leftover cow dung, dry it, and keep it for fuel for the winter. The whole *kolkhoz* was involved in the wheat harvest. We had to separate the wheat from the chaff, which was very difficult work. The machine that used to clean the grain spat out such dust that, despite having her mouth covered while she was working, Mommy coughed for the rest of her life.

I was responsible for looking after the calves which were separated from their mothers so that they would not feed on their mothers' milk; it was need-ed for butter and cheese-making. I had about 100 calves in my care. We used to walk them quite far away so that they would not be tempted to return to their mothers. We would leave at about 4:30 in the morning and, as payment, received milk without the cream; basically fat-free milk which they could not use. The locals sometimes fed us a type of pasta. We had very little clothing and, while we received some parcels from Poland, we traded clothing for food. For example, my mother traded one of my embroidered nightdresses for some eggs which, she was told, would hatch.

We were moved to another *kolkhoz* because ours had, apparently, gone bankrupt. My mommy and brother were sent to a local town to find work. However, in order to ensure that they did not escape, we were kept behind as hostages. It was getting cold and we could no longer work so were sent to school. I was always a good student but just couldn't learn in Russian. This was the winter of 1940-41. My mother wrote that she had found work in an orphanage and would not be escaping. She wanted us to join her so that we would be together. Initially, they did not want to let us go because we could work again in the spring but, at the end of March, we were taken to join her. I worked as a babysitter; the cradle was hooked up to a spring in the ceiling so that, each time the baby made a sound, we could rock it. I was given food as payment which I brought home to share with the family. You become like an animal in these circumstances, gathering and hoarding food.

Aniela Bechta-Crook

b. 1936, Borszczów
February 1940, deported to the Soviet Union
1943-49, Africa
1949-51, England
1951-62, Argentina
1962-68, USA
1968-present, New Zealand

My parents had a small parcel of land in an ex-servicemen's *kolonja*,[131] Wołkowce, near Borszczów, Tarnopol, in what was then eastern Poland, where my grandparents and 24 other Polish families settled after the Russo-Polish War. The farm was too small to be self-sufficient so both my parents had to work. Our lives changed forever after Hitler and Stalin signed the Molotov-Ribbentrop Treaty of Non-Aggression. Germans attacked Poland from the west and, two weeks later, Soviet boots marched in from the east.

My dear mother had a strong foreboding when friends begun to disappear. She started to stockpile food, and even killed a pig on that fateful evening. At 4 AM on February 10, 1940, two militiamen burst into our house, held my father against the wall at the point of a bayonet and ordered Mother to pack.

---

131   *kolonja* (Polish): colony.

It was a freezing winter so she packed warm clothing, a feather eiderdown, (which later saved our lives), and the still-warm pork meat we had just cooked. Together with my five-year-old brother, Emil, and 11 other members of our extended family, we were led out to big sleighs and taken to Borszczów train station. With 2,000 others, we were all loaded onto a cattle train. For some unexplained reason, my mother's sister and her family were left behind.

We traveled for three weeks with no idea of our destination. Every so often the doors would slide open and we'd be given some thin gruel, bread, and coal for the small stove. There was no toilet in the wagon, only a hole in the floor. One old man died and his body was left behind. When the train finally stopped somewhere in Altai Kraj, we transferred to sleighs and, for a further three days, traveled deep into the wilderness. Our *liesnoje chozjajstwo*[132] consisted of several old and freezing barracks full of hungry bugs, scattered within 8 kilometers of each other. Our family was separated. Within a day or so, the adults were marched off to the forest to collect pine resin while the very young attended a small pre-school where speaking Polish was forbidden. Older children were sent to a Russian village school. Personally, I have only a few sporadic flashes of memory from those times.

There was no escaping the forced labor and when my father caught pneumonia following a snowstorm, Mother had to work twice as hard to make his quota as well as her own. There was no medical care. *"Poland is lost forever; you are here to work until you die,"* was their motto.

Sometime in July or August 1941, Mother gave birth to a baby boy and, soon after, we were given 'amnesty', a move prompted by the German invasion of Russia. On September 2, the family gathered in our barrack, the closest to the village, and began the long walk to the station. The aim was to go south and find an assembly point for the incipient Polish Army. *"Where there's an army there's food."* We traveled three weeks through the Central Asian territories, with thousands of other ragged, hungry families, sleeping on crowded station floors and in ditches where our eiderdown saved us from freezing. When we got to Gorczakowo, all my five uncles managed to enlist but my dear father was rejected due to his poor health. Mother took him to a hospital and only saw him there twice. We asked the Red Cross to help us find my father but he was never heard of again and we do not know his fate. It is hard to imagine that there could be a place worse than Siberia but, for my mother, this was so. It was a constant struggle to find shelter, work, and food; even a dog would do! But, somehow, she managed to get us out of there, and even found a priest to christen baby Guscio.

---

132 *liesnoje chozjajstw* (Russian): forest operation.

Józef Kałwa

b. 1928, Nowogródek
February 1940, deported to the Soviet Union
1942-47, Iran, Iraq, Palestine
1947-62, England
1962-present, USA

My parents had about 42 hectares of land in Nowogródek in 1939, so we were comfortably off. There were seven of us in the family. Relations between the Belarus population in our settlement and the Poles were very good, as they were suffering the same treatment as we were and they were also worried about their future. In fact, some of them sent us parcels after we were deported.

On February 10, at 2 AM, we were awoken and told that we were being 'moved,' but they didn't tell us where. We stayed in cattle wagons at the station for three days and, then, traveled for two weeks. After a further two days' travel by sleigh, we reached a labor camp that had been built especially for us. There were eight families per building, though each family had its own 10-foot-square room. The three youngest of us had to attend Russian school, while my three older brothers (aged 14, 15, and 16), and Mother, worked from 6 AM to 6 PM cutting down trees, pulling them to the river and floating them down to the nearest town.

In April of 1941, the Camp Commandant told our mother that, since she could not keep the three youngest sons healthy, we would be moved to a special school in September. She couldn't refuse; we were destined to be separated but as soon as Germany attacked Russia they forgot about us. Psychologically, I don't think the experience touched me; it was like being in a Boy Scouts' Camp. 10 million Ukrainians had been thrown into the forest in 1932 with nothing; those who survived showed us what was edible in the forest. Nature was rich and we were on a lake so we went fishing. We supplemented our diet with things that we picked or caught; this was crucial to our survival as the standard daily diet of soup and two slices of bread would have killed us. Those who worked relied upon us for food supplements to survive. Survival in the area was possible for a maximum of five years because of the diet and hard work. It was a form of extermination.

Julian Ciupak

b. 1935, Bartków
February 1940, deported to the Soviet Union
1942-48, Iran, India, Africa, England
1948-present, Canada

My family came from the Rzeszów area, but moved to the Lwów area in the 1920s, and I was born in Bartków. We were Poles living in a predominantly Ukrainian area so, when the Russians moved in, we were treated like squatters as opposed to settlers in reclaimed lands.

I remember our farmstead and how my mother had to take the cow to the town, crying as she walked along the road. I later found out that the Russian Army requisitioned animals from the farmers, though the farmers did receive some payment. We prepared food for the winter by digging a hole in the ground, lining it with straw and, then, covering it with straw. When the snow came it covered the hole and insulated it for the remainder of the winter. I remember a steam tractor plowing the road so we could be taken out of our homes. I remember the night that we were taken away there was a lot of confusion and commotion. It woke the calf which started to cry. My mother said, *"Who is going to look after the calf?"* She was told, *"Look after your children and not the calf, woman."* I knew there was tension but I couldn't pin it down to anything specific. War did not factor into my mind. There was movement of people but I did not connect it to war.

We were taken away very early in the morning, having been given one or two hours to pack. They were making the rounds of the village. My whole family was taken together; my parents and older brother, my grandparents, and my grandmother's family. We traveled in freight cars; these were not cattle cars as cattle cars are different and made with slats which let the wind through. Freight cars are solid. We had platforms on each side of the wagon for sleeping. I remember the telephone wires going up and down as we traveled; it was white and I couldn't figure out why the distant objects moved slower than the ones closest to the train. I remember people using words that I was not supposed to hear. My mother or grandmother had a little sing-song every time the train started: *"sakum, pakum, jeźdź do Rosji...."* [133] I remember a muddy place where we were put into a carpenter's shop and we looked under the tables for blocks of wood to play with. This must have been the spring of 1940.

Eventually, we arrived in the labor camp. My family went to work in the forest; I was too young. My grandfather and sister did not join us; I have no

---

133 *"Sakum, pakum, jeźdź do Rosji..."* (Polish): "sakum, pakum, ride to Russia...".

memory of them at all though I know that my sister died of pneumonia during the journey. I picked mushrooms and blueberries in the forest and watched the men put a chopped log onto the creek which became a large river in the spring. I remember that I had just received a gift of new rubber boots and one of the men dropped his long pole onto the side of my boot; the pole bounced and cut my left calf. I thought I had done something wrong so I hid under the bed at home. My parents looked at the wound and I wondered what would happen next. My mother said, *"Please tell me, my dear son, how you have a cut in your left foot but a hole in your right boot?"* Everybody started laughing which broke the tension.

The Light of the Candle

A cold, frosty window against the darkness of the night
A lonely candle burns with a small flickering light
A small boy watches the flame with curious eyes
Babciu, you lit this candle, can you tell me why?

I lit this candle to remember someone I never knew
Somebody I just heard about when I was as little as you.
This is for my grandparents who never got the chance to see
Their homeland again and a new world with just me.

They lived in a time when their Polish freedoms were taken
On a cold February winter night, all humanity forsaken.
I only knew them from the many stories that were told
How they struggled to survive with hunger and bitter cold.

They never had the chance to get back what they knew
Their lives were destroyed and there was nothing they could do
Their last steps on earth were struggling to return
And I try to remember this as the memory candle burns.

I missed the warm hugs they might have given me
If they had just been given another chance to see
But in my heart I always felt their love stream thru
And from my heart I give *Babunia* and *Dziadek* to you

They were warriors of faith and loved their land
Their fate was unnecessary and hard to understand
They were proud people, gentle and strong
Trapped in a world where so much went wrong.

When the 10th of February comes, remember this light
And the story I will tell you about them tonight.
May the candle burn bright and their memory survive
As their spirit touches us as if they were here and alive.

When I light the candle it is because I hope they will see
That their story will be passed on down to you, thru me
I can feel their smiles from the warmth of the flame
I hope the lit candle will always make you feel the same.

© Hania Kaczanowska, 2007

Since the fall of Communism in Poland, a new tradition has emerged.

On February 10 of each year,
people all over the country place a lit candle in their window
to commemorate the first of four waves of deportations (in 1940)
of approximately two million Polish citizens to Siberia.

I ask that you also light a candle in their memory and in the memory of all those
who suffered through this Russian genocide of the Polish people,
and of the many other citizens of the Baltic countries.

A Candle Loses Nothing by Lighting Another Candle.
Please Keep This Candle Going!

Thank You.

Hania Kaczanowska, 2007

LIFE IN TRANSIT

CHAPTER 7

Amnesty

Fleeing the Soviet Union
1941-42

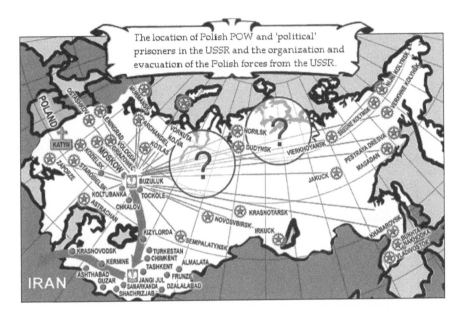

Figure 45. Fleeing the Soviet Union, 1941-42[134]

134   Lt.-General Anders, W. (1949). *An Army in Exile*. Nashville: The Battery Press, p.57.

Location of Poles who fled the Soviet Union:
approximately 115,000, or 7% of all deportees

- June 1941, Germany attacked the Soviet Union.

- July 1941, Sikorski-Maisky agreement signed: Stalin agreed to issue an 'Amnesty' to deported and imprisoned Poles and allowed the formation of a Polish Army on Soviet territory, under the command of General Władysław Anders.

- By December 1941, 44,000 Polish servicemen reported for duty at reception centers; rations issue by the Soviet General Staff deliberately maintained at 26,000. 15,000 officers were missing.

- By March 1942, the Army numbered 70,000. Anders was given permission to evacuate the Polish troops via Krasnovodsk to Pahlevi, Iran.

- During March 24 - April 4, 33,039 military personnel and 10,789 civilians passed through Krasnovodsk on their way to Iran.

- In May and June 1942, more able-bodied men and women of military age were transferred to camps in Palestine to prepare for active service; those underage joined the '*Junak*' units and prepared for service later.

- During August 8-30, a further 44,832 military personnel and 25,437 civilians arrived in Krasnovodsk for evacuation to Iran.

- 37,000 civilian refugees and dependents (including approximately 18,300 children) temporarily distributed among camps throughout the British Empire and Dominions, and Mexico.
  - Persia - Tehran, Achwaz, and Isfahan.
  - India - Chela, Jamnagar (Balachadi), Kolhapur (Valivade), and Karachi.

- Mexico - orphans, mothers with children to Santa Rosa.

- March 1943: Poles remaining in the Soviet Union were forced to accept Soviet citizenship.[135]

---

135   Hope, M., op. cit., pp. 36-40, and Piotrowski, T., op. cit., pp. 8-10.

Zygmunt Kopel

b. 1934, Mołodeczno
April 1940, deported to the Soviet Union
1942-47, Iran, Iraq, Palestine
1947-present, England

My parents' generation was a wounded generation, and my generation didn't have a childhood. A terrible thing that happened to me was that I was sent to the *Junacy* School[136] when I was only 10 years old. The school maintained army discipline so you could not go to anyone if something was bothering you. We used to get beaten but, overall, it did me good as it prepared me for life. In comparison, my parents lived through two World Wars.

I remember well the Russian invasion; how they marched through our town all day and night. We were deported on April 13, 1940. There were four of us, including my sister. My father was taken as a prisoner by the Russians and escaped but was recaptured. He received a sentence of eight years of hard labor, which was common. He was in Trzeblik.

In 1941, we knew nothing about the outbreak of war between Germany and Russia. My father was released in July of 1941 and found us; I have no idea how he managed that. Later, my mother told me that my father met someone who had a wife in the same *kolkhoz* that we were in and that's how he found us. We did not have to endure hunger. My mother was arrested just before my father arrived, so I was left alone with my 13-year-old sister for only eight days. I don't know how we took care of ourselves; perhaps my sister used the packages that we received from our family in Poland. My father knew the direction in which to travel to join the Polish Army; others had no contact with the Army and stayed behind.

In March of 1942, we learned that the Polish Army was being transported to Persia from southern Russia. We went by train to Krasnovodsk from where we sailed to Pahlevi, arriving on April 1, 1942. We had scarlet fever and jaundice, though we were fortunate that my family did not suffer from typhoid. All our belongings were taken and burned in Pahlevi; we were disinfected with DDT,[137] which, today, is forbidden. I don't know how my mother managed to hide our photographs but I'm so glad she did, as they provide a 'hook' to the past.

---

136   *Junacy* (Polish): Cadet School. *Junacy* schools in Palestine were located in Baszit, Qastina, Barbara, Nazareth, Sarafuand, Beit Nabala, Kiryat, and Motzkin. In Egypt, in Te-el Kebir, Mena and Heliopolis.

137   Dichloro-Diphenyl-Trichloroethane: the agricultural use of DDT was banned in the US in 1972 and in Britain in 1984.

Julian Ciupak
b. 1935, Bartków
February 1940, deported to the Soviet Union
1941-48, Iran, India, Africa, England
1948-present, Canada

I keep telling everyone that Hitler did us a favor by attacking Russia as, all of a sudden, we became Russia's allies. In our camp somebody was told that we could leave. This man traveled for two weeks to confirm the news. It was the winter of 1942; shortly afterwards, we left by sleigh for the nearest railway station.

I don't remember much about the trip south, however, I do remember that at one point we lost our mother. When the train stopped at a station there were local people selling food on the platform; my mother got off for a second time with some other women to get more soup and the train left without them. When we stopped for the night we hoped that they had managed to jump on the last wagons. There was much crying and sadness.

We were asleep in a warehouse when, suddenly, at midnight, there was some shouting. It was only four or five years later, when I was old enough to understand, that I found out what had happened. Mother told us that they jumped on the next train, which was a military train. The conductor tried to get the women off but they refused to leave. He told them that the train was not stopping at the station they needed. The train stopped two stations beyond ours, but the conductor told them to get off and showed them where to get a passenger train back. The conductor was worried that she might be shot for stopping the train, but the women knew that if they didn't stay on the train they would never find us again. All they knew was where our train was stopping for the night.

We arrived in Uzbekistan on January 1, 1942. This was probably the most miserably hard time that we'd ever had. They had no accommodation for us so we stayed in sheds until accommodation was found for us on farms. We lived in mud huts. The Soviet Government made no provision for our care so we scrounged what we could from the local collective farms. I remember picking wild sorrel for soup in the spring. It was the most delicious soup I'd ever tasted. Father left us to join the army, so we were on our own. I remember the place crawled with turtles. Once, Father came back on leave; he was carrying a turtle on which he had stepped and broken its back. He told Mother to make turtle soup from it; the whole army was living on turtle soup. Then, our diet improved; we were there through the harvest because I remember my mother and the other women collecting the leftover straw and grain from the fields. The straw was used for the roof of our huts.

Figure 46. The Ciupak family, Tehran, Iran, 1942

I remember nothing about the journey across the Caspian Sea. We finally got to Pahlevi in Iran; we lived on the beach all day and night, with little canopies to keep out the sun. I was very sick at this time. The English doctors would check us regularly to see if we were fit enough to be put on a lorry and taken to Tehran. My mother told me to rub my cheeks so that they would be nice and rosy; then we'd be selected. I remember that my insides were coming out of my rear end, (it may have been dysentery), and I remember a woman in a white coat coming to see me. She gave Mother some pieces of soap and told her to soak them so that the rough edges would be removed. Then she cut them into little pieces and used them to push my insides back up inside me again. My insides revolted and came out again. She rinsed them and put them back in. After a few attempts my innards stayed inside. Mother was told to keep one piece of soap for the future.

My mother got typhoid; she walked to the hospital and came back two weeks later. She would walk for a few minutes and then lie down for a rest. People would touch her; if she moved, they'd keep walking. Finally, a man with an ox and cart took her near to the hospital. My grandmother died in Uzbekistan. Mother and Father looked for a church or mosque (there were no Roman Catholic churches) where she could be buried in sacred ground; they were refused everywhere. The women wrapped *Babcia*[138] tightly in a sheet. My mother told me to sleep next to *Babcia* because she loved me very much. The next day they dug a grave outside our hut and buried *Babcia* in a grove of apricot trees.

138 *Babcia (Polish)*: grandma.

We made it out of Pahlevi to Tehran. The road to Tehran on the narrow winding roads had a drop on one side and mountains on the other; I found the drive very exciting. In Tehran we stayed in the Shah's stables, the best accommodation we'd had so far. Supposedly, the Kaiser had built the stables for the Shah to persuade him to join the Central Powers during World War I but, after they had been built, the Shah changed his mind. We were there for 11 months. They tried to establish a school but could not because we had no teachers.

I Lay Down On The Shores Of Pahlevi

I lay down on the shores of Pahlevi and wept
My body could not stop shaking from the dysentery
My emaciated frame of bones hugged the sand in gratitude
As my frail loose skin blew in the sea breeze
And the salt water flowed over my filthy remains.

How I shuddered with convulsive tears
And delight at the gentle warmth of the sun
Amid the coolness of the sea and the wind
And I didn't care if I lived or died.
I was so very happy
To be no longer in the Soviet Union.

Free to die free, at last
If not to survive
As if that were possible
But no, to die was enough,
Free in the caring hands
Of the British, the Persians,
And oh – how I'm crying again –
My Polish soldiers,
My own folk.

Look at them, in proud uniform
And health, their skin tight
And love on their faces
As they look to help me up.

I'm sorry I am crying so much,
To be helped by my people
And they so well
Who only weeks before must
Have been, like me, rags and bones.

Fit only for the grave

And yet, look, they positively shine health.
Perhaps, oh don't get excited,
It may be too much,
I may die of hope
That I might live yet

That I might live
And even feel again.
Look at me,
I'm in a state,
Beyond control.

The irony.
For days I had no water
Now I'm pouring it out of my eyes.

And orange juice!
The British bring me orange juice
On a tray my God, a tray.

I have not seen a tray for…
For, my, I don't know the years any more
Since Poland, since home
Since Mama and Papa.

Oh, Mama.

© **Martin Stepek, 2005**

Figure 47. Arriving in Pahlevi, Iran, 1942[139]

Maria Pawulska Rasiej
b. 1927, Lwów
April 1940, deported to the Soviet Union
1942-47, Iran, India, Africa
1947-51, England
1951-present, USA

The Germans invaded Russia. I remember that this was a time of red sunsets, the color of which I had never seen. The local women would look at the sunset and say it was a sign of impending war. My mom worried about how we'd survive the next winter. Then, we heard about the Amnesty but we were not allowed to leave until October.

All we knew was that we had to head south. We traveled on a cattle train heading south, only getting off the train to buy *kipiatok* and to go to the toilet. We had to stop along the way to work and earn more money. The war between Germany and Russia did not make much difference to us, though we did see Russian refugees on the move. We would see trains with wounded soldiers, so it was even harder for us to get a place on a train. My mom bought a ticket for Dzamboum,[140] in Kazakhstan. We had to travel with our metal utensils in order to purchase *kipiatok* on the journey. We were not allowed to enter some

---

139   *The Story of the Second AGPA,* a souvenir booklet belonging to Hania Kaczanowska's father.

140   Dzamboum, renamed Taraz on January 8, 1997.

of the towns on the way as we had no passes, or because somebody told us that we were 'prisoners' and, therefore, could not enter. There were, maybe, 2,000 people on each train looking for temporary work and for somewhere to live. At one point, my mother and brothers found lodgings in a corner of a steam bath, but there was no space for me there. I remember looking for a place where I could sleep. After finding lodgings, we had to find work.

My mommy found work in a private home, embroidering bedding. Then, the landlord told me that we had to leave because his son and family were coming to stay and would be using the bathroom which was our home. My mommy was out, walking and looking very worried, when she was stopped by a woman who asked her in for tea and she explained what was wrong. We were sleeping at the station at this time. The woman, a Tartar, tried helping us and gave someone a deposit so that we could stay there. She hated Russians because they had occupied Kazakhstan and persecuted her husband who, then, had committed suicide. She hated the Communists and had a good heart and wanted to help us.

We heard that there was a Polish Army in Yangiyul, in the vicinity of Tashkent, Uzbekistan. The only people allowed go there were Army families. They did not encourage other civilians as the conditions were very hard; there was disease and the starved, weak refugees were easily impacted by disease. Fleas were the national animal of Russia. We heard that people were dying and, later, that they were dying from dysentery due to the overly rich diet fed to them by the well-intentioned army;[141] after years of starvation they could not digest the food they were given.

I also worked at this time, making boots. I worked in a unit separating dirt from the wool. The state factory went bankrupt; I was 15 years old and had to work in order to have a card for bread. You had to have work and lodgings, though having a card did not guarantee bread, as you could stand for hours to get your portion and then find that they had sold out. I was then taken to work in road construction, collecting stones from the river and taking them to where they were building the road. This was terribly hard and exhausting for me.

By this time, Mommy had made contact with delegates of the Polish

---

141   Polish cemeteries in Iran: Tehran, Dulab-Polish Cemetery has 1892 graves (408 military); Bandar-Anzali-Polish Cemetery has 639 graves (163 military); Tehran-Polish section of the Jewish Cemetery has 56 graves (13 military); Ahwaz-Polish section has 102 graves (22 military); Mashad-Polish section of the Armenian Cemetery has 29 graves (16 military); Isfahan-Polish section of the Armenian Cemetery has 18 graves (1 military); Golhak-British War Cemetery has 10 military; Khoramshahr-Polish section of the Catholic cemetery has 5 military. http://polandiran.blogspot.com/2007/09/polish-cemeteries-in-iran.html

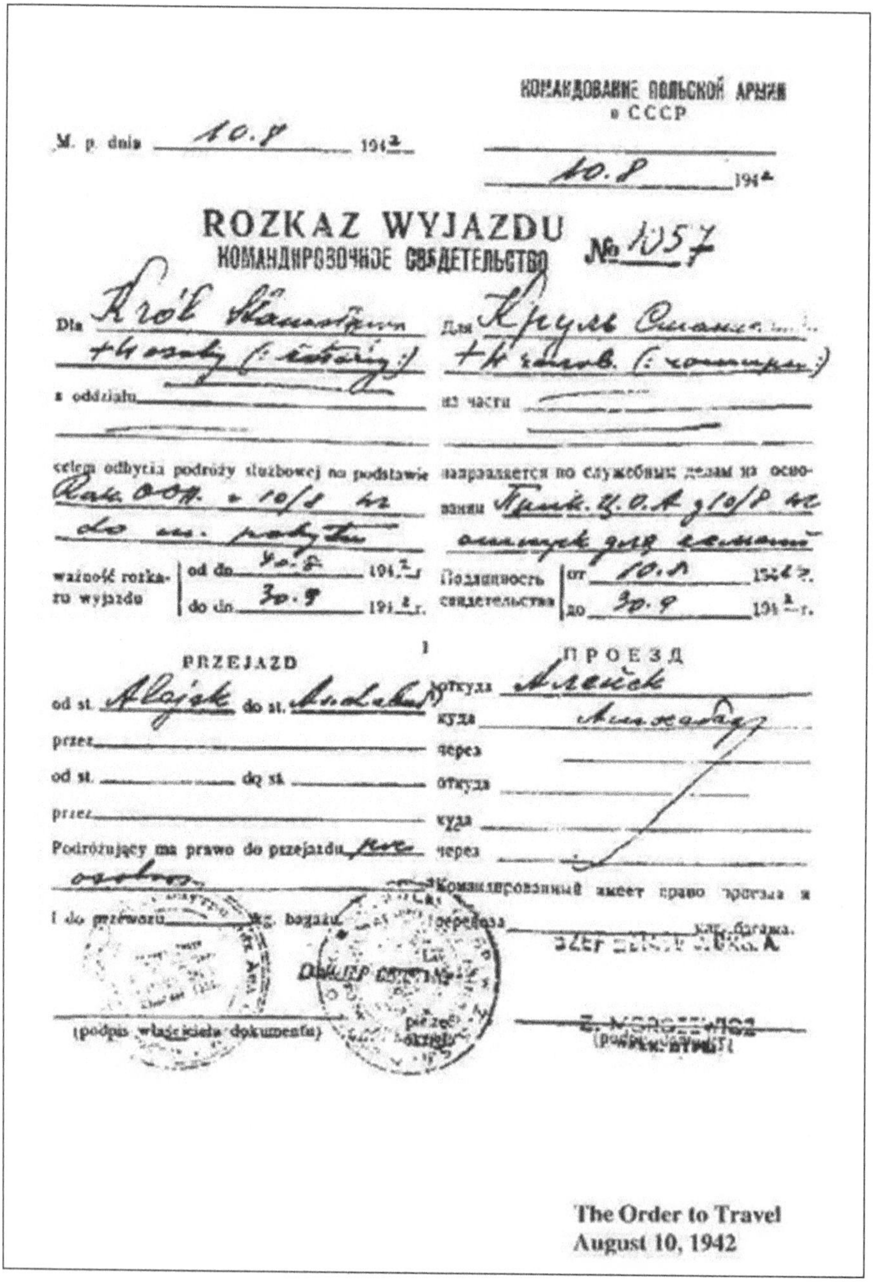

КОМАНДОВАНИЕ ПОЛЬСКОЙ АРМИИ
в СССР

M. p. dnia 10.8 1942 — 10.8 1942

ROZKAZ WYJAZDU
КОМАНДИРОВОЧНОЕ СВИДЕТЕЛЬСТВО № 1057

Dla Król	Для Круль
z oddziału	из части
celem odbycia podróży służbowej na podstawie	направляется по служебным делам на основании
ważność rozkazu wyjazdu: od dn. 10.8 1942 r.; do dn. 30.9 1942 r.	Годность свидетельства: от 10.8 1942 г.; до 30.9 1942 г.

PRZEJAZD — ПРОЕЗД

od st. Alejsk do st.	откуда Алейск
	куда
przez	через
od st. do st.	откуда
przez	куда
Podróżujący ma prawo do przejazdu	через
i do przewozu kg. bagażu	Командированный имеет право проезда и перевоза кил. багажа.
(podpis właściciela dokumentu)	(подпись)

The Order to Travel
August 10, 1942

Figure 48. The order to travel to leave the Soviet Union, 1942

Government-in-Exile in town. We would see Polish men heading to the Army and injured Polish servicemen coming back to recuperate in the town. The Polish Government had a soup kitchen in the Delegation; it was always busy since those with no food, lodging, or work, would come to eat. I would walk from wagon to wagon looking for Daddy. Some people tricked us and said they had seen my father just so we'd give them food. While searching a train for my father, I came across a man whose responsibility it was to produce lists of civilians who were to leave with the Army because they were related to soldiers. I stared at this man with his red face and pince-nez. I didn't ask him anything but went home. I didn't want to tell my mommy that we had no hope of getting out, but when I said his name and described his appearance, she said that he was a friend of my father. She said this man used to visit us and she wrote to him; he listed my mommy as his sister just before they closed the list. My brother, Tadzio, joined the *Junacy*, so Mommy, my brother, Jerzy, and I were left. Tadzio went south with the transport. We had no contact with him; everything was learned by accident.

We went 180 kilometers to Yangiyul to join the transport. The town of Yangiyul was closed and the Polish Delegation, accused of stealing, had been arrested. The rumor was that the Delegation received clothing for the Poles but that many of these items were being sold on the black market. This was a pretext as, at this time, all the Polish Delegations were closed. So, how could we leave legally with the town closed to us?

Fortunately, Mommy remembered someone else she knew who was a pawnbroker and thought that she might have a truck that could be used for our journey. But before she finished telling us this, our neighbor came to see us. He was a cobbler who offered us his truck so that we could join him. He wanted 500 *rubles* for the journey. We had only 400 but he still took us. We had to leave during the night so as not be caught by the police. Someone borrowed a NKVD uniform and drove us out of the town. We pretended to be migrant harvest workers. That's how we got to Krasnovodsk. We got there on June 26. Some people left their families behind and walked to Krasnovodsk, believing that the train would pass through Yambol. Yet, when we passed through Yambol they had closed the train station and would not allow people to board the train. I will never forget the cries of those who were left behind; they wept and knelt before the Russian officers begging for admission but they were not allowed to board the train. So, children and older people who could not walk were left, behind the metal gate. There were loud cries when the train pulled out of the station.

The same thing happened in Krasnovodsk, Turkmenistan, where people were not allowed to board the container ship. They were sitting with their legs dangling through the balustrade as there was no space. There was no light and no space; we traveled like this for two days. The oil tanker could not moor in Pahlevi because the port was too shallow, so we had to board smaller craft and then used trucks to take us to the camp.

Barbara Kocuba Bik

b. 1929, Lwów
February 1940, deported to the Soviet Union
1942-46, Iran, Iraq, Syria, Lebanon
1946-51, England
1951-present, USA

We were moved to Maromnice Camp, which was under military control. The living conditions were a bit better, but the food was still inadequate. The work was still in the tundra, the only difference from our previous camp near Oparino being that, here, children under the age of 14 could attend Russian school. Nobody, not even the children, was allowed to speak in Polish. In this camp, we had our first contact with Poland and we occasionally received parcels from the Red Cross.

Here, we also heard about the Amnesty, thanks to the negotiations of the Polish Government-in-Exile with Russia. But hope of improvement came to nothing. We traveled from Oparino to Kirov in dirty, frozen cattle trucks. The Russians threw the dead out of the train along the railway tracks, probably as a meal for wild animals. We were traveling south to Saratova, on the other side of the River Volga and, each day, there were fewer of us. There, three more wagons were attached and we were left on the sidings for a few days without any help. Then, the transport went to a *kolkhoz* called Ekaterina, where heavy labor was no longer in the tundra but in the fields. Many more Poles began to arrive; they were deportees from all over Russia. After two years in Russia, we saw our first Polish soldier and, from this time onward, we were in Polish hands.

The Sacrament of the Division of Bread

My Aunt Zosia relates the tale
Of Janka
Whom she met
When they shared a mud hut in Uzbekistan
In terrible times

Darling Zosia
Fretful with worry
That her mother
Whom she had had to leave
Without anyone to care for her
Mother Janina
Alone, ill, fading away.
Might die,
Zosia praying to God
To keep Janina in his loving embrace

Met Janka
Tall, brunette, eyes that knew life,
Self-controlled.

Janka
When the spoonful of sugar
And small chunk of bread
Was handed out
With the pea soup
- the food for the day –
Would divide her bread
Into two equal halves
And dry one half for a later date

When starving Zosia
Asked in disbelief
How Janka could be so
Disciplined
How she could abstain from eating every last crumb
In a flash of need, of desperate need
She replied

"I dry the bread so that
If I get the opportunity
I can send it to my mother.
She is in the Uzbek village
And is suffering hunger."

Zosia fell ill
And was taken to a mud hut
That was used as a hospital.

When she returned from the hospital
Janka was not there
She had died from hunger.

Zosia does not know if Janka's mother
Ever received the bread
Which this teenage girl had kept aside
To keep her alive

The bread of a life
Sacrificed by a daughter
For her mother
In terrible harsh times

Just as Zosia had shared
Her meagre rations
With her precious mother
Janina
In previous months
Ready to die
So that the other might live

The truest testimony of love
The miracle of breaking bread
The sacrament of holy communion.

© **Martin Stepek, 2005**

Persia/Iran, 1942-45
115,000 refugees

Maria Pawulska Rasiej
b. 1927, Lwów
April 1940, deported to the Soviet Union
1942-47, Iran, India, Africa
1947-52, England
1952-present, USA

Figure 49. The Dining Room,
The Polish Orphanage in Tehran, Iran, c1943

In Pahlevi we lived in the so-called 'beach camps'. There were several camps; the disinfectant camp, and the one where you got used to 'regular' food. My mommy got very ill but she told no one; she would sit in the sea because she hurt less in the water. She was scared that we would be separated. Here, we found my brother; he had left the Soviet Union for Tehran before us. My mommy was almost unconscious; she had pneumonia and two types of typhoid for 4 months. Our roof was a blanket balanced on four sticks. When we got to the main camp, it was better. First, my mommy was taken to a small hospital and, then, to the main one, so I had to take care of everything. She left the hospital in December. When she was returned to the camp she was so weak that she had to crawl on all fours to get to our barrack.

We were in Tehran Camp Number 2, in hangars, and we sat on bricks in school; we had no books so everything was dictated by the teachers. These were very primitive conditions with the oppressive heat and the absence of all equipment needed for teaching, but we could see that things were improving slowly. We had very good, professional teachers from Poland.

Usually, the food comprised beans and greasy soup; it was cooked using some meat. I got very sick with pneumonia and spent almost a year in hospital; first, I was in the civilian hospital and then in another. My friend bought me homework from school so that I would not fall behind.

The barracks were very simple but clean. There were about 80 people, head-to-head, in each barrack. Then my brother, Tadzio, got sick. I thought the *Junacy* were treated very badly by their officers who used them as gofers. I got Tadzio out of the Army by writing the request and having my mother sign it but she was so ill that her signature came out as one line; I'm not sure if she even knew what she was signing. We spent the next two-and-a-half years in Tehran.

**Figure 50. The Classroom,
The Polish Orphanage in Tehran, Iran, c1943**

Then came the time of departure to the British Dependencies and, every day, people would come by, announcing who was leaving and who had to pack. I don't remember how they transported us, but we got to Achwaz in the autumn of 1943. There was no one left in these camps other than civilians who were the relatives of Army personnel.

Romuald Lipiński

b. 1925, Brześć
June 1941, deported to the Soviet Union
1942-45, Iran, Iraq, Palestine, Egypt
1945-46, Italy
1946-53, England
1953-present, USA

After the Amnesty, we were free to travel wherever we wanted, except to the big cities like Moscow. My father heard that a Polish Army was being organized so he wrote to the Polish Army HQ and said he wanted to volunteer as a doctor, that my mother was a certified midwife, and that I would be a volunteer. They replied that the Polish Army was being evacuated to the south of Russia, and that we should go to Tashkent, in Uzbekistan. My father organized a group of 54 people to go there. We had to buy tickets and rent two boxcars to travel from Barnaul to Tashkent. Two hours before we were due to leave, the railway man came to tell us that the deal was off; Father knew that they wanted a bribe, so we collected some more money and sent a good-looking woman to plead for the two boxcars. After two hours we were told everything was in place.

We got to Tashkent, but there was no Polish Army, so we went east to a town called Kokany, where we rented a small room and waited for the Polish Army. In the meantime, the Russians came and transported us back to Novosibirsk. The train stopped somewhere on the tracks and we stayed there for 10 days. They were giving us some food and, all of a sudden, they moved us back to Tashkent and then to Osh, the last station on the line, in Kyrgystan, close to China. Then, they put us on trucks and took us on a three-hour drive through the mountains and gave us rooms with Kyrgystani families.

We did not know what to do; we didn't know anything about the Polish Army. We had a large room which we shared with four other people; we had no privacy and conditions were very primitive. Once a week, we went to town to buy bread. We weren't working, and it was winter. The host family was very sympathetic but they could not supply us with anything; they also hated the Russians. We stayed there from November 1941 to March 1942, when news came that the Polish Army was in the area, recruiting soldiers. I ran from home and wanted to join the Army. I found a Polish officer and was told that I was too young to be a soldier but I could join a semi-military organization called the *Junacy*. Two hours later I saw my parents coming; they created quite a scene, and I was very embarrassed. We stepped outside, and they promised me that we would go to the Army together.

There was Polish doctor who ran the local dispensary. He was also an army Major; when he joined the Army my father took over the dispensary. Then, we received a telegram calling us to HQ. My father used to play the violin and I played the guitar. Sometimes the Kyrgyzstanis got us out of bed to play for them. My father would tell them that my stomach was empty so they brought me food so that I would play.

We were heading towards the Army base when I got a fever. I remember traveling with a fellow who slept above me and who had terrible lice. Each time he moved the lice would fall on me. My father told me I couldn't go, so he went by himself. We were sent to Gorchakovo; the Polish Army was nearby, east of Tashkent. My mother rented a room and we stayed there for a few weeks. Then, the first evacuation to Persia started. My father came with the soldiers to pick up our things. That was the day I noticed the rash on my body and we immediately recognized it as typhoid. They had a big decision to make. My father was under orders to go. I was half-conscious and don't remember much of what was going on around me but my parents told me later that they had a choice. They could try to smuggle me, but would I survive the trip? My father went to the Commandant and told him about the situation. There were thousands of Polish civilians in the area, seeking help from the Polish Army. A group of soldiers was left to take care of the civilians; this was the 'liquidation company'.

My father pleaded successfully to be allowed to stay and the Army sent the liquidation company doctor to Persia in his place. My father had with him a big box of medical samples which he had brought from Poland. He found good medicine for me and I probably got the best care in the whole of Russia. So, the three of us stayed together; once you were separated from someone in Russia you never saw them again. It was Easter, 1942, when I was finally strong enough to sit up. We celebrated Easter with the Russian family who had rented the room to us. The son of the widow worked in a slaughter-house; he stole bulls' testicles. My mom exchanged clothing for flour from which was made some bread and soup; my father brought some sausage and sugar from the Army; that was our celebration of Easter.

The first evacuation from Uzbekistan to Iran was in March, 1942; the second was in September. My father got me a job as a nurse in the dispensary and I was getting a regular ration of soup. I cleaned the dispensary. We left on the second evacuation when I was in better shape; we went through Krasnovodsk. My father was with the Army and we were with the civilians. We arrived in a big field, a flat place, and were there for a day under open skies. There was one faucet for water, and there were a couple of thousand people there. We sat on our things, waiting to move. I didn't see my father during the transport; he was with the troops. Finally, the train arrived and took us to the docks where we had to wait a couple of hours to board the ship. It was packed with people, squashed like sardines. I don't know how to describe it; we waited for a day on the ship and, then, during the night, started to move. A day and a night later we arrived in Pahlevi, Iran. The harbor was too shallow for the ship so we were brought onto the shore by smaller boats.

We lay in the sand on a beach about half a mile long with just a straw roof over our heads. The army was not far away, but we were all civilians. The British gave us heavy food, such as lamb, which was full of fat. Our stomachs were not used to that and the effect was terrible. The latrines were at one end of the camp; people were sick there and they didn't bother to go home, they just lay there on the sand. We stayed for a few weeks after which we were put on trucks; the Persian drivers drove at break-neck speed through steep mountains. The road was just a shelf cut out from the rock, with only a few places where the trucks could pass each other. There were no barriers and there were often accidents. We stayed overnight in a town between Pahlevi and Tehran, in what appeared to be a school; we slept on the floor.

Figure 51. The Polish School, Tehran, Iran, 1942

In Tehran our home was what looked like a big plane hangar which housed at least 500 people; we stayed there for several weeks. We didn't know what they were going to do with us. This was Civilian Camp Number 2 and next to it was a military airport. This is where I went back to school, at a level equivalent to the American tenth grade. The school was in a big garage with compartments for trucks; each compartment formed a classroom. We stayed there from September 1942 to Jan 1943, when I joined the Army and went to Iraq.

Figure 52.   Paramedics, Tehran, Iran, 1942

Figure 53.   Romuald Lipiński and friends,
Civilian Camp #2, Tehran, Iran, 1943

Figure 54. **Romuald's High School Graduation Certificate issued while he was in the Polish Army, 1945**

My father was discharged from the Army because of his age, so he found a job as a civilian doctor in the hospital in Tehran. My parents stayed behind when I went into the Army; I wrote to them. They were supposed to go to Africa, but my brother's wife, who was in Scotland teaching Polish diplomats English, managed to persuade my parents not to go to Africa but had them sent instead to Lebanon. I was in Iraq, my parents were in Lebanon, while another brother was prevented from leaving Russia when the border was sealed and was conscripted into the Russian Army. The commandants in this Army were Russian while the troops were Poles who had been left behind in Russia. He remained in Russia permanently. I joined the 12th Podolsk Lancers Regiment and went to Jordan and Palestine for training. In Julis, Palestine, we were in the Army but also studying. We were supposed to be in the Officer Cadet School for 5 months but, after a month, on December 21, 1943, we were shipped to Egypt. They needed officers, so from October 1944 to May 1945, I was in the Cadet Officer's School. I saw action in Italy in 1945, and remained there until 1946.

Stella (Stanisława) Synowiec-Tobis

b. 1928, Brantowce
February 1940, deported to the Soviet Union
1942-46, Iran, India, Mexico
1946-present, USA

It was my first day of school in Tehran. I had no paper or pen. The teacher noticed that I came empty-handed and said, *"You can tell a good student from the first day."* I started crying as my mommy came to my mind. The teacher ignored me completely all day. The next day my sister and I came again and, once more, I had no paper or pen. She asked where everybody was living. I said, *"Block 28"* (i.e. the orphanage). She turned pale but said nothing. I started crying again. She tried to make things better but I could never feel good towards her because she had hurt me so much. I had always loved to study, so this treatment hurt my ego greatly; all I could do was cry. When I think of my mommy, I always start to cry. Nobody ever managed to find my mommy; I tried the Red Cross but had no luck. The teacher did not know much about the orphanage; she never apologized for criticizing me for not having paper and pen but, later, she showed me favor to compensate for her behavior. But I was very cold towards her. Yet, since the majority of the children were with their mothers, how could she have known?

We were told to go to the class in which we had been in 1939. My sister only had one outfit, so she was very, very, cold. The teacher told her that she had to dress better. But we had nothing else to wear as all our clothing had been burned when we arrived in Iran. However, I had insisted on not parting with some possessions such as my First Holy Communion book. So my sister also had a hard time.

We thought we'd be sent to Africa, not from Tehran, but from Istfahan, a town for orphans, *Miasto Polskich Dzieci.*[142] The locals gave up their own homes so the orphans could live there until they went to Africa. About 5,000 orphans were in Istfahan[143] until 1945. We arrived there on February 11, 1943, and went on to the port of Khorramshahr where we were placed on board a British ship, *Emperor*, and crossed the Persian Sea and Indian Ocean to Karachi in India.

---

142   *Miasto Polskich Dzieci* (Polish): Town of Polish Children.
143   Istfahan, also known as Esfahan.

Zdzisława Bilewicz Korniłowicz
b. 1926, Dolinóków
February 1940, deported to the Soviet Union
1943-47, Iran, Palestine
1947-53, England
1953-present, USA

We heard that we were free to leave. My daddy wanted us to leave as soon as possible and head south. We left in November, 1942, not yet knowing about the formation of the Polish Army in the south, but we knew that we had to head south in the direction of Tashkent. My daddy said that there was no other direction in which we could go, as to the west there was war. Before we reached Tashkent we came across a Polish military mission in Vorenburg where there were masses of people fleeing the Soviet Union.

I remember that we traveled for a week on rafts and reached a cotton-growing area where we stayed until the Polish authorities heard that the river would freeze; they quickly ordered us to return to the port so that we could get out. It was a nightmare journey and people drowned. My father went into the Army. My older sister and I entered the Cadet School so that we could support our family. My younger sister, grandmother and aunt all died and, then, my older sister got ill. She got typhoid and then dysentery; we had to leave her behind in a Soviet hospital. We never heard from her again. Being an adult, if she had survived, I am sure that she would have found a way to contact us. The British were fantastic to us in Persia; when we arrived in such a terrible state they already had everything ready for us. Our clothes were burned, we were disinfected, and our hair was cut off; they were concerned about the spread of disease.

Since my father was in the Polish Army, we were allowed to move to Palestine where I finished high school and was accepted to study pharmacy at the University in Beirut. However, at this time the unrest in Palestine reached a point that required us to leave. In reality, I was not eligible to come to England with the Polish Army as I was over 18. What the Polish Army did in such situations, in order to get people into England, was to allow them to enlist into the Polish Army. I was then able to come to England as a member of the Polish Army with the Cadet School from Nazareth. I have the best of memories from England and would not have left if my fiancée had not already arranged to come to the USA before we met.

Palestine, 1942-47
5,000 refugees

Zygmunt Kopel
b. 1934, Mołodeczno
April 1940, deported to the Soviet Union
1942-47, Iran, Iraq, Palestine
1947-present, England

We stayed in Pahlevi for a short while and, then, were moved by trucks to Tehran. For six weeks we lived in a deserted factory. I remember people being removed every day by ambulance. Some of the men weighed only 5 stone.[144] I remember that the mother of a friend of mine came to see us and told us that my friend had died. We went to the mortuary and I saw him lying there like a skeleton, with glassy, open eyes. This was the tragedy; people had managed to escape from Russia but the results of their suffering continued to manifest themselves. People also had dysentery; they were so malnourished that they could not cope with any illness. Everything was organized very well here and we were vaccinated for lots of things and received American help. My father visited us briefly.

We went through Iraq and Jordan to Palestine; on May, 1942, we arrived in Rehovoth where the Third Division of the Carpathian Artillery was stationed. The official language here was English, as Palestine was under the control of the British. Some refugees from Persia went to India, others went to southern Africa; we were taken to Palestine. Here, we began elementary school. Every few months my father was able to come and visit us. We lived within a sea of tents for 2 months until my father was able to find a private room for us to rent. After 2 months we were moved to Abo Kabir where there were many Polish families. I remember we were near St. Tabitha's supposed grave, where a light burned all the time. We did not ask why we were moved; we trusted everything would be alright.

I was eight years old at this time and could neither read nor write. Our teachers were teachers from Poland. We'd already had some English lessons in the previous camp from both English and Polish teachers. In Abo Kabir, all the teachers were Polish and were under the care of the Delegature of the Polish Government-in-Exile. We had books as, by 1941 there was a Polish publishing house in Jerusalem. My sister was in a different school, one for girls. We also had

---

144   5 stone = 70 pounds.

pastoral care. We had our First Holy Communion and Confirmation there and spent the Christmas of 1942 in Bethlehem.

I saw this as the land of milk and honey. We had everything we wanted. The housing was somewhat primitive as there was no running water but we were never hungry. We knew that the Polish Army was being trained in Iraq, and that there were some Polish administrators in Palestine. We did get news, as we had a Polish newspaper published in Jerusalem, and I remember that we learned about the death of General Sikorski in 1943.[145] Tehran was the first step but Palestine was much better; Tehran was about disinfection and vaccination.

I visited Tel Aviv where everything was in Polish; you could get Polish food everywhere and everyone was very good to us. The locals liked us more than they liked the British. In 1941, a Polish secondary school was established in Tel Aviv, and I went there. Half of my class in Abo Kabir was Jewish. We had lessons together and they recited all the Polish nationalist poems with us. We just had separate religion lessons. I thought nothing of this; I thought this is how things were supposed to be. They would come to us for recreational purposes as well.

In 1944, my sister and I were finally together in school in Tel Aviv. That's where I was when the War ended and my father came to see us. We lived in a Polish house in Jaffa. Of course, I was not consulted because I was only 10 years old but, all of a sudden, the family was moved to Nazareth and I was sent to the *Junacy* School! My sister was sent to a young volunteers' school for women. This was the end of my childhood, as these were real barracks with army discipline and there was no going home to Mom every night. I was only able to visit my parents from time to time, on Sundays. My father stayed with us until about July 1945, when he returned to Italy. My mother worked for a Catholic organization in Nazareth called *War Relief*. I remember the presence of British soldiers who were always asking for tea, and the standard reply was, *"With milk or lemon?"* Milk was not really a good option as it was condensed or evaporated and completely unsuitable for milk tea, so English soldiers had to learn to drink tea with lemon.

I hated the army discipline and didn't tolerate it well. We had a doctor with a monocle; I remember feigning heart problems. As the doctor would not confirm that I had a heart problem, I decided to escape. One night, under the pretext of going to wash my hands, I ran away. Of course I could not walk along the main road so I had to take the back roads to reach my mom. I got to her between midnight and 1 AM, expecting her to receive me with sympathy. Instead she

---

145 General Władysław Sikorski died on July 4, 1943, when his plane crashed into the harbor in Gibraltar. The precise circumstances surrounding his death are still being questioned today. An exhumation of his remains in November 2008 revealed no signs of his being shot or poisoned.

said that I could spend the night but had to return to school the next day. Of course, I was punished for leaving without permission and was obliged to wash pots and pans. There was no other school in Nazareth for me; this was seen as the best solution to the situation. I am sure my parents were concerned about our future, especially after Tehran and Yalta,[146] but we all believed that we would eventually return to Poland.

The *Junacy*, or Young Soldiers, as we were known, moved with the older *Junacy* to Barbara in early 1946, and I was moved into the *Junacy* Cadet School there in 1947. In August, 1947, when we moved to England, there were 350 boys in the Cadet School but over 1,250 boys went through the School. Boys aged 17 and up were automatically sent into the Armed Forces. I remember that Communist Polish Repatriation Commissions were active, but they were generally not well received. Those servicemen and women who had family were allowed to remain in the Middle East, in Egypt or in Palestine. But this did not last very long. When the Polish Second Corps was moved from Palestine to England in October 1946, we had to follow and, in the summer of 1947, the evacuation from Palestine to England occurred.

Three nationalist Jewish organizations, Irgun, Haganah, and Stern,[147] were active in Palestine at this time. Irgun blew up the King David Hotel in Jerusalem, where the British Armed Forces HQ was located. The explosion was heard as far away as Barbara. Jewish legions came to Barbara to play football with the British, and the Italian POWs were allowed to come and watch. However, we had no contact with the Germans. In 1947 we saw German POWs at Port Said as we were leaving for England. Someone went up to the German POWs to talk to them; immediately the principal of our School said, *"Absolutely no fraternizing with the enemy."* We were friendlier with the Italians.

Being eleven-and-a-half years old, we did not fear the future, yet the British did not encourage us to come to England. Bevin's speech that we should return to rebuild Poland was well known, but our Poland no longer existed as we came from the eastern part now incorporated into the Soviet Union. From Port Said we traveled to Southampton and then, as we were under the guardianship of the Third Carpathian Artillery Division, we accompanied them to their camp in

---

146   The Tehran Conference: the meeting of Joseph Stalin, Franklin D. Roosevelt and Winston Churchill between November 28 and December 1, 1943 in Tehran, Iran. It was followed by the Yalta and Potsdam Conferences. At the insistence of Stalin, the borders of post-war Poland were determined along the Oder and Neisse rivers and the Curzon line. Poland, despite being a major Ally, was not invited to the talks that determined her future.

147   Irgun, Haganah, and Stern: paramilitary Zionist organizations in Palestine, with the goal of driving the Arabs out of Palestine.

Bodney. We were allowed to wear their emblem of a pine tree, but not the cross, as we were not real soldiers.

As it turned out, my whole family went to England by separate routes. My father, mother, sister and I; none of us knew where the other was. There were separate transports; for the school, the army and for civilians. I first heard of my family's whereabouts at the end of 1947 when my sister, who was in Foxley Camp, sent me a box of *Black Magic* chocolates. My father arrived in November, 1947, and took me to Rivenhall Camp where my mom was living. Today, I would be very concerned about how everyone would make it to England but, at that age, we assumed that there were older people who would take care of everything.

Józef Kałwa

b. 1928, Nowogródek
February 1940, deported to the Soviet Union
1942-47, Iran, Iraq, Palestine
1947-62, England
1962-present, USA

In the fall of 1941, we were told about the Amnesty: all the guards from our camp left and we could move wherever we wanted. We were asked to join the Russian Army to help in the conflict, but about a third of the camp left for the railway station to head south to where the Polish Army was forming. On January 3, we walked for 2 days and 2 nights to get to the nearest railway station. We stayed at the station for 3 or 4 days while the train was prepared. We then traveled for 2 months to reach the Polish Army.

On February 28, we reached the Polish Army Center in Husara. Four of us were under 16 so we joined the cadets, whereas Mother and my older brothers joined the regular Polish Army. In our group there were 123 adults and children; seven died during the 4 months of travel. During the journey we received tokens which we could exchange for bread and soup. If we knew the train was going to be at a station for 3 to 4 days, we would to walk to the village to beg for food. We were never refused. In February, 1942, the United Sates sent trains full of arms to Russia. With them came the Salvation Army. In every town in southern Russia, the so-called 'Blue Angels' were there and gave out things like dried milk and powdered eggs. We used to circle around them a few times to get more, until we were caught.

Our government insisted we boil everything we ate, as local diseases were rampant. Of a group of 117 Ukrainians, only eight arrived in the south; they had pretended they were Polish in order to get out of Russia but they did not maintain the same level of hygiene. If somebody died on the journey they were just thrown out of the train and covered with snow; there was no time or place to give people a proper burial. Looking out from the train, we often saw dead bodies just lying on the ground.

During the second and third weeks of March, the Army was loaded onto three ships in Pahlevi. The Russians did not give permission for the junior army (*Junacy*) to be taken out of the country but, as the Polish authorities were determined that we should not be left behind, we were woken up at 2 AM, smuggled onto a ship, and hidden between the legs of soldiers who had already loaded onto the ship. This way, General Anders was able to move the junior army school out of Russia. It took three days to get to Pahlevi. Upon arrival we were disinfected, given new clothing, and moved to the British Zone in Tehran.[148]

Tehran was like heaven on earth. Things changed for us overnight; we got food and clothing. After two weeks in quarantine, we traveled to Iraq, Syria and Palestine, near Gaza. Army camps were prepared for us. The Polish Army engaged my mother as a manager of the officers' mess. My oldest brother was in northern Africa and went to Italy where he was wounded during the Battle of Monte Cassino. After that, he went with the Army to France but never recovered his health. We were moved to the Cadet School; the juniors stayed in one place while the older ones, including myself, were sent to a school for older boys where we stayed until 1947. So, my family was divided. My two younger brothers were in one school, I was in another; one older brother was with the Polish Air Force in England, and one was with the Polish Army in Italy. Meanwhile, my mother stayed in the same camp as the Cadet School until 1947, when everyone was moved to England.

---

148   Persia was occupied by Russia and Britain.

Stanisław Milewski

b. 1930, Bagrów
February 1940, deported to the Soviet Union
1942-47, Iran, Palestine
1947-59, England
1959-present, USA

**Figure 55. Stanisław Milewski at
the *Junacy* School, Palestine, 1944**

We learned about the Amnesty in November, 1941, when the Commandant told us that we were free. The Poles immediately started to build rafts so they could float downriver to Archangel. It was winter and we could not leave as our clothing was in rags and it was impossible to leave without the right clothing. Fortunately, through an uncle in Poland, my Father sent us 1,000 *rubles* which we used to buy clothes.

We left on January 6, 1942. We were stopped at Pinegi where Mom bribed an official and we were able to get away; those who came this way before us were not allowed to leave. Two weeks later, we reached Archangel where there was a Polish Consulate. We were given food, clothing and a ticket to go south, almost as far as Moscow. Halfway to Moscow we had to leave the train. On every station we encountered prisoners from Russia who had been freed in order to join the Army. You had to run and jump on the train. We reached Kuybishev where the Polish Army was stationed but they had already left; we slept on the station. We met a Polish officer who knew our father and helped us get away on the next transport. On March 6, we reached Govoluj; the whole journey had taken us 2 months.

In Wugovoje, my father met us; I remember it was terribly muddy and I had no boots left. My father and brother left for Krasnovodsk before us. It was hard to get onto the ship which was overloaded. It took all day and all night to get to Pahlevi. We were given kippers to eat so people were vomiting and dying as they could not digest such food. In Pahlevi our heads were shaved and we had special disinfected showers. They burned all our clothes and we received English Army uniforms. We saw open shops for the first time; they sold figs and oranges. There were no shops in Russia. We reached Tehran at the beginning of April. We were on one of the first transports and were placed in a former Persian Air Force base. We slept on the floors with a blanket, with many of us in one hall. People continued to die and, as my mother was a nurse, we were moved to the hospital. We were in Tehran for two years. There were 5,000–7,000 people. They built a tent city consisting of about 500 tents. Then they built barracks. This was a transit camp and, after a few weeks, people were moved on to India, Africa, and Palestine. That was hard for me as I would make friends and then people would leave. I stayed with my mother in the hospital. We finally left in October, 1943.

The views from Tehran were beautiful. The Polish military attaché was a friend of my family so, sometimes, we were taken by car into town to eat in a restaurant. When the Russians closed their border we got ready to leave Tehran as they were closing the camps.

The Polish scouting movement played a huge role in our lives. My father and brother were in Iraq at this time, after which they went to Italy and fought at the Battle of Monte Cassino. My mother was given the option of going to India or to Africa, but my parents decided that we should go to Palestine; we went by train and truck. In Jerusalem, my mother was sent north to Nazareth, to a young volunteer girls' school, and I was sent south to Barbara and, in November, 1943, was accepted into the *Junacy* School there. There were about 500 boys there, from 13 to 18 years of age. I spent the years 1943-47 in the School.

I have good memories, as we finally regained our health but, it was a military school with all the rigor of military training. We had to get up early in the morning to march and, as I was the youngest one in the School, I was always last in line. The older boys would leave and go into the proper army. I spent the holidays with my mother in Nazareth. I remember hearing the Muslim call to prayer. It was beautiful there. Palestine was very primitive then, just like in the time of Christ. There was a boys' school on top of the hill from which you could see Haifa.

**Figure 56. Motto of the *Junacka Szkoła Kadetów*
(*Junacy* Cadet School), 1942-47**

Jerzy Kozłowski

b. 1929, Łuck
February 1940, deported to the Soviet Union
1942-47, Iran, Palestine
1947-present, England

We had been deported to Russia under the pretext that *"our neighbors were not happy with us so, in order to keep us out of harm's way, we were being resettled."* They didn't take my father, just my brother, my mother, and me. As young boys, we had no idea what was going on and what we should take. I remember that one of our servants had trimmed our sheepdog's hair, and we still had the hair. My mother took this with us and later made gloves from this hair in Russia. They turned the house upside for two hours while we packed food and clothing. In 1942, after the Amnesty, we went to Palestine where I entered the *Junacy* School.

There were food shortages during our journey out of Russia: they gave small portions to the Polish Army and these portions had to be shared with the civilians. I remember that we received condensed milk which tasted wonderful. My father had been warned that we might be deported and, even, gave food to friends to send to us in case we were taken. Unfortunately, none of that food ever reached us. When the Russians first crossed into Poland they took our horses, so my father demanded a receipt. The Russian sergeant could not write so he marked the receipt with an 'X'; I still have that receipt.

In Palestine, we were in Baszit. There were about 2,000 boys and girls. We were divided into schools; a cadet school, a mechanical school, a communications school, and an elementary school. I had attended school in Russia but was thrown out with a friend because of an incident that occurred. One day the Commandant's wife came to the school (it may have been Stalin's birthday), and wanted us to beg for sweets. We refused, so she tried to take my friend somewhere but he refused. Trying to grab him she fell and, being pregnant, was rushed to the hospital where she gave birth to a healthy baby. However, we were not allowed to return to school. Instead, we had to go to work, cutting peat for fuel.

In Baszit, we lived and had our lessons in tents pitched on the sand. We had no books, chalkboards, or other basics. Eventually, we had benches and tables made for us from sacks filled with sand. We decorated the wall of the tents with shapes cut out of metal cans. My brother went to school in Heliopolis as he wanted to join the Air Force. During 1942-47, I was in Palestine and, eventually, left with the mechanical school, not the *Junacy* School. When the War ended, we planned to go to England. My brother left first with the Air Force. My mom traveled with the young female volunteers, my father with the HQ, and I, separately. So we were all split up. In England the *Junacy* schools were disbanded. I was sent to a Polish school for boys in Dorset, England.

CHAPTER 8

Refuge

India, Africa and Mexico

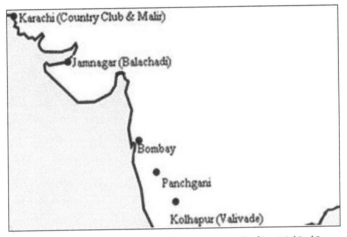

Figure 57. Location of Polish camps in India, 1942-48

India, 1942-48
5,000 refugees

Figure 58. The Polish Orphanage in Jamnagar, India, 1942

Danuta Suchecka Szydło
b. 1925, Wilno
June 1941, deported to the Soviet Union
1942-47, Iran, India
1947-present, England

We were deported on June 16, 1941, when I was 16, my sister was 13, and my brother was 9. My daddy was a civil servant; the Russians arrested him immediately and took him away; we didn't know where. The rest of us, my mom and three children, were deported. Fortunately, we were in Russia for only a short time because of the Amnesty, after which the Poles and Polish Jews were allowed to leave and go south. Native Lithuanians were not allowed to leave.

We traveled for 3 weeks until we reached Uzbekistan where conditions were terrible. All the little children were dying from dysentery. My mother dug graves and I wrote the children's names on wooden crosses. She died from typhoid;

we had to leave her behind, not knowing what happened to her body. She had planned to go into the Polish Army and had put us into the Polish orphanage.

At this time, the first transport of a limited number of orphans left for India (the Indians would take only a few). My sister was still in hospital, ill with typhoid, but we got her out; then my brother got sick with typhoid. We got to Ashgabat[149] on the Russian/Persian border where there was a Polish orphanage; I was detained there because I got typhoid, jaundice and dysentery a few times so I didn't go until the second transport. There was so much poverty and hunger in Krasnovodsk. My brother used to sell potato pancakes on the street to earn money but people didn't always pay him. We slept outside; I remember it was December because we awoke covered in snow. There was no contact with Poland. We never thought that we'd get out of Russia.

My sister and brother arrived in India but in an area ridden with malaria. My journey was made hair-raising by all the winding, narrow roads in India; it was so hot, and dry, and dusty. The plan was to join my brother and sister but, because the River Indus burst its banks, we had to stay for three months in an English settlement where the English Viceroy lived in the Himalayas. We lived in tents, waiting for the river levels to go down so we could leave and continue our journey by truck. It was a fantastic place and we had school with Polish teachers, doctors, and a priest. We had no books so everything was taught from memory; later we got books. I remember seeing a barefoot policeman! We got to Jamnagar and I was reunited with my brother and sister. I was one of the oldest; there were about 10 of us so they sent us to an English convent school in Karachi. I was there for two years. I knew no English but, in 2 years, I learned. The younger children had schools in Jamnagar.

Through the Red Cross, we discovered that my father was trying to find us. He joined the Polish Army but was given medical leave because he got TB. There were 5,000 people in the Polish camp; mothers and children and orphans from Russia. I was in an English school and my sister was sent to another location to get help with her lungs; my brother was elsewhere. My sister did not know that my mother had died; she read about it in my diary before I had a chance to tell her. My father came to India and I could not believe how bad he looked. He found out through the Red Cross that Mommy had died. People died en route and they used to just throw the bodies out, so some people's fate was never recorded.

The Polish camp at Kolhapur (Valivade) was very well organized and was paid for by the Polish Government-in-Exile stationed in London. There were five middle schools, an orphanage, a kindergarten, and a vocational school. We

---

149   Ashgabat is now the capital and largest city in Turkmenistan.

were not in the orphanage because we had our dad. We all went to school. In 1946, India got her independence so, by 1947, the Indians no longer wanted the Poles. There were many Polish transit refugee camps in Karachi. The majority of people left from there to go to Africa and to Mexico; my father returned to the Army. My brother had an opportunity to go to school in the USA, but my father refused to let him go.

When we were in India, we were encouraged to write to soldiers in order to help maintain their spirits; I wrote to some officers. Because Father was in England, we had a right to go there too. One of the soldiers returned to Poland and gave my name to another officer and suggested that he write to me. He wrote and we met in England and got married. My sister also married someone to whom she wrote from India. My brother-in-law returned to Poland and she followed him. He was very disappointed with the Communist Government.

When the War ended and they had to liquidate the Polish camps, Polish delegates tried to convince orphaned children to return to Poland but the majority would not return. I had nobody to return to, as Wilno was no longer in Poland. My brother finished his education in a Polish school in England. In 1945 my father was in England, in hospital, and died 10 days after my wedding. And that's how our history finished.

Franciszek Herzog

b. 1931, Lubaczów
April 1940, deported to the Soviet Union
1942-47, Iran, India
1947-52, England
1952-present, USA

We knew that there was an Amnesty and that there was a Polish Army forming in southern Russia; we even received some American parcels. Mother died in January and we left for Tashkent in March. We joined the orphanage in Ashgabat while my older brother got off the train to join the Polish Army. So, my middle brother and I joined the orphanage and arrived in India at the beginning of April, 1942. From Ashgabat, in Turkmenistan, we went to Mashhad, in Iran; then, across Afghanistan to India. America took no refugees while Mexico did. I had no choice about where we were going; we joined the orphanage and that was it.

Figure 59. The Scouts, the Polish Orphanage, Jamnagar, India, 1942
Figure 60. Dining Room, the Polish Orphanage, Jamnagar, India, 1942

Figure 61. The Dormitory, the Polish Orphanage, Jamnagar, India, 1942

There was a big transit camp in Karachi and there was a smaller camp for the orphanage in Balachadi, built by the Maharaja Jonahed of Namangan. The story goes that during World War I his uncle, the previous Maharaja, had an estate in Switzerland next to Paderewski[150] and they knew each other. He became interested in Polish affairs and when, in 1942, he heard about the children in Russia, he said he'd build a camp to house up to 1,000 people. As he was the head of the council of all Indian Maharajas, he then persuaded the other Maharajas to also pay for some of the children. The camp for 5,000 was supported by the Polish Government-in-Exile and by the British Government.

---

150   Ignacy Jan Paderewski, (1860-1941), was a Polish pianist, composer, diplomat and Prime Minister of Poland (1919).

Initially, we stayed in Bombay for 2 or 3 months until the camp was complete, then stayed there for four-and-a-half years.

A few years ago, a private high school in Warszawa was named after Maharaja Jonahed of Namangan. I was in the orphanage until 1946, then I spent a few months in Kolhapur (Valivade), after which I joined my brother in England. He was in the Polish Army so he was able to bring us to England. We were too young to be concerned about the future. The Polish Government in Poland insisted that all Polish orphans belonged to the state and that we should return to Poland. Neither we nor our guardians wanted to do this. The Maharajah said that he would adopt all the orphans so that they would not have to return to Poland. He did all the legal paperwork to make this possible. I have not seen the document but I am sure that there was nothing included about us inheriting the Maharaja's wealth! Some of the orphans did return to Poland; some were not true orphans but those whose mothers who had put them into care in the orphanage. These mothers and their children were reunited in Poland. Some went to Africa and some to Australia. We could have gone to a seminary in America, just to get out of India. My brother was unaware that I had arrived in England and gone to a Polish High School in Bottisham Polish Camp.

25th July, 1947

Mr. Calwell, who had been in India recently, confirmed that the vessel Manoora was going to India to pick up emigrants. The number of British (European) emigrants had not been so great as he had originally anticipated.

He was therefore prepared to allot 400 berths to Poles. He would like to give preference to single men who could work on the Tasmanian or Darwin schemes. He only wanted to accept Polish orphans as a second choice. It was explained to Mr. Calwell that the majority of the Polish refugees in India were women and other people not fit to undertake hard manual labour. At this, Mr. Calwell said that orphans could go anyway.

Mr. Hankey[151]

---

151   *Question of Poles in India, 1947*. Mr. Calwell, the Australian Minister for Immigration. Extract from Mr. Hankey's minutes. FO 371/66226. Political Departments: General Correspondence from 1906-1966, National Archives, London, England.

Figure 62. General view of the Camp, Jamnagar, India, 1942

Figure 63. The children's host, the
Maharaja Jonahed of Namangan, Jamnagar, India, 1942

Figure 64. The Hospital, Jamnagar, India, 1942

East and South Africa, 1942-51
19,000 refugees

About 30 camps comprising:

- 3,500 older men who were unfit for military service,
- 6,000 women,
- approximately 9,500 children, including 1,500 adolescent girls.

Figure 65. Location of Polish camps in Africa, 1942-49[152]

---

152 http://www.immi.gov.au/media/publications/refugee/langfitt/images/map2.jpg

Emilia Kot Chojnacka

b. 1931, Bartesowa
February 1940, deported to the Soviet Union
1942-50, Iran, India, Africa
1950-present, England

India was heaven; we were clean, our teeth were brushed, and we even had tooth-cleaning powder. This was fantastic. In the morning and during the day, we had a table full of food, including white bread. Our beds were clean, and we had clean linen next to our skin.

We traveled to India in open army trucks so we were covered in dust and oil. We got to Delhi where they put us on trains; then, things got better. The cooks were amazing and we got wonderful food. We reached Bombay where we stayed for 2 months. I wanted to know everything. We heard that there were amazing hospitals where they looked after you, so I told everyone that my throat was hurting me. Then, I heard about x-rays and so I asked for an x-ray, which was fortunate as they found out that I had advanced tuberculosis. There were four girls with tuberculosis at first; we were treated for free. I was in the sanatorium for 2 years and 7 months. It was primitive treatment but they cured me. They treated me with lime, raw eggs and cod-liver oil. It was horrible. I now have fossilized lungs in two places due to the lime. They also used air-pumping treatment, whereby the air was pumped out between your ribs to immobilize the lung so it could heal.

**Figure 66. Emilia Kot Chojnacka's home,
Tengeru, Tanganyika, 1944**

My brother was sent to a Polish orphanage in Jamnagar, India. There were close to 172 people there. My father went there with the healthy children. At this time we found out that my mom was alive. After the Amnesty she was released from prison and went back to our camp only to find us gone; our aunt had put us in the orphanage. She was selected for the transport for Africa, though we were in India. We knew nothing about one another's whereabouts. Auntie and Grandmother were still in Uzbekistan. Grandfather and uncles were in the Army and, then, Auntie and Granny were taken across Iran to Africa.

I got the first letter from Mom in 1944, saying that she was in Africa. Travel was very dangerous as it was still wartime and there was no transport. As soon as there was a transport from Karachi, we went to Southern Rhodesia,[153] then, to Tanganyika.[154] I came with my brother and met him again in Bombay, two years and seven months later. We traveled in army trucks to Tengeru. We saw a lioness during the night; we arrived at midnight near a shop at the camp and asked for *"Kotowa."*[155] The woman ran and banged on the door yelling, *"Get up, the kocięta have arrived."*[156] We had been expected to arrive later in the day. My mother had been looking for us through the Red Cross, and my brother found my other brother in Poland in this way. He had no knowledge of our whereabouts after Russia. The Red Cross re-established contact for us. I next saw my sister in 1945. She was in a convent school. My father had siblings who were nuns, priests or monks. We were in Northern Rhodesia[157] for 2 months; then we went to Kenya and onto Tengeru, a camp of about 6,000 people.

Although we lived in very primitive conditions, life in Africa was good. We had three beds, sisal mosquito nets, a table, three chairs, and a cupboard for our food. There was a kitchen where we got food; later, they gave us provisions. Four columns supported the roof which was made from corrugated metal. We had a stove with a chimney; we also had a baking oven and some sort of iron-framed door. The breads and biscuits we baked were amazing. We had a plank of wood on which to sit. I went to Polish School; we had books and exercise books that came from Palestine and England. In the sanatorium we did not have books; the teacher taught from memory. We didn't have 'real' teachers until later.

---

153 Southern Rhodesia was recognized as an independent country in 1980, and renamed Zimbabwe.

154 Tanganyika is now known as Tanzania.

155 Woman whose last name is 'Kot.'

156 *Kot* is the Polish for cat, so the woman was yelling *"Get up; the kittens have arrived."*

157 Northern Rhodesia is now Zambia.

As I said, the conditions were very primitive and we had no electricity. To find out what was going on in the world we had to go to the common room. We had lanterns and studied by their light as it was dark by 7 PM. We got some world news. I don't remember there being any newspapers; news came from outside the camp and I'm not sure how. We received letters and photographs from my father. I was 12 or 13 years old and was not that concerned about what was happening in the rest of the world, but we did hear things. I was more interested in gossiping with my friends. We were happy when the War ended but terribly disappointed about the Yalta settlement.

Figure 67. The Polish Settlement in Tengeru, Tanganyika, 1943

Figure 68. Home in Masindi, Uganda, 1947

The first transport for Poland was in 1947. In 1946, I remember my dad wrote to ask if we were coming back because my grandfather was returning to Poland. *Babcia* had died in Tehran. Since Stalin was still alive, my brother and I did not want to return; we had no guarantee that things would be okay in Poland. As a result, my mother did not return. My grandfather did, and died after three days; in addition, he was robbed. In 1947, the transports for England started. We were the last ones to leave for England; the orphans left after the entire Army, their immediate families, and fiancées had gone. The Communists wanted to take all the orphans back to Poland but Father Królikowski[158] scattered the orphans among traveling families and smuggled them to Canada.

**Figure 69. Making bricks for the church,
Masindi, Uganda, 1944**

---

158   Królikowski, L. (1983). *Stolen Childhood: A Saga of Polish War Children.* (Translated by Kazimierz J. Rozniatowski.) This is the story of 150 Polish children who, in 1949, were rescued from being sent back to the Soviet Union by Father Królikowski, a Franciscan priest. He was branded a 'kidnapper' by the Soviet Government.

Maria Pawulska Rasiej

b. 1927, Lwów
April, 1940, deported to the Soviet Union
1942-47, Iran, India, Africa
1947-52, England
1952-present, USA

We left Tehran in October, 1943. My brother was ill but we did not want to leave without him, so we went into town so that we would not have to leave. This was not punished; our departure was just delayed. When we saw that Tadzio was due to leave, we also left for Ahwaz. I was not well again. My mommy found work on the American Army base. Many women went to do this, not for the pay but for the food. Very often, the food left over was untouched and my mommy would bring this to me in the hospital. Eventually, we went to Basra where we got on a ship which was surrounded by a British Navy flotilla as we left the Persian Gulf. We were crossing by Oman and Japanese submarines would not let us leave, so we had to follow the Arabian coast to avoid them and get to Karachi. The Japanese forced us south to Bombay. There, Polish authorities were organizing camps in India and Africa. Many camps were full so we had to go to Zanzibar where we could not disembark because they also had no space, so we went further south, only this time without the British flotilla. We were sailing to Mozambique; before we arrived, there was a terrible storm which blew us off track and we went much further south to Durban, South Africa. They told us that they were neutral and did not accept refugees. However, they allowed us to disembark and we went by train to Southern Rhodesia. There were a number of camps there; our first was Marandebal.

We were housed in traditional African huts made from clay, with straw roofs and no windows. A middle school was organized, but I was too old, so I went to Digglefold, near Salisbury (Hara), where a grand building functioned as a school, with other buildings for housing. I think there were about 180 female students. My mommy joined me as a physical education teacher and dormitory parent. The house had belonged to an English couple until their son was bitten by a snake and died. They had left their property to the state and the British gave it to us for a school. We had a lot of work to make up for the years that had been lost in Russia. We had to complete two grades in just over one academic year.

My brother was in Palestine at this time, in the Fourth Company of Cadets and, also, in secondary school. My uncle was in Lusaka, in Northern Rhodesia. There were many Poles, mainly older people, living near Victoria Falls. My uncle worked as an administrator for the British, and we moved to Lusaka to be with him. There was a large co-educational secondary school there and a boarding school. I started high school there. Again, we had very good teachers. There were also many Polish organizations, such as the Scouts. We received some general news from Poland; letters started coming after 1945, and people started finding one another. The first transport to Poland was in 1947. My mommy was in contact with Daddy's brother who wrote and told her that it was a difficult situation as the children of those who had returned were being taken to Russia to be trained as officers in the Russian Army. Mommy did not like this idea and did not offer to return.

There were also lists of people going to England to join the Polish Army which was being demobilized there. My brother's cadet school was moved to England and he went with them. There was also a Captain Tadeusz Pawulski who was allowed to bring his family to England, and they only realized on the ship that we were the wrong Pawulski family, since cadets did not have the right to bring their families to England. The message reached Lusaka too late; we were already on the ship and arrived in Southampton, England.

Helena Jopek (Jopeck) Zasada
b. 1925, Wołyń
February 1940, deported to the Soviet Union
1942-48, Iran, Africa
1948-52, England
1952-present, USA

We went with the first transport to Africa; the journey from Russia was terrible. We were traveling into the unknown but were happy to be leaving wretched Russia. We wondered about what was before us. In comparison to Russia, Africa was like heaven on earth. We felt totally safe; there were no bombs dropping on us out of the sky. We were *"U Boga za piecem"*. [159]

We had no choice as to whether to go to India or to Africa, but were not afraid. People on the ship were ill; we slept under blankets on the deck. We were among the first in Africa. About 900 of us arrived in a small camp in Morogoro where, unfortunately, there was malaria which we all got. We were taken to Ifunda where most people recovered. It was good; we had a communal kitchen where the women prepared meals. We also had a school but, for me, it was a wasted year educationally. We caught our breath and got better nourishment.

---

159   *"U Boga za piecem."* (Polish): *"Behind the stove in God's house."*

There were about 15 of us who needed a higher-level school. We were offered a school in Tengeru. We were 2 years behind because of Russia, and they were not sure where to place us, so we worked through our vacations in order to catch up. We were added to the orphanage. We had half a barrack; it was primitive but, in comparison to Russia, everything was wonderful. The orphanage had children ranging from babies through to age 16. We had some professors from Poland and we studied Latin and English, though we were taught English with a Polish accent; when we got to England, nobody could understand us.

Meanwhile, my mother and younger brother remained behind in Ifunda. There was no room in Tengeru for them; we were there, without our mother, for 2 years before space was found for her.

Our professors constantly told us that it was important that we study because Poland was occupied and at war; there were few schools and there would be a need for educated people once we returned. We believed that we would return to Poland, even though it would not be what it had been. The professors were excellent; I must emphasize how hard they worked to expand our knowledge, yet, they received a minimum stipend. At the beginning we had no books; the teachers dictated and we wrote. We didn't know shorthand so we used to gather and compare notes until we had the full lecture written out. After two years we started receiving books from Egypt, so we had one book for four people. When it was my turn to have a book, I worked hard to make most use of it. There were only about six or seven boys in our class, and 30-35 girls. We listened intently. The fatherless boys (two in particular) tried to play up or play truant in the jungle; generally, we all studied well.

Then, malaria came again. I had malaria for six years. You could not see the mosquitoes but you had to wear appropriate clothing. We slept under nets, yet, they managed to bite us. It was in our blood all the time so I took pills for this which turned my skin yellow. It also harmed our hearts; it was a very bitter pill. A few people did not have malaria; those who had it got headaches, developed anemia and suffered from loss of memory. We started fainting just before our high school graduation exams. We'd faint two or three times a day. The studies were very demanding. We were not children at the time; I was 20. One of my friends lost her memory completely and was taken to the hospital. I was frightened that the same thing would happen to me. I was determined to succeed. The exams, both oral and written, were very difficult.

The Red Cross reconnected me with my brother but not with my father. We also corresponded with soldiers. Two of my friends were brought to England as 'cousins' and they married; there were others. My mother had no contact with Poland. There was no work after you graduated so, as I was good at history, I was given a history class to teach, even though I had no qualifications. I taught the youngest class. I was so exhausted because of the malaria that I would come home after teaching and rest. I never regained my health after this malaria. Some of us had scurvy in our teeth, and they were all extracted. There was a doctor in the camp; he worked with one eye, under a lantern, and saved what he could. A young boy broke his leg; the doctors tried to set it but did it incorrectly. This doctor tried everything he knew to help; he broke the bones again and re-set them but that did not work either. There were some nurses from Poland and also some trained assistants.

Our Commandant was American and he tried to do what he could for us. They used to send us canned milk, oil, and the Red Cross sent us clothing. We shared this between us.

Stanisława Robaszewska Woźniak
b. 1927, Kobylnik
April 1940, deported to the Soviet Union
1942-46, Iran, Africa, India
1946-present, England

Figure 70. Stanisława's mother, Tengeru, Tanganyika, 1943

We had no choice where to go from Iran; we had to go where we were sent. Our destination turned out to be Dar-es-Salam, in Tanganyika.[160] I remember that the four ships traveled in convoy and they made contact by sirens, not lights. When we landed in Dar-es-Salam, we were taken by truck to a transit camp where about 400 of us stayed for 6 months. That's where I got my first attack of malaria. I remember that there was an outside radio and the priest announced something about an Uprising, but we didn't know what he was talking about as

---

160   Dar-es-Salaam, formerly Mzizima, is the largest city in what is now known as Tanzania.

we were really cut off from the outside world. We knew that Father was in Iraq.

During 1944-45, we lived in the Tengeru settlement, a beautiful area with mountains and a lake. Our schooling was organized here, with vocational schools for the older children. We had barracks, desks, and books from a Polish publisher in Palestine.[161] The teachers often taught from memory, yet the curriculum was rigorous and I graduated.

Figure 71. Stanisława *(second from the left)* **marching with her fellow students, Tengeru, Tanganyika, 1943**

The camp had an English and, also, a Polish Commandant. Our neighbors knew the English Commandant who helped me get a job as the secretary's assistant. My English was not very good but I knew enough to manage. The wife of the Commandant helped older girls to travel to Nairobi, in Kenya, to work as au pairs. My mother encouraged me to go; she said that I should go and see the world as so much of my life had been spent in camps. I was keen to go so I could improve my English. I was placed with an English family; both of the parents worked and I was left to look after their little girl whom I loved very much. They also had a black woman to do all the dirty work in the house. I, therefore, didn't have an opportunity to practice my English as much as I would have liked. There were other Polish girls in the area looking after children and we used to meet up. I was there for 6 months and, then, heard that my mother was ill with depression again so I returned to the camp. This was when they began sending people to England; I was engaged to help teach English to young girls. My father came from Egypt after a stay of 2 years; this also caused my mother to fall into depression. Every shock, whether good or

---

161 *Polska Macierz Szkolna* (Polish): Polish Educational Society. This organization remains active in England where it has over 100 Polish Saturday schools under its care. Among other responsibilities, it provides these schools with teaching materials.

bad, caused this. She would lie in the dark thinking about her life and about what she could have done better. There were no medicines for depression in those days; this lasted for months. It was very hard for my father. In 1948, the UNRRA[162] directed people to go to Poland, whereas others were leaving for England. We could go to England because we were an Army family. To be honest, there was a tremendous amount of confusion as to what was happening.

**Figure 72. Stanisława's teachers outside the school,
Tengeru, Tanganyika, 1944**

Aniela Bechta-Crook

b. 1936, Borszczów
February 1940, deported to the Soviet Union
1942-49, Africa
1949-51, England
1951-61, Argentina
1961-68, USA
1968-present, New Zealand

Fifteen members of our extended family's uncles, aunts, and grandparents, were deported on that fateful night of February 1, 1940. I acquired a baby brother in Siberia but lost a father in Uzbekistan. The journey to Pahlevi, with so many people crammed on deck, was an ordeal. Emil got very ill from eating rotten fish in Krasnovodsk but a few swigs of vodka and a long sleep soon cured him. In Pahlavi every inch of our body hair was shaved; we were 'disinfected' and all our clothes were burned. We had to make a choice from a very eclectic range of clothes and shoes donated by the good people of the world.

---

162   The United Nations Relief and Rehabilitation Administration, 1943-47.

**Figure 73. Aniela Bechta-Crook with her mother
and brother, Koja, Uganda, 1943**

Next stop was a camp in Tehran where my baby brother died; then a move to a transit camp in Ahvaz and, eventually, on to Karachi by ship. There, we almost lost our mother to dysentery. Several countries offered asylum and Polish evacuees were dispersed all over the world, including New Zealand, Mexico, India and the British colonies in Africa.

Figure 74. Going to church, Koja, Uganda, 1943

We were assigned to Uganda and, in December, 1942, travelled by ship to Mombasa, then, by train to our Polish settlement, Koja, by Lake Victoria. The settlement had about 3,000 people, mostly women and children for whom this was an idyllic place. In spite of frequent bouts of malaria, our education continued; we had a jungle to play in and the inviting waters of Lake Victoria in which we were not allowed to swim. However, we almost lost my brother, Emil, to the lethal strain of encephalitic malaria. It left him with memory lapses and deafness for a long time. Mother worked in the gardens and on road-building to help her sister in Poland. We sent dolls stuffed with a coin, ring or watch. This tight community was almost self-sufficient by the time it had to be liquidated in 1951.

Figure 75. The Polish Camp, Koja, Uganda, 1943

Mexico, 1943-46
1,450 refugees, of whom 450 were orphans

Julek Płowy
b. 1940, Soviet Union
February 1940, his family was deported to the Soviet Union
1942-46, Iran, Mexico
1946-present, USA

When the Soviet Union invaded Poland in 1939, I was not yet born; my brother, Tadeusz, was 17, and my sister, Helena, was about 12. My father was a farmer and we were well off. Our settlement of Lechutka was one or two miles outside Przemysł. In our settlement were about seven or eight families, all of whom were deported.

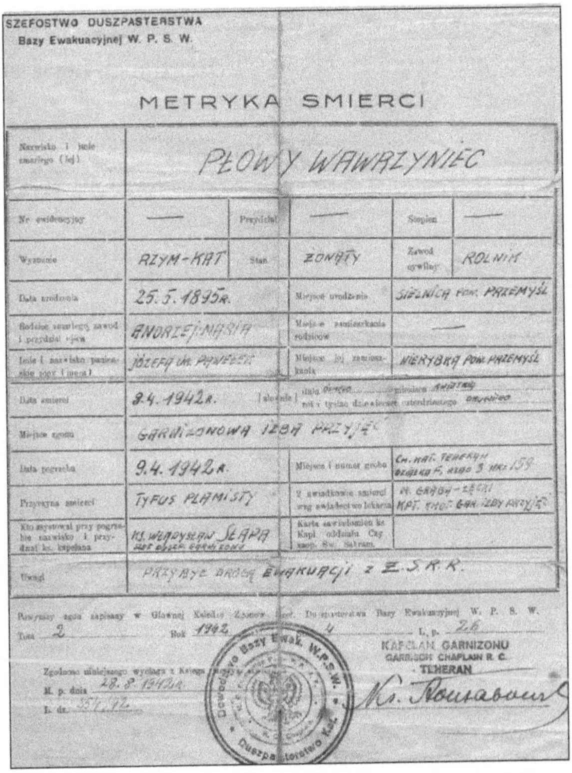

Figure 76. Wawrzyniec Płowy's death certificate, Tehran, Iran, 1942

My mother was 7 months pregnant with me when we were deported in February, 1940. We were in Russia for two-and-a-half years. My brother and my father worked in the lumber yards in the Ural Mountains. My sister was also forced to work and my mother worked after I was born. When my brother worked in a grain mill he used to stuff grain into his boots so that we would have more food. Temperatures used to drop to -45 °F. The year I was born was a particularly bad winter. My mother breast-fed me and another child because its mother's milk had dried up; both of us survived. My mother refused to talk about those years so I don't know the details, but she did tell me that the guards used to tell my mother to pray to Stalin as Stalin would give her food, whereas her God had given her into Russian hands.

We found our way to Tehran, where my father died from typhoid. I cried when I got my typhoid shot in Tehran; I ran to the front of the line to get it so that I wouldn't die. My brother joined the Polish Army-in-Exile and got us extra food this way. They were taking civilians out of Iran; my mother decided to attach us to the Polish orphanage going to Mexico. She was afraid of the animals in Africa and would not go there. We went to Mexico by the second transport; there were 1,500 of us whereas there should have been 25,000. However, because of the Poles' anti-communist leanings, the Mexican Government (which was pro-communist at the time), decided to limit us to a far smaller number.

Figure 77. Helena, Julek and Józefa Płowy
at the grave of Wawrzyniec Płowy, Tehran, Iran, 1942

Figure 78. Julek Płowy *(front row, center),*
Colonia Santa Rosa, Mexico, 1943

We traveled through India, New Zealand and, then, California, USA; we stayed in a camp where the Japanese were interned.[163] Then, we went by train to El Paso where we switched to a Mexican train to Santa Barbara. The Polish camp was one large hacienda in a state of disrepair. Those of us who had a parent or parents were separated from the orphans. However, I went to school with the orphans, while my mother worked in the orphanage. My memory starts in Mexico. I was told to eat raw onions to get my health back.

Figure 79. Orphanage staff, Colonia Santa Rosa, Mexico, c1944

By then, we were in contact with Poland. My mother was a very forceful woman which, probably, is how she managed to save photographs from being burned in Iran.[164] My brother was a communications radio operator in Italy. We didn't see him for about 10 years though we had contact. He told us that, at the Battle of Monte Cassino, when they fell asleep in the cold, their hair would often freeze to the ground and they had to cut it off to get up. He went to England with the Army after the War and we finally got him to join us in the USA.[165]

We got to the USA because a former neighbor, who had left Poland before the War, sponsored us to come to New Jersey. We eventually settled in Buffalo, New York. My brother considered returning to England as he thought it was better there but, eventually, he married and settled down in the USA. My

---

163   Poles were not allowed to leave the camp; their arrival was kept quiet in order not to upset the Soviet Union.

164   All possessions were burned during the disinfection process, in order to prevent the spread of diseases brought from the Soviet Union.

165   The majority of the Poles in Mexico subsequently settled in the USA.

mother wanted to return to Poland but would not consider returning while Poland was under Russian rule. She knew of families who had returned only to be deported again to Siberia.

Anita Paschwa-Kozicka

b. 1929, Rokitno
April 1940, deported to the Soviet Union
1942-46, Iran, India, Mexico
1946-present, USA

**Figure 80. Anita Paschwa-Kozicka in her
Girl Scout uniform, Colonia Santa Rosa, Mexico, 1943**

The day came when we were told to move again; it was September, 1943. A very small ship took us from the seaport in Karachi to the main seaport in Bombay where we embarked on a huge ship, *US Hermitage,* which carried many wounded American soldiers. Out of the 728 Polish refugees on the ship, 408 were young orphans. We knew that we would reach California, USA, after six weeks. However, once, our ship had to turn back for a few days since Japanese mines were placed in the Indian Ocean. Somehow, I was not afraid of this at all. I knew that God would not let us down. We were witnesses to the crimes committed in Russia. I always wanted to tell the whole world how we were left to die in that terrible land.

Finally, we reached Melbourne, Australia, where we stayed for two days. On our way to California we passed the island of Bora Bora and arrived in Los Angeles, California, on October 24, 1943. We stayed at Camp Santa Anita, California, in wooden army barracks. After 2 weeks in the army camp we had to move again. We took a train to the border city called Juarez and transferred from an American train to a Mexican train.

I received an American half-dollar in Santa Anita and wanted to buy an orange after we boarded the Mexican train. I saw a Mexican man selling oranges and, not knowing the language, pointed to the oranges and gave him the money I had. He walked into our compartment and emptied the whole bushel onto the seat. I did not know what to do or say; in the meantime, he left the train. Everyone laughed at me because I had purchased a whole bushel of oranges instead of just one orange.

We arrived in Leon, Guanajuato, on November 2, 1943, and were immediately transported by bus to a place called Colonia Santa Rosa. We were the second transport of Polish refugees to this place. Altogether, there were 1,432 people living there, including 408 orphans. In addition to our regular schooling, there were many extra-curricular activities in Colonia Santa Rosa. In our high school program, we had Latin, English, and Spanish as foreign languages, and Polish as our main language. I was in great trouble for signing up for as many extra-curricular activities as possible while not having much time available for study. So, after lights out at 9 PM, and when all 25 girls in my dormitory were fast asleep, I studied by the light of a candle.

In 1944, the nuns from the American National Catholic Welfare Council took over the running of the orphanage and I was allowed to play the piano. I got up at 5 AM to practice. How much I wanted to tell both my sisters of my success in playing the piano but one of them was, at this time, a prisoner in Berlin, serving as a railroad worker, while the other was a nurse in Palestine. None of my family knew that I was in Mexico, playing piano on the stage in the same way that I had listened to piano recitals in Poland.

When we arrived in Santa Rosa we were first placed in barracks with bunk beds while a new orphanage was built. Each one of us got a doll as a bed decoration from our principal, Zygmunt Ejchorszt. We had to place it sitting in the middle of the bed. It was a beautiful flamenco dancer, with a red lacy dress and a high tiara. When I got this doll I realized that this was the first doll I ever had in my life. I was such a happy girl but my thoughts were with my family, especially little Nina whose grave I could never visit. I wondered if someone had stolen her scarf and the sticks which we had placed there. How gladly I would have given her this beautiful doll. We always went to school; in Tehran, on board the ship going to California and, of course, in Mexico.

My teacher in Mexico hanged herself; her husband was in England and, since he had a girlfriend, he wanted a divorce. The teacher had an 8-year-old daughter by him and believed that if she was dead then the husband would have to look after her. The daughter was sent to England to be with her father.

Figure 81. Stella Synowiec-Tobis and Anita,
Colonia Santa Rosa, Mexico, 1944

Figure 82. Anita and an orphan boy,
Colonia Santa Rosa, Mexico, 1944

Soon, we were assigned to the younger children as 'big sisters'. Our duty was to take care of the little ones and play with them after school. I had a little four-year-old boy called Bolek. Every time I played with him, out in the field, I thought about my brother, Nicolas, who was almost seven when he was adopted by his new family; they didn't want to adopt me because I was a girl. It was so terrible to be separated from him and I hated those people for a long, long, time.

After the War ended, we were stuck in Colonia Santa Rosa with no place to go. Then, the American National Catholic Welfare Council asked American organizations if there was anyone who would sponsor 408 orphans. We had no support from European governments because they were busy rebuilding their own countries and had no money to help us.

**Figure 83. The Dining Room in the Orphanage,
Colonia Santa Rosa, Mexico, 1944**

While I was in Mexico I searched for my older sister but the Red Cross could not find her; it finally found her when I was already living in the USA. She was in England and we had not seen each other for eight years. My two older brothers were killed on the Eastern Front; their wives waited for them for seven years after the War but they never returned. So many people are just finding out today that their husbands and sons were murdered in Katyń. A lady I know, after 50 years of waiting, found out that her husband was killed in Katyń; they were identifying the remains and they found photographs of her and their family in the sole of his shoe. He was expecting to die so he hid these photographs.

Maria Zak Szklarz

b. 1926, Nowogródek
February 1940, deported to the Soviet Union
1942-48, Iran, Mexico
1948-present, USA

We were supposed to go to Africa but, in Karachi, we were offered the opportunity to go to Mexico, which we accepted. We spent 3 months on a ship, during which time my mother was worried because of the US-Japanese War. We had no contact with my father or family in Poland. We arrived in Mexico on July 1, 1943, having left Bombay on May 15, 1943. There were a few orphans on this transport but about 500 came on the second transport. The conditions in Mexico weren't great but, at least, we were not dying from hunger.

When we arrived I only had one skirt and blouse so, when my mommy washed my clothes I had to lie under a blanket and wait for them to dry. Eventually, the Red Cross supplied us with clothes. Mommy helped in the kitchen while I went to school where I learned to sew. We lived in barracks, three or four families to a room. Later, more accommodation was built so we had some privacy. There were communal bathrooms and a communal kitchen.

Figure 84. Maria Zak Szklarz *(first from the left)* **and her family, Józefa and Helena, Colonia Santa Rosa, Mexico, 1945**

At this time we started receiving information abut what was happening in the world and in Poland. But we did not know what had happened to my father; my daughter found this out quite recently through the Red Cross. After the War some people returned to Poland, but my uncle in Poland advised us to go to the USA. Families in Poland discouraged us from returning. However, we needed a sponsor to get to the USA so my uncle in Poland asked someone he knew to sponsor us. He sent us the papers but, then, we had to wait three years to get a visa. Those who had family in the Polish Army went to England; many returned to Poland and only a few went to the USA. The orphans did not have to get visas as they were helped by Polish-American organizations, so they went to the USA. Nobody helped us; we had to earn our own keep. I worked in a textile factory in Mexico City. I also worked as a nanny and typist; in total, I had about 20 jobs. Later my sister worked with me in a factory. My mommy worked for the American Army; we lived separately from her.

We finally arrived in the USA; I knew nothing about the USA. The sponsor did not expect us to work for him (he was in Minnesota) so we rented a bus and travelled for three days in October, 1948, and had to start looking for work from scratch. My friend had arrived in Chicago and she knew somebody who helped us. We stayed in Minnesota for 1 month but could not find any work but eventually my mommy repaid the sponsor for his sponsorship. I found a job in a factory and, later, we found accommodation. We were not always well received; people called us names. This was the first time I heard *"DP"*.

Stella (Stanisława) Synowiec-Tobis
b. 1928, Brantowce
February 1940, deported to the Soviet Union
1942-46, Iran, India, Mexico
1946-present, USA

We did not step onto American soil until October 24, 1943, at the port of San Pedro. American Army trucks drove us to Camp Santa Anna, where we were kept under close guard. Everywhere were soldiers with guns. Again, we felt like we were not welcome here. We were not allowed to go anywhere outside the camp. Yes, we were given good and rich food, but a child needs more than that; a child needs love and that was forbidden. We had suffered so much in our short lives that, it seems, we would not have known how to accept it. Still, there was no attempt. At least, it was not permitted by the government of the USA to those who were willing to give us love. They would not allow the 408 innocent children to stay in their country.

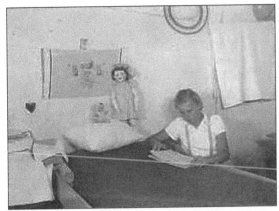

Figure 85. Stella in her dormitory, Colonia Santa Rosa, Mexico, 1944[166]

---

166   Note the dolls on her bed.

After five days and unsuccessful attempts by Polish organizations in the USA to grant us permanent stay in the USA, we departed by bus to the train at San Pedro station, guarded by soldiers with guns and bayonets. Locked trains carried us to El Paso, Texas, on the Mexican border. There, we crossed the border on foot after going through customs.

It was late in the afternoon on October 31, 1943, when we boarded a Mexican train which was waiting for us. We noticed the contrast right away. The train was not as clean as the one we had just left, but the people were very friendly and courteous. As the days passed, we became more and more excited about our trip coming to an end. We were tired and stiff from not being able to move around but the humor of some of the children was inexhaustible and they entertained the others. Our train kept going, night and day. The Sierra Madre Occidental Mountains moved in front of our eyes, at times close by, at other times far away on the horizon. The clock seemed to run slower than ever. Finally, on an afternoon at the end of November, we arrived at Leon, in Guanajuato State. Leon is a city almost 400 years old, located five miles away from the camp in which we were going to live. A few buses were ready to take their passengers on the last segment of the guarded trip.

On a dirt road, through the fields of a large valley, our buses carried us to the gate of the Colonia Santa Rosa. Our first impression was scary. On both sides of the gate there was a barbed wire fence which showed us where the borders of our freedom lay. The gate was guarded by a Mexican policeman. It opened up and we were brought in to the middle of the camp where a huge, four-story building called *Molino*[167] towered over the rest of the small, Spanish-style flat-roofed buildings. Every one of us carried our little bundle of possessions to the storage buildings in the back of the camp.

This was the site of the orphanage. The buildings, a cold gray on the outside, looked more inviting inside. The walls were white and freshly-painted. The blue double bunks were covered with clean sheets and blankets. A little picture of the Blessed Mother lay on each bed. We found out that the preparations had been done by the existing Girl Scout troop at the camp, who had arrived at Colonia Santa Rosa with the first transport of 706 people on July 1, 1943. With our transport of 726, there were now 1,432 refugees in the camp. Our orphanage consisted of 265 children; there were also 537 children with their mothers. 600 of the children attended school.

During the first day at the Colonia Santa Rosa, we realized that our life at the camp would not be as bad as on first impression. We had good meals prepared by our own cooks and, with a pass people were allowed to go to Leon.

---

167   *Molino* (Spanish): Mill.

The next day we were instructed to go to school which was held in the park. For a few weeks we had to study outside until the reconstruction of the school building was finished. Gradually we noticed how, as the reconstruction went on, the younger children's classes disappeared from the park into the school building.

There were prizes given to the best students, sent from Polish organizations in the USA. All the prizes were dolls. One would think that, at the age of 15, I would be embarrassed to receive a doll as a prize, but it was just the opposite. I was very happy and proud when my name was called. This was my third doll and the largest of all. I did not play much with my dolls but I made new clothes for them and I enjoyed having them on my bed. They reminded me of my dolls from before the War; dolls that had been thrown on the floor by the NKVD when they arrested us in Poland on February 10, 1940.

At Colonia Santa Rosa, there were 13 children under the age of five who had been infants during the deportation. They were like my brother, Jureczek. Whenever I saw a little boy, I thought, *"This is how my brother would look."* At that time, I did not cry any more for Jureczek or for my mom, I just prayed. Prayer had given me more relief than tears could.

Those were our fun times, but they lasted only until we heard about the outcome of the Yalta agreement between Roosevelt, Churchill and Stalin. After that treaty, our happiness ceased; our hopes for returning to our homeland were buried. It made of me a permanent immigrant.

CHAPTER 9

Post-War Europe

Betrayal of Poland

- In February, 1945, Joseph Stalin, Winston Churchill and Franklin D. Roosevelt met in Yalta, in the Crimea. With Soviet troops in most of Eastern Europe, Stalin was in a strong negotiating position. Roosevelt and Churchill tried hard to restrict Soviet post-War influence in this area but the only concession they could obtain was a promise that free elections would be held in occupied countries.

- Once again, Poland was the main debating point. Stalin explained that, throughout history, Poland had either attacked Russia or had been used as a corridor through which other hostile countries invaded her. Only a strong, pro-Communist government in Poland would be able to guarantee the security of the Soviet Union.

- Poland was, at this time, under the control of the Red Army. It was agreed to reorganize the Provisionary Polish Government that had been set up by the Red Army through the inclusion of other groups such as the Polish Provisional Government of National Unity, and to have democratic elections. This effectively excluded the Polish Government-in-Exile that had evacuated in 1939.

- The eastern border of Poland would follow the Curzon Line, and Poland would receive substantial territorial compensation in the west from Germany, although the exact border was to be determined at a later time.

Polish Armed Forces:[168]

- In 1945 about 250,000 Polish troops were in exile (92% of these were in Britain).

- 105,000, or 42%, of these troops returned to Poland.

- Britain established the Polish Resettlement Corps in 1946 to *"help those Polish troops who felt unable to return to Poland, to resettle in civilian life in Britain."*[169] About 20,000 of these were pre-War intelligentsia.

- 123,000, or 49%, of these troops stayed in Britain (the majority were evacuees from the Soviet Union).

- 21,000, or 8%, of these troops returned to Poland from communities around the world (e.g. India, Africa, Palestine and Italy).

- There were approximately 41,000 dependants of the Polish Armed Forces in Britain, Italy, Africa, New Zealand, India, Palestine and western Germany.

Displaced Persons Camps In Europe:[170]

- In 1946, approximately 330,000 people who declared themselves as 'Polish'[171] were in DP camps in Europe.

- 1,600,000 Poles made their way back to Poland from DP camps by the end of 1946.[172]

---

168   Ostrowski, M. (2006). *History of the Polish Armed Forces.* PhD thesis, http://www.angelfire.com/ok2/polisharmy

169   Sword, K, Davies, N. & Ciechanowski, J. (1989). *The Formation of the Polish Community in Great Britain, 1939-50.* London, University of London, p. 246.

170   Ostrowski, M. op. cit., Chapter 8, p. 8 *(each chapter starts with p.1).*

171   Some declared themselves to be 'Polish' in order to avoid forced repatriation to the Soviet Union.

172   Ostrowski, M. op. cit.

**Resettlement of Polish DPs from post-War Europe involved
quotas and labor needs of the host countries[173]**

- In 1946, the Belgian government sought refugees for work in the coal mines; 10,378 Poles went to Belgium.

- In 1947, Australia accepted 60,308 Poles from the DP camps in Germany.

- In 1950, 200 Poles from the Lebanon moved to Australia.

- Canada admitted 46,961.

- France admitted 11,882.

- Netherlands admitted 2,969.

- Argentina admitted 6,563.

- Brazil admitted 7,770.

- Paraguay admitted 1,433.

- Venezuela admitted 2,814.

- United Kingdom admitted 35,780.

- USA admitted 110,566.

- Israel admitted 54,904 refugees who listed Poland as their country of citizenship.

- 1946-48 Britain accepted 35,780 Polish 'European Volunteer Workers'.

- 1947-48 approximately 40,000 Polish family members were moved to England from Europe, India, the Middle East and Africa where they had been left behind in refugee camps, cared for by the International Refugee Organization.

---

173   Jaroszyńska-Kirchmann, A. op. cit., Table 3.1 *Resettlement of Polish Refugees, July 1, 1947 – December 31, 1951*, p. 108.

- Commonwealth countries such as the Union of South Africa, Northern Rhodesia and Southern Rhodesia (Zimbabwe), Ceylon (Sri Lanka), Kenya and Tanganyika (Tanzania) took more than 1,500 refugees.

- In 1948, there were over 160,000 Poles left in DP camps in Europe.

Italy, 1945-46

Stefa Kowalczyk Bączkowska
b. 1924, Baby
1942-45, Germany
1945-46, Italy
1946-present, England

and

Celina Kabala Wojciechowska
b. 1923, Warszawa
1944-45, Germany, Austria
1945-46, Italy
1946-present, England

Stefa Kowalczyk Bączkowska: We knew the War was coming to an end because there was a lot of unrest. In May, we were liberated by Moroccans under American command. The Red Cross organized for us to move in to Austrian homes; the Austrians had to move out. I knew nothing about the future except that the Germans had lost the War. We were hungry and I remember once walking with some other girls looking for food when an envoy of officials and reporters drove by. They gave us pea soup and canned pears which tasted so good!

I remember that the Polish girls who had dated French men had a hard time because many felt that the French hadn't shown sufficient resistance to the Germans. Any Polish girl who went out with a German or a Frenchman had her hair cut off, right to the scalp.

Celina Kabala Wojciechowska: At dances, Polish boys would take Polish girls who had dated French men to dance and then leave them in the middle of the floor, alone. No one would dance with them.

Stefa Kowalczyk Bączkowska: Innsbruck was a collection point where we were assembling to be taken somewhere, but we didn't know where. Then came American cars and they didn't tell us where we were being taken. There were about 30 of us, boys and girls I heard one of them say that we were near Brenner, which I knew was south, near Italy. We eventually stopped in Bologna and I saw Polish soldiers for the first time. These soldiers gave up their beds for us. Then we went to Verona and Predappio, where there were a lot of people. We still didn't know what would happen to us.

One of the older ladies said, *"We're probably being sent to Africa to chase monkeys."* We were quartered in a beautiful old palace which had once been the home of Mussolini. However, the palace was badly damaged as the Italians had taken their revenge on Mussolini. Italian women cooked for us; I remember we had a good dessert from raisins.

We were taken to Trani. Some of the young people were saying that they wanted to go into the Polish Army. I remember one of the officers saying, *"The War is over: you are going to study!"* At first there were no books, papers, or pens; you had to memorize everything. The mathematics teacher had no chalk board or chalk so he wrote on the dirty wall with his finger; we just had to imagine what he was writing. He also used students to represent numbers and symbols in equations. This was my first encounter with algebra.

Celina Kabala Wojciechowska: When we first arrived, the Director of the school had us all write an essay so that he could ascertain our level for class placement; after all, we were a variety of ages and from different schools and had all had our education interrupted. He personally checked all our work and said that he was surprised at the high standard. This was the *"country of our childhood years."*[174] For the first time, we felt nurtured and safe.

Stefa Kowalczyk Bączkowska: We were in Trani for a whole year. In 1946, there was pressure for us to return to Poland. Our teachers, however, were in touch with General Anders; he told them to discourage us from returning. He knew about the imprisonment and beatings received by returnees at the hands

---

174   *"The country of our childhood years"*: *"Kraj lat dziecinnych."* (Polish) This is a translation of a quote from the Polish writer Adam Mickiewicz's epilogue in *Pan Tadeusz, or the Last Foray in Lithuania: a History of the Nobility in the Years 1811 and 1812 in Twelve Books of Verse.* (1834).

of the Communists, but some still chose to return.

We left Trani on a train that was also carrying Polish troops, and headed for Calais, France. We were due to have supper at 8 PM, yet, at 8 PM we were still in Germany and the train had stopped; 10 o'clock, then 12 o'clock passed and we were still standing, very hungry. Someone told us there was a problem. The English train driver knew that we were supposed to be in western Germany but he realized that we had landed up in eastern Germany. The tracks had been sabotaged to divert us to the east and force us to return to Poland. Thanks to him, we eventually got to Calais and, then, across the English Channel to Dover, England, from where we went to a school in West Chiltington.

Figure 86. Celina Kabala Wojciechowska,
Barletta, Italy, 1946[175]

Celina Kabala Wojciechowska: We were separated at this time; I was sent to Maghull, then to Doddington where we had classes and, then, to school in West Chiltington. We were there for a year. Then I spent a year in school in Stowell Park[176] but, because we were older, they didn't want to keep us any longer to get us ready for higher education. They wanted us to find jobs and leave. I left to get married.

---

175   Celina is in the second *(crouching)* row, first on the right.
176   Stowell Park: a former POW camp which became a school for Polish girls.

Figure 87. Polish women liberated from Nazi POW and labor camps, Italy, 1946[177]

Figure 88. Celina Kabala Wojciechowska, Maghull School for Girls, England, 1946[178]

---

177   Celina is in the nearest row, fourth from the left.

178   Celina is in the front row, fifth from the left. See also Koło Byłych Wychowanek Gimnazjum i Liceum im. i. Paderewskiego w Stowell Park. (2000) *Drogami świata do Stowell Park*: Circle of the Former Pupils of the I. Paderewski School in Stowell Park. *Roads from the World to Stowell Park*. Sussex, Caldra House.

Romuald Lipiński

b. 1925, Brześć
June 1941, deported to the Soviet Union
1942-45, Iran, Iraq, Palestine, Egypt
1945-46, Italy
1946-53, England
1953-present, USA

We arrived in Italy on December 21, 1943. I participated in the Battle of Monte Cassino. In October 1944, I was sent to the Officer Cadet School because I had passed tenth grade, and was there until May 1945.

Many former labor camp inmates made their way to Italy, including my brother from the Krupp[179] factory. He found out where I was. When he identified himself to Polish soldiers as my brother they took care of him. That was the atmosphere in the Second Polish Corps; we were like brothers, like a family. After the War, I went to a school for soldiers in Matino to finish twelfth grade. All 300 of us were from the Third Carpathian Division, The Army had an education division; I'm not sure about the background of the teachers, but instruction was in Polish. We finished 2 years' work in 6 months. We didn't have books and everything was memorized. School ended for me in October 1946.

I went back to the Regiment with my high school diploma thinking there would be war. In the meantime the Army started organizing all sorts of vocational courses. I knew that I had to learn something practical. I didn't think I was prepared to go to university, but I applied for a chemistry degree and was admitted to Turin where there were about 300 Polish soldiers. About 75 were officers; I was a corporal officer cadet. There were also some privates.

We started to attend lectures in Italian during the time the Italian Government recognized the Lublin puppet government of Poland. In the meantime, representatives of the new Polish Embassy in Italy came to the Italians and questioned how it was they could recognize our high school certificates since they had been issued by a government that was no longer recognized. So the Italians told us that we had three alternatives: to produce a 'valid' Polish high school diploma, to take the Italian high school diploma, or to go back to the Regiment. About 40 of us decided to pursue the second option. We hired an Italian professor to teach us all the required courses such as Italian language,

---

179   During WWII, Krupp produced submarines, tanks, artillery, naval guns, armor plate, munitions and other armaments for the German military. The firm is particularly famous for its 88 mm anti-aircraft cannon.

literature, history of art, philosophy, and physical education. Those who had shrapnel wounds were exempt from physical education. After a couple of months we went for our exams. I spoke Italian fairly well. Whenever we occupied a city during the War, I would find a book and teach myself Italian grammar.

I wrote an essay on the comparison of Garibaldi and Mickiewicz.[180] This moved my examiners to tears, as I talked about the desire for freedom. It was a well-written essay. I had connected the ideas of freedom of the Italians and Poles very nicely. I scored a six on all my subjects; in Italy the maximum score was seven.

Our generals implied that there would be a war so, if we returned to Poland, we would be fighting against them. The commanders were trying to tell us to stay to wait to see what would happen. I completed a degree in engineering at the Polytechnic in Turin.

**Figure 89. Romuald Lipiński's Diploma from the
Polytechnic of Turin, Italy, 1946**

Because my parents were in Lebanon and wanted me to stay with them, I also went to the University in Lebanon. At my interview, the Director spoke to me in French and I answered in Italian. I was admitted and stayed there for about a year, but the Polish military began to enquire as to what had happened to Lipiński, since the Polish forces were being taken to England. The joke was that, *"Lipiński went to the Lebanon for 2 weeks and got lost."*

---

180   Garibaldi, G., (1807-82): Italian hero, soldier and explorer. Mickiewicz, A., (1798-1855), regarded as the greatest Polish romantic poet.

I was told to go to England to be discharged, so I left the Lebanon and was discharged. In England I was placed in the Polish camp at Sudbury. I didn't know what to do with myself so I started a draughtsman's course. In the meantime, I applied to 16 universities and one answer came, from my eighth choice, Leicester College of Technology, that I could be student of the University of London and attend lectures in Leicester. I got a stipend of 18 pounds a month from the Polish Education Committee and enrolled at Leicester.

My brother came to join me and we shared the expenses, which meant sharing the 18 pounds a month; we had one pair of pants between us. This was the most difficult time of my life. We took my discharge savings and whatever money he had and bought two beds, two pillows, one table, two chairs; that was our furniture. I was admitted to an English university but I didn't know any English and so I hired a tutor. My first lecture in Leicester was physics and was given by a Scotsman who even the native English had difficulty understanding. He was talking about surface tension. The only word I associated with the English word 'surface' was 'service,' and, to me, 'service' meant military service so, for hours, I was trying to figure out what military service had to do physics!

Germany, 1945-51

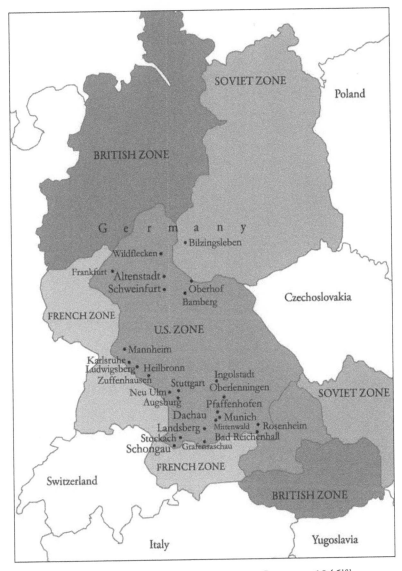

Figure 90. Location of DP Camps in Germany, 1946[181]

---

181   Referred to in this text. There were 762 DP centers in post-War Germany and Austria in June 1947. Wyman, M. (1989). *Europe's Displaced Persons 1945-51*. On p.47, Wyman writes: *"...as 1945 ended there were still 737,375 DPs in Europe receiving aid from the UNRRA - almost 60% of them Poles - and this total ignored thousands of 'free livers.' The total receiving UNRRA aid by March 1946 jumped to 844,144."*

George Hayward, (born Jerzy Maciej Siennicki)

b. 1938, Poland
1944-52, Germany
1952-present, USA

My father attempted to escape Poland with his children in 1944. I remember we were on a train going to Czechoslovakia and landed up in Germany where we were captured and placed in a labor camp. I think my father was hoping to go to France or Morocco; I am not completely sure as he did not share everything with me. I remember how we celebrated Christmas in 1944; we managed to get a Christmas tree and made some paper decorations. I don't recall much about my experience in those years but I remember being hungry.

Figure 91. George Hayward, his sister Maria Siennicka, and her daughter, Germany, 1946

The Americans liberated us in 1945, and we went to live in numerous DP camps. In May and June 1945, we were in Bamberg, in June and July we were in Wildhof, July to September in Frieman, near Munich, September to March 1946 in Nilligan, and March to May in Mannheim; this being the first camp I really remember. This was a good-sized camp and we were introduced to various dried foods like milk, fruit, and potatoes; everything was dried and none of it tasted very good at all but we ate it. I recall people cooking their own meals outside.

The camps were former German barracks which had been converted to house DPs. Because of the large number of DPs, usually three or four families were in one room, divided by a wire on which was hung a cloth to provide some privacy. There were communal baths and showers; however, within a very short time, normal life resumed. Schools were formed, but I got very little education because we moved so often. Nevertheless, I learned enough to read and write in Polish, and my math was always very good so that when I got to the United States I was placed in sixth grade.

I had a very good friend in Mannheim. Toys were not available but life goes on and, somehow, we began to make our own toys. Among the very popular things were scooters, in Polish called a *hulajnoga*. We made our own *hulajnogas* out of wood, leather straps, and ball bearings, things that were available because the Germans just abandoned a lot of that kind of stuff. We made our own guns out of wood because that was what we were exposed to. We played soldiers and had races on these *hulajnogas*. Bicycles were not available at all, especially for kids our age. I don't know how people obtained bikes but some had bikes with a crossbar. We were not tall enough for these bikes so we learned to ride the bike under the bar.

From May to October 1946, we were in Karlsruhe, October to November in Zuffenshausen, November 1946 to September 1948, in Ludwigsburg, September 1948 to December 1949, in Heilbronn, and between December 1949 and April 1951, in Landsberg American Base near Munich. As my father spoke English as one of his seven languages, he got a job as part of a Polish squadron that was hired by the Americans to guard various American bases in Germany.

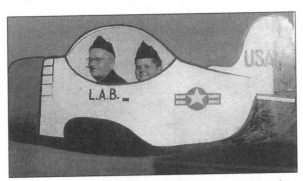

Figure 92. George and his father, Roman Siennicki, Landsberg American Base, nr. Munich, Germany, 1950

In 1949 my father got sick and was badly paralyzed. Unable to work, he was persuaded to give me up for adoption. The emigration document reads as follows: *"I hereby certify that I relinquish all claims to any rights and benefits attaching to my relationship to the said child and declare that my reasons for consenting to the said child's emigration are as follows: I am paralyzed and have no chances to recover, therefore, I am not able to give my minor son proper care and education. My chances for emigration are nil."* The document was witnessed by my half-sister and my father.

My visa was issued in January 1952, and I got to New York on board a US military ship on February 22. These decisions were made by me; my father simply consented. He was paralyzed and his mind was not good so I don't know what he felt. I had only five years with my mother, and 12 years with my father, but values were instilled in me so that, when all of this happened, I knew I wanted a good life for myself and that I would do whatever it took on my own to bring this about.

I was sent to St. Joseph's Home for Boys in Pennsylvania in 1952. The Catholic Charities knew I couldn't live with my sister and asked me if I wanted to be adopted as I could stay at the home for a few more years and then be an independent adult. I wanted to experience a real family so I was adopted by one in Iowa the same year. The Catholic Charities bought me a suitcase and some clothes and put me in a taxi. I made my way by plane to Iowa, all the while speaking very little English. It was unusual for a family to want to adopt an older child, but my adoptive family sought a replacement for a son they had lost who had been about my age. My new family changed my name. They provided me with almost eight years of stable life and a good education, which led me to college.

My sister was in Philadelphia. I think we both got very busy with our own lives so we had little contact. I also wanted to assimilate as quickly as possible into the American way of life. I remember my adoptive mother asking me, in 1953, if I wanted her to buy me a Polish-English dictionary so that I wouldn't lose my Polish. I was not interested. I lost contact with my sister. I never thought of contacting my father. I was in a small town in Iowa where there were no Polish people at all.

Rita Wolf Robinson

b. 1941, Poland
1944-51, Germany
1951-present, USA

A normal stay, as far as we were concerned, would have been about one year. On a Sunday night a truck with a loudspeaker would go by saying you had to be packed and ready to leave by six o'clock in the morning. At 6 AM, the army trucks would come and pick you up and take you to the next camp, usually within one day's travel. You would get picked up in the morning but at night you would be sleeping in your own bed again. As they condensed the camps and shut them down, the trips got shorter and the stays got shorter too.

Figure 93. Rita Robinson *(circled)*, **DP camp, Germany**[182]

I was an old lady at the age of 12. I didn't play with kids, I was always with adults; when I was 10 years old, I took care of the rest of my brothers and sisters. I went from being a kid to being a grown-up. I didn't have any of the growing-up years, the teen years, the dating years, or the get-to-know-yourself years after which you got married and left home.

Andrzej Zdanowicz
b. 1938, Białystok
1939-45, Warszawa
1945-50, Germany
1950-present, Canada

After the War, in the town of Bilzingsleben, we saw some American troops but they left the area because of the impending division of Germany.[183] So, to avoid the Russians, we got on a train again to escape. We saw a red flag on the platform. At this point my mother gave up and said *"what will happen will happen"*. But the train stopped, reversed, and went west, somewhere. We eventually disembarked and went by French trucks to the Wildflecken DP camp. I was there from 1945 to 1950. The only way you could emigrate anywhere was if there was a man in the family.

---

182   Rita lived in the following DP camps in Germany: Siegen, Bockhorn, Carl, Sande and Tirpitz.

183   West Germany and East Germany came into existence as two separate entities in 1949.

Zbigniew Haszlakiewicz
b. 1922, Przecław
1943-50, Germany
1950-present, USA

The Allies didn't know what do with us; they wanted us to return to Poland so they put pressure on us to do so. They gave us difficult living conditions and, while UNRRA was supposed to be looking after us, they constantly reminded us that the best way to solve our problems was through repatriation. Meanwhile our Polish organizations were opposed to this. We knew what communism was and what was waiting for us if we returned. So there was continuous war between the Allies and our Polish organizations.

We had three 'plants' at the polytechnic who tried to convince us that 'heaven on earth' was waiting for us in Poland. Some of these 'students' were not real students at all. They enrolled at the universities and, being Polish, joined our organizations. Once in, they would privately try to persuade people to return. There were 70 of us and three of them.

For practical reasons we fought to have a Polish dormitory as there were very few places to live; the buildings were in ruins and it was hard to find anywhere to live privately. The authorities wanted to keep us in the DP camps but camp conditions were not conducive to studying, as we'd live in large wards. The worse the conditions for us, the better for the authorities, as they wanted to be rid of us. The wives of students resident in dormitories were not allowed to live with their student husbands, as this was a 'student' dormitory; they had to live separately, which was a great problem. The women and children received free food in the camps; it was basic, but nobody died from hunger. The Germans were obliged to supply food, and the Red Cross and other charitable organizations also supplied food, particularly for the children and sick.

In order to get married you needed documents such as a birth certificate, but we had none. Among us were priests and they opened chapels in all these camps. They gave us spiritual care. We went to one such priest and said we wanted to get married. He took our word for it that we were free to do so. He asked for no proof and he believed us. The priest had to take everything on faith and believe us. However, a Catholic wedding like this was not valid in Germany; it had to be conducted by a civilian. We lived our lives in the camps not thinking about this; we thought that, after a few years, the Soviets would be chased out of Poland. After a few years, we realized this was not going to happen so we had to get a civil wedding. Consequently, my sons attended our wedding.

The education of the children was in the hands of each of the national groups. Polish children living in the DP camps received an education organized by the Polish Government-in-Exile. Polish education was well organized by London; there was an educational organization that provided teachers and books, the supply of books from the West particularly annoyed the Communists who were trying to push their own books with Russian literature.

With medical care it was more difficult. We were short of doctors as many had been exterminated in the camps. There were more from other nationalities who had not been as persecuted by the Germans and who, sometimes, even cooperated with them. Most of the medical care was provided by UNRRA who sent doctors, all of whom were volunteers, from western countries like Belgium, France, and England. If there was an area with many DPs, then there was a hospital just for DPs. Our children were born in just such a hospital. When I compared this to the help I had in the concentration camp, it appeared a luxury. The most important thing is that it was sufficient; very few people died from lack of medical care.

When we finished our studies, where we went was a matter of accident as opposed to a rational decision. We didn't care if we went to Canada, America, or Australia; just so long as we were outside Europe; anywhere in Europe was too close to the Communists for us.

Stanisław Sagan
b. 1926, Anin
1944-45, Germany
1945-46, Italy
1946-56, England
1956-present, Canada

I was in Poland until the Uprising of 1944. We tried to sneak into the center of Warszawa to join the fighting and got caught, not by the SS but by the regular German Army. My twin brother was arrested with me. For that, we were sent to Oświęcim concentration camp. I was there for 10 weeks. My mother and one of her sisters were also taken to Oświęcim. My sister and my twin brother escaped and stayed in Poland.

I was eventually taken to Dachau which was liberated by the US Army on April 29, 1945. We were locked up in barracks and didn't know much about what was happening outside. The Americans could not believe what they saw when they arrived. Apparently, they started killing the SS. Some of the German cadets started saluting the Americans and telling them where their superiors were; the Americans couldn't stand this. The Germans shot at the Americans when they came to the gates and the Americans shot back. We were kept in Dachau for a while because of the diseases that existed among the inmates; after this we were moved to DP camps in Germany, and German guards were replaced with American guards.

**Figure 94. Stanisław Sagan's work permit issued
by the Nazis, Warszawa, Poland, 1943**

After liberation I did not want to stay in Germany a moment longer than I had to. I had to bribe my way into General Anders's Army as they didn't want people like me who were half-dead. I was first driven to Murna, a Polish POW camp and, then, to Italy. If not for Anders I don't know how many young people would have perished in Germany. I got to England with the Polish Army. I did not see Churchill as having betrayed Poland; they couldn't stop the Soviet Army. Also, Churchill had to look out for Britain. After our liberation from Dachau we knew what was happening in Poland and many people in the Army were waiting for a third world war. I wasn't thinking about another war as I was in the Polish Army. I had not finished high school in Poland because of the War. I attended the Polish University in Liverpool and studied Architecture. After my experiences, and despite rationing, conditions in England were wonderful.

My brother wrote to me from Poland asking me to write to his military address; he had been called up to the post-War Polish Army medical corps. I though he was crazy and didn't. When we met in 1963 he told me that he hoped that a letter from me would be enough to get him discharged from the Army. I had also hoped to be a doctor, just like my brother. I worked as an orderly in Dachau hospital; it was very hard work as I was with patients who were dying.

Copy of statement by Polish women from the dissolved concentration camp at Ravensbruck.

"During the night from 4th-5th of May of this year, between 12 midnight and 2 AM, two lightly intoxicated Russian soldiers, members of the active army, entered by force to the room where we stayed overnight in a deserted farm about half a mile from Wismar. This interruption in our march was ordered by a Russian officer commander of the troops by the barrier between the American and Russian occupation territories. The mentioned two Russian soldiers tried at the beginning to ensure us of their kind intentions, but after refusing them delivery of young girls to play with, and spend with them the rest of the night, threatenings began – backed by shooting up, and finally they concluded, "Go with us or you will be shot" whereafter three shots were fired, which killed Miss Danuta Pawlak, 19 years of age, and Mrs. Helena Piotrowska, 45 years of age, who heroically stood for the former girl.
Both ladies were buried in a park in a place known to us, by their friends and with the assistance of drivers of the Swiss I.R.C. and some French P.O.W.
We have to point out that the Russian Military authorities showed no interest in this case and did not take any proceedings."

For a true report (signed) Joanna Lipska, Bogna Piatkowska, Wanda Gatarska, Helena Zachemska, Alfreda Wszelaka, Genowefa Zielinska, Helena Augustyniak, M. Aniołkiewicz.[184]

Janie Suszyńska Micchelli
b. 1952, Germany
1952-present, USA

My parents, Hipolit Suszyński and Feliksa Jakubowska Suszyńska, were farmers from Horochów, in the Kresy area. They married in 1940 and were taken as slave laborers to Germany in 1944. The first papers I could locate were dated June 1944, showing that they were brought to a camp for de-lousing and assigned to work. The remaining members of their families were not taken out

---

184   Copy of a statement by Polish women from the dissolved concentration camp at Ravensbruck. (1945). HS4/21, M19/MS/BM/173/3, marked 'Secret.' National Archives, England.

of Poland. I heard that each family had to send their eldest child to work in Germany. My father was the eldest in his family; my mother, an orphan living with her uncle, was also the eldest.

My brother, Józef, was born in Oberhof in September 1944. I have his birth and death records; he died of diphtheria in January 1945. I don't know when they got to Wildflecken, but my sister, Kazimiera, was born there in February 1946, and died of seizures in October 1946.

Figure 95. Feliksa Jakubowska Suszyńska and Hipolit Suszyński with their deceased daughter, Kazimiera, Germany, 1946

Figure 96. Janie Suszyńska Micchelli laying flowers at her sister's grave, Wildflecken, Germany, 2002[185]

Figure 97. Family life in a DP camp, Germany, 1945-50

185   Kazimiera was buried along with 427 other Polish children. http://www.camp-wildflecken.de/dp-camp-wildflecken/janies-return.htm

My brother, Adam, was born in Wildflecken in 1947; my sister, Sofia, was born in Schweinfurt in 1949, but baptized in Wildflecken. After that, they were at some other camps including Bad Reichenall. I have a postcard addressed to them in this camp. I was born in Schongau; after that, we were moved again to another camp, the final one, before we went to America.

I was a baby when we got to America, so I have no personal memory of conditions in the DP Camps. However, I heard my parents say how crowded the camps were and how families were forced to keep moving from camp to camp, and how their future was unknown. My dad worked in the forest, while my mom worked in the Camp's communal kitchen.

Wanda Larkowski
b. 1949-51, Germany
1951-present, USA

When the War ended, my father, Józef Larkowski, had no documentation to prove who he or my mother were, so they had to find two witnesses to testify to their identity. My dad, apparently, had two sisters and two brothers who had not been deported to Germany, in Kraków. He had been trying to escape deportation and was caught and beaten very badly. My mother, Stefania Fudala,

Figure 98. Polish slave laborers in Germany[186]

---

186   Wanda's parents were slave laborers in Germany from 1940-45.

was born in Germany as her parents were Polish migrant workers. She was 14 when the War broke out. Her father was dead. Her whole family, mother, two sisters and a brother, were deported. They were taken out in the middle of the night and traveled by train for days, with standing room only.

When they reached some sort of clearing house, they were forced to strip so that they could be de-loused. This was in Neu Ulm. I remember my mother saying how embarrassing this was, particularly for the older women. After that, the family was separated. They were in the same area but were sent to different farmers, maybe 7 to 8 miles apart. When the War ended she was in the DP camp in Neu Ulm. Often, the labor camps became DP camps.

My mother told me that the farmer at the first farm where she worked was very mean to her. She was very hungry and stole an egg. She was responsible for the laundry and planned to cook the egg in the boiling water. The farmer's wife caught her, cut off all her hair and beat her so badly that she was semi-comatose for two weeks. The *Burgermeister* was supposed to ensure that the slave laborers were treated well, so, when she felt better, she was moved to another farm where the people were very good to her and didn't insist she wore her 'P'; they even took her to church. She stayed there for the rest of the War.

**Figure 99. Wanda Larkowski's nursery class,
Wildflecken, Germany, 1951**

From Neu Ulm, my mother went to Ludwigsberg where she met my father, then to Forstein. In Ludwigsberg, the family was together but the authorities began to split them up. My mom went to Altenstadt. The authorities wanted them to return to Poland, but they didn't want to. The authorities placed them in huge hangars with only curtains for privacy.

My mom was once on a train when the IRO told them they were going to a different camp in Germany; they were, in fact, going back to Poland. Everyone on the train revolted so the train had to turn back. Many people were afraid that they would be killed if they went back. Rampant rumors flew around the camp and she believed what she heard. The Red Cross tried to reunite families; even when they were in different camps, at least they knew where they were. The DPs were promised money and clothes to go back to Poland as there was no space for them in the camps.[187] The German people did not want them; they were not only a defeated nation, they also had insufficient food for themselves.

My mother said that when camps were first established, they were very bad; Red Cross packages were not getting through; people working in the warehouses were stealing and selling them off on the black market. She said that the Americans would often give them chocolate and cigarettes, and that they would trade the cigarettes for milk for their children. My father went to prison for doing this: he was trying to get food for the kids. My mother told me how cruel the nurses in the hospital were; when my brother was sick he was taken to the morgue, yet he was not dead. My mother did not believe he was dead and went into the morgue. A lot of children died in the DP camps.

People had no plans for the future as they weren't told anything. They didn't even know the scope of the War. They knew they had to black out their windows, but not much else. Certain countries were opening up for DPs; for example, Belgium was taking couples, and England took single women as nannies. My mom wanted to go to Australia (not that she knew where Australia was); she had heard that it was beautiful. However, the family was not accepted for emigration due to the absence of official paperwork for my father.

During his life, my father would periodically relive the War. In the nursing home, he would lock himself in the closet because he was afraid the Nazis were after him, just as when he was deported, and they beat him on the head with the rifle butts. Sometimes he would say to me, *"Wandzia, I can't think; it hurts."* They damaged him permanently.

---

187   The IRO put 60 days supply of food rations in their windows to tempt the people to go back, knowing that the former slave laborers were always hungry.

Bolesław Biega

b. 1922, Warszawa
1944-46, Germany
1946-50, England
1950-present, USA

After liberation it took us three to four days to reach the American lines. As DPs, we were in German barracks. I made it known to the US Army that we were officers from the Polish Army. When I told them that I spoke English, the US officers were delighted to have me as an interpreter. This was May 1945 and I found out from another interpreter that this area was to be given up to the Soviet Union; even the US Army did not know that. This had been decided in France. I was then appointed to help with the evacuation. After that I was sent to London in mid-July and then back to Germany two weeks later as a liaison officer. I was working in the DP camps. Until the situation in Poland was clarified we had no intention of finding ourselves under Soviet domination.

The camps were initially operated by the occupying army in their own zone: British, American and French. It wasn't until roughly June or July 1945 that UNRRA took over. But UNRRA depended on the Army to transport food and supplies to the DP camps. In general, by August 1945, the camps very well supplied with food. People were not living well, but there was no hunger. Most of the camps were former German Army camps. Some were located in former German POW camps, or in schools; in other words, in permanent buildings. Families lived in one room; single people shared a room.

There was a lot of pressure on people to return to Poland, though it depended on the local UNRAA authorities as to how much of this pressure was applied. As a liaison officer I had to step in, two or three times, to prevent forced repatriation. There was a group of us with an office in Frankfurt; my area was from Stuttgart south to the French zone, and east as far as Ulm. When we learned of an attempt to force repatriation, I would call the commander of the local unit and protest; if that did not work I would call the headquarters in Frankfurt. In every case the repatriation was stopped. These were efforts by a zealous local unit commander, or arbitrary decisions by some colonel, to solve a problem by placing people on trains and having them go away.

Most people were hoping to get to the United States or Canada. Polish organizations in the USA were working on this, but the USA government placed severe limitations on how many people were being admitted.[188] In the meantime, other countries, such as the Canada and Belgium, were recruiting. Efforts were being made by DPs in the British zone to go to England but the British were resisting this as they already had hundreds of thousands of Poles in England, the military and their families, and some Polish orphans. When the US Government withdrew its recognition of the Polish Government-in-Exile, our role was ended and Poland sent its own Mission with a goal of repatriating people to Poland. In fact, in 1946, there were two Polish Missions in Germany attached to the US Army; we were the Polish Mission for Welfare, and the Polish Mission from Poland was the Polish Mission for Repatriation. That's how the Army distinguished between us.

Andrzej Zdanowicz
b. 1938, Białystok
1939-45, Warszawa
1945-50, Germany
1950-present, Canada

We were taken by the French Army to the DP camp in Wildflecken, where I was between 1945 and 1950. To get out of a DP camp you needed a man in the family and, since my mother and grandmother and I were together, nobody would take us. My aunt married somebody in Wildflecken and, once he got a job in Canada, she joined him; a few years later, she sponsored us to come to Canada. My grandmother went to her son who was then in England. My mother worked as a midwife.

The camp at Wildflecken was fantastic for a child. You went to school but still had enough time to play. There were 50,000 people there and all of them were Polish. Later, it changed to being a transition camp but, in the beginning, it was all Polish.

We first lived in a well-camouflaged building on the top of the mountain; it was not on any map. The Americans did not know about it until they

---

188   15,000 Polish Quota immigrants were allowed into the US, 1939-45; 17,000 more, 1945-48; as a result of the 1948 Displaced Persons Act and its 1950 amendments, 140,000 Poles came to the USA. Between 1940 and 1954, 178,680 quota immigrants born in Poland arrived in the USA. The National Origins Act, 1924-65, set the annual quota for Polish immigrants at 6,524. Jaroszyńska-Kirchmann, A. op. cit., pp. 9 & 245.

stumbled on it by accident. You couldn't see it from the valley or from the air: it had a black slate roof and had been an army camp for the Germans and the SS. Accommodation was very good, except that we couldn't cook; there were six or seven kitchens from which food was handed out. We used to say: *"Daje, aż w gardle wstaje. Potrawy zimne i gorące."*[189] That was the song.

My mother went to work in the hospital as a midwife's aide. Eventually, she took the test and qualified as a midwife and delivered 210 babies; many babies were born in the camp. I also remember there being a riot when Poles from Poland came to try to pressurize us to return to Poland. The police had to come and protect us. People who had gone through Russia would never go back, as they knew what awaited them. Other people didn't. They also gave incentives of food supplies for a few weeks.

The Germans didn't want us as they did not have enough to support themselves. Often, the men found jobs and left for overseas and were later followed by their families. Many countries needed farmers so many men suddenly became 'farmers.'

---

189   *"Daje, aż w gardle wstaje. Potrawy zimne i gorące."* (Polish): *"(They) give until it sticks in your throat. Hot and cold meals."*

THE NEW POLISH DIASPORA

CHAPTER 10

The Road of No Return

> *"...why was the most faithful of the Allies sacrificed, an ally who could not be accused of any breach of promise, of any denial of his obligations, or of any neglect in making the supreme effort? It was done to appease Russia. It was done because Russia demanded that Poland be sacrificed as the price of her further co-operation with the West. Under Soviet pressure no place was left for Poland even in the political thought of the Western Allies. On the day of the armistice with Germany, on the V-Day of the Western world, the Polish soldier became once more what he had been since the end of September 1939, since the days of the joint attack of the German and Soviet forces on Poland: a soldier without a country, to whom the road to his home was barred."*
>
> **Lt. General Władysław Anders**[190]

---

190   Lt.-General W. Anders, op.cit., pp. 307-8.

The total number of Poles who were demobilized from the Polish Armed Forces were:

114,000	Polish Resettlement Corps
86,000	Returned to Poland from United Kingdom
12,000	Returned to Poland from Italy
5,000	Returned to Poland from Germany
2,000	Returned to Poland from Middle East
8,000	Disbanded without joining PRC
1,000	Recalcitrants ineligible for PRC
14,000	Repatriated to countries other than Poland
7,000	Settled in France
=======	
249,000	

From the nearly quarter of a million Polish Armed Forces, 105,000 returned to Poland. The above figures do not give a clear indication of how many Poles began new lives in Britain. According to Zubrzycki,[191] the peak of Polish settlement in Britain was in December, 1949:

91,400	Polish Resettlement Corps
2,300	Ex-Polish Forces not in PRC
31,800	Dependants of the above brought to UK by War Office
2,400	'Distressed Relatives' brought to UK (Poles married to UK Citizens)
29,400	Polish 'European Volunteer Workers'
=======	
157,300	

In 1949, according to the Commissioner of the London Metropolitan Police, Poles made up well over a quarter of the aliens in the Police District: 37,819 or 27.2% of the total.[192]

---

191 Zubrzycki, J., op. cit. p. 62.
192 Ostrowski, M., op. cit., Chapter 8, pp. 19-20.

Mieczysław Juny

b. 1913, Lwów

1939-45, Hungary, Yugoslavia, Greece, Lebanon, Syria, Palestine,
Egypt, Iraq, England, South Africa, Sierra Leone, Scotland

1945-present, England

Figure 100. Mieczysław Juny, Ilford Park, England, 2006

We received a letter from the Ministry of Foreign Affairs, from Bevin, en-
couraging us to return to Poland,[193] now that Poland was free, but the Poland
I knew no longer existed; home was now part of Ukraine. Poland was under
Soviet Communist rule. We had news of those who had returned to Poland
and what had happened to them. Thankfully, Churchill realized what had
happened and it was thanks to his initiative that the Polish Resettlement Act
was introduced in 1947.[194] We all had wanted to return to Poland; that is, after
all, why we had been fighting. Unfortunately it became apparent that this was
impossible.

---

193   This was known as 'Operation Keynote.' Between March 20 – 21, 1946, all
members of the Polish Armed Forces received a letter from Ernest Bevin strongly en-
couraging them to return to Poland. He presented this as their patriotic duty and in
Poland's best interest. See p.279.

194   After the Second World War the majority of Polish troops who had fought alongside the Western Allies preferred not to return to a Communist-dominated Poland; they
were allowed to stay in Great Britain. A Polish Resettlement Corps was established,
which offered vocational training and discharged the troops from the Polish Armed
Forces. Wives and dependent relatives were brought to Britain to join them, bringing the
total estimated number of cases to over 200,000. The Polish Resettlement Corps (PRC)
was raised as a corps of the British Army into which Poles were allowed to enlist for the
period of their demobilization. The PRC was formed in 1946 and disbanded in 1949.
http://www.nationalarchives.gov.uk/familyhistory/guide/migrantancestors/polish.htm

Józef Kałwa
b. 1928, Nowogródek
February 1940, deported to the Soviet Union
1942-47, Iran, Iraq, Palestine
1947-62, England
1962-present, USA

When I graduated from Commercial College (near Cambridge, England) three teachers asked for a meeting with us and presented themselves as having been sent from Poland by the Polish Government. They wanted to recruit us into Foreign Trade in Poland. Two volunteered and sailed to Gdynia in Poland. We had already managed to communicate with their families as to who was arriving. The boat arrived, their families saw them there, but they never got off. The next stop was Kalin, in Russia. To this day we have no word of what happened to them.

Witold Mazur
b. 1936, Kołodno
February 1940, deported to the Soviet Union
1942-48, Iran, Iraq, India, Africa
1948-58, England
1958-present, Canada

When my father went back to Poland to visit his brother, Antoni, he learned that a lot of people who were left behind in south-eastern Poland had been slaughtered by the Ukrainians. In 1946-47, the Poles from the Kresy region were moved to the 'reclaimed lands' in western Poland; that's how my uncle moved. He was told that my father was a 'traitor' because he did not return to Poland, and was a 'subversive'; that if he went back to Poland he would be arrested and tried. My father and grandfather talked to people in the village who were all of the same opinion, seeing us as traitors who did not want to come and build a new Poland, and that we were against the 'People's Poland'. My uncle did not, himself, believe this, but his wife was very adamant. She said *"The Government of Poland will look after you; they gave us such a beautiful farm with brick buildings, and all the barns and everything."* Our correspondence ended when my uncle died.

In 1956, when still in England, I received a letter from the Polish Government stating that, because of my activities to start a Polish organization which was anti-*Polska Ludowa*,[195] if I went to any countries that had an extradition treaty with Poland, I would be arrested.

Zbigniew Haszlakiewicz

b. 1922, Przecław

1943-50, Germany

1950-present, USA

Figure 101. Zbigniew Haszlakiewicz, USA, 2006

The decision not to return to Poland was not difficult to make because my family and I knew the Bolsheviks[196] very well. The fact that they were ruling Poland was enough for us not to consider returning. When Churchill announced the existence of the *Iron Curtain*,[197] because he had, at last, realized what he was dealing with, the pressure on us to return ended. People knew that

---

195 *Polska Ludowa* (Polish): Polish Peoples' Republic, i.e. Soviet-controlled Poland.

196 Communists who seized power in 1917 Russia and founded the Soviet Union.

197 The '*Iron Curtain:*' In a speech on March 5, 1946, Winston Churchill, the Prime Minister of England, announced the existence of an *Iron Curtain* between the western powers and those countries controlled by the Soviet Union, *"From Stettin in the Baltic to Trieste in the Adriatic an iron curtain has descended across the Continent. Behind that line lie all the capitals of the ancient states of Central and Eastern Europe, Warsaw, Berlin, Prague, Vienna, Budapest, Belgrade, Bucharest and Sofia; all these famous cities and the populations around them lie in what I must call the Soviet sphere, and all are subject, in one form or another, not only to Soviet influence but to a very high and in some cases increasing measure of control from Moscow."* Modern History Sourcebook: Winston S. Churchill: *'Iron Curtain Speech'*, March 5, 1945. www.fordham.edu/halsall/mod/churchill-iron.html

we were right in not wanting to return to Poland.

We were totally indifferent as to where we would go; it was usually by accident rather than as a result of any informed decision. We just excluded the European countries as they were too close to the Soviet 'paradise'.

Andrzej Sławinski
b. 1929, Łodowa
1944-45, Germany
1945-46, Italy
1946-present, England

We didn't trust the Soviets and for obvious reasons. The NKVD officers came and told us to stay put and wait for transportation to Poland. We thought, *"Poland? Hello; how about Siberia?"* Half of our group (of 40) decided to return to Poland on their own, so they stole tractors and lorries from the local Germans, looted whatever they could, and went to Poland. The second half of us decided to go to the Americans. It was very risky because, of course, we were in uniform, and very funny uniforms too; they were American uniforms of World War I vintage. We were stopped many times by Soviet officers who asked us who we were; we told them we were Polish prisoners heading east, going back to Poland. We then proceeded to go west, but not a single Soviet soldier or officer knew where east or west was so nobody stopped us. After 3 days we reached the American lines. The first American said, *"Why are you going west? Poland is in the other direction!"* Most people thought it was too dangerous to return to Poland. Maybe it was naïve, but they were hoping that things would change, either through gradual pressure by the Allies or through another war.

Everybody was waiting; nobody knew what for, but something had to happen. Actually we were bored, waiting for something to happen.

> ### Speech in House of Commons
> ### by Foreign Secretary Bevin, March 20:
>
> *"I recently told the House that I hoped shortly to be in a position to make a statement on the problem of the Polish Armed Forces under British Command. I have explained the principles underlying the policy of His Majesty's Government in this matter. While we will not use force to compel these men to return to Poland, I have never disguised our firm conviction that in our view they ought to go back in order to play their part in the reconstruction of their stricken country...... For this reason His Majesty's Government have for many months been urging the Polish Provisional Government to clarify the conditions which would apply. Agreement has now been reached with the Polish Provisional Government and we have arranged to issue a document in Polish to every individual member of the Polish Armed Forces. The men will receive it today."*
>
> ### Rt. Hon. Ernest Bevin[198]

Lech Hałko

b. 1925, Warszawa

1944-45, Germany

1945-46, Czechoslovakia, Italy

1946-53, England

1953-present, Canada

Propaganda was written that tried to persuade us to return to Poland. Even Churchill told us that it was our responsibility to return. We struggled with our consciences as to whether or not to return, but the news from Poland was very, very unfavorable. We heard that our friends had been arrested, especially those from the Home Army, and deported to Russia; living conditions created by the Communists were hard.

---

198   Speech in the House of Commons by Foreign Secretary, Ernest Bevin. Hansard, House of Commons Parliamentary Debates, UK. March 20, 1946.

Jadwiga Krzysztoporska Piasecka
b. 1935, Warszawa
June 1940, deported to the Soviet Union
1942-44, Iran
1944-68, England, Scotland
1968-present, USA

My parents knew they would never return to Poland. Once the War ended and Poland was joined to the Russian block, they knew it was impossible; this was very difficult for them. After their experiences in Russia, they couldn't endure Russian rule again. My uncle, imprisoned in France for the duration of the War, did return to Poland.

Maria Pawulska Rasiej
b. 1927, Lwów
April 1940, deported to the Soviet Union
1942-47, Iran, India, Africa
1947-52, England
1952-present, USA

I always missed Poland a lot; I never left the emigrant 'limbo', though you can't call this 'emigration' because the departure to Russia was not 'emigration'. We were forced out of our country. I never settled down; a short visit to Poland for vacation was always accompanied by great emotion.

Zygmunt Kopel
b. 1934, Mołodeczno
April 1940, deported to the Soviet Union
1942-47, Iran, Iraq, Palestine
1947-present, England

With our sense of having been harmed, we were, to the British, a totally unknown entity. They knew nothing about Russia; they thought it was heaven on earth as described by George Bernard Shaw in the 1920s. There were communications with our relatives in Poland; they knew that the Polish authorities in Poland were hunting down Polish officers. We were cadets but the Communist authorities called us *'Anders' pawns'*.

The British didn't want us, they wanted us to return, especially after Bevin's speech; they said it was our duty to return to rebuild Poland.

Roma Michniewicz King

b. 1939, Wilno
1940, deported to the Soviet Union
1942-46, Persia, Lebanon, Egypt
1946-51, England
1951-59, New Zealand
1959-present, USA

Figure 102. Roma Michniewicz King, USA, 2006

The British were not happy to have so many Poles in Britain. They really were not very nice, saying, *"Go home, why don't you go home."* They were very happy to have us help them; our Air Force worked with them, our Army fought alongside them but after the War, all you heard from every side was, *"Why don't you go home?"* I met that so often. *"Why are you training your troops to stay here? Tell them to go home, send them home..."* But home was Communist so they would not have fared very well if they had gone. My father would have been put in prison because he was a political prisoner during the War. He was even afraid when, at the age of 19, I went to visit Poland for the first time. He was afraid for me. He said, *"You know, they have our name, and I just don't feel easy about you going to Poland."*

Józef Szkudłapski

b. 1925, Lwów
1940, deported to the Soviet Union
1942-43, Iran, Palestine, South Africa,
1943-45, Scotland
1945-present, England

We all planned to return to Poland. I got a letter from my mother telling me not to be stupid and return (I could read between the lines). They had a very hard life in Poland. They got an apartment and my sister got a job in an office, but was fired when she refused to join the Communist Party.

Romuald Lipiński

b. 1925, Brześć
June 1941, deported to the Soviet Union
1942-43, Iran, Iraq, Palestine, Egypt
1943-46, Italy, Lebanon
1946-53, England
1953-present, USA

Figure 103. Romuald Lipiński, USA, 2005

Everybody was hoping there would be war between America and Russia so we could return to Poland and take part in a victory parade. Everything was considered temporary. Later, our dreams were shattered and there was complete chaos in the Corps; people didn't know what to do or where to go. There were suicides as all this sacrifice had been in vain. When we got to England, we suffered from complete despair.

Charles Lesczuk

b. 1916, Siedlec
1939-42, the Soviet Union
1942-46, Iran, Iraq, Italy
1946-present, England

I got a letter from my mother asking me to return to Poland at once. Then I received another letter from a relative telling me not to come, that the previous letter had been dictated, and that my mother was forced to write it. She told me to think about what I had left behind, and what I may not find upon my return.

Stanisław Milewski

b. 1930, Bagrów
February 1940, deported to the Soviet Union
1942-47, Iran, Palestine
1947-59, England
1959-present, USA

Figure 104. Stanisław Milewski, USA, 2006

When the War ended we could not return to Poland because my father had been a great anti-Communist before the War. In 1945, he came to see us in Nazareth and lived with Mom there until 1947; I believe those were the happiest years of their lives. He was still in the Army; from Nazareth he went to Egypt and then to England. My sister and mother left and, 2 months later, I also left for England with my school. We were in Horsley Camp, Mom was in Brantington. I cycled from Horsley to the port of Southampton[199] when I heard that there were some Polish servicemen arriving; indeed, my father was on the ship.

---

199   Horsley to Southampton: a distance of 25 miles.

CHAPTER 11

England

> *"In their note of the 8ᵗʰ August, 1946, my Government made a proposal to call into being, in place of the Polish Resettlement Corps, another organisation in Britain for training for civilian life of these, soldiers who, in the meantime, had not decided to return to their country. However, this proposal was not accepted by His Majesty's Government.*
>
> *The course of events during the last two years confirmed fully the correctness of the forecasts and reservations of the Polish Government. Both the Polish Resettlement Corps and the hitherto not demobilised centres of the former Polish Armed Forces under British command, bound personally and financially with the political apparatus existing in Great Britain and beyond her frontiers, which is centred around the so-called 'London Government', were used by certain factors for warlike agitation, development of propaganda based on slander against the return to Poland, and for the conducting of diversionary, subversive and intelligence activities directed against the Polish Government.*
>
> *The émigré Press, paid for by social funds of the former Polish units under British command, has also been used as a tool for war agitation and propaganda against the return to Poland."*
>
> *Z. Modzelewski*[200]

---

200   Modzelewski, Z. Polish Government (in Poland) representative. Hansard, Commons Parliamentary Debates, 12 May 1948, vol. 450, cc216-9W.

Danuta Banaszek Szlachetko

b. 1929, Warszawa
1944-45, Germany
1945-46, Italy
1946-present, England

**Figure 105. Danuta Banaszek Szlachetko,
Northolt RAF Base, England, 2006**

Everyone felt humiliated, because we had been humiliated, and we had to accept menial jobs. Those were difficult times, the post-War years in England, but we were a real community. We helped each other; you would lend money and help others however you could. Eventually, we all landed on our feet. For some, it did not turn out well, especially for the men; maybe because of the War and all the hardship, they got sick and died early.

We had a lot of wasted life. Our youth was difficult and so we did not experience the joys you would expect; we couldn't go anywhere we chose, or do anything we wanted, or have fun. We had no freedom to choose our education. Not everyone could get the education they wanted because there was no help. Our youth was not really youth; there was no family. There were language difficulties, you were always on your own among strangers, and being on your own was very difficult. Many women today find themselves in the same situation and we understand each other as we have experienced the same things. We will always help each other because we know how difficult it is.

Danuta Mączka Gradosielska

b. 1925, Równe
February 1940, deported to the Soviet Union
1942-46, Iran, Palestine, Iraq, Egypt, Italy
1946-present, England

When we bought our first house we had no furniture; we slept on the floor, only the baby had a bed, and there was a washing machine. I went to the greengrocer and brought home some wooden crates which became our chairs. I had a radio and listened to *Mrs. Dale's Diary*.[201] She would give her maid detailed instructions as to what to buy when shopping; she spoke slowly and that's how I learned English. I also learned English at the camp school I attended.

When my second baby was due, the visiting midwife said I couldn't give birth on the floor and that I had to have a bed. At this time, my husband was compensated for the overdose of penicillin given when he was injured at Monte Cassino. With the 70 pounds[202] we bought some bedroom furniture. He also got some civilian clothes to replace those he was issued when he was demobilized. I went to the local market and bought myself some cloth remnants for 10 shillings[203] and made myself a couple of outfits. So, I had a bed too but the baby was born in hospital, as was every child after that.

Józef Szkudłapski

b. 1925, Lwów
1940, deported to the Soviet Union
1942-43, Iran, Palestine, South Africa,
1943-45, Scotland
1945-present, England

The Polish Resettlement Corps was a joke; they pushed us towards the worst jobs. Many worked in the mines. I was just a Corporal. They sent us to a camp near Cambridge. Many of my friends were being demobilised and I was still a secretary in the Polish Army. I went to report to the Officer and he told me that I would stay in the Army as long as he saw fit. I replied that I would only stay until I got a job. I found a job with the British American Optical Company. It was terrible work.

---

201   *Mrs. Dale's Diary*: BBC radio serial drama which ran from 1947-69; 1962-69, it ran under the title of *The Dales*.
202   70 British pounds: in 1945, £70 would have the same spending worth as today's £1,810, or $3,350.
203   10 British shillings: half of a British pound, equivalent to $23 today.

Charles Lesczuk

b. 1916, Siedlec

1939-42, Soviet Union

1942-46, Iran, Iraq, Italy

1946-present, England

**Figure 106. Charles Lesczuk's Polish Resettlement Corps
Registration Document, 1948**[204]

The English were such 'good' allies that they would not allow us to follow our vocations. We were only allowed to work as laborers,[205] so we went where we could find work. I was a carpenter and, then, an army mechanic. In Kensington, London, there was a Polish Rehabilitation Office at the *Polskie Ognisko*.[206] We, servicemen, were together in the Army and, together in the Russian *kolkhoz*,; when I asked for help with finding accommodation they said there was none, yet, when a corporal asked, it was found. There was no help for the rank-and-file. I realized early on that I could only rely on myself so I lost touch with Polish organizations.

---

204   The document reads: *"Finally discharged from R.C. on 19.2.48"* (February 19, 1948).

205   Note in Polish Resettlement Corps Registration Document, Figure 144, p.259: *"Permission granted for employment as labourer…"*.

206   *Polskie Ognisko* (Polish): Polish Hearth, one of the centers for post-War Poles in London. It functions to this day and is best known for its old-European atmosphere and high quality restaurant.

Kazimierz Bączyński

b. 1920, Bielsko Biała
1939, deported to the Soviet Union
1939-45, Hungary, Yugoslavia, France, Morocco,
Gibraltar, England, Scotland
1945-present, England

Russians were the heroes at the time; the British saw Stalin in the cinema, and applauded. They called us fascists, saying, *"Why don't you return to Poland?"* It was not pleasant for us; there was a strong Communist Party in England.

We set up our own organizations, especially churches; everything happened around the church; this was most important to us. Restarting life in England was difficult, especially for those from Anders's Army who did not speak English and, while the English intelligentsia were especially well-disposed to us, the general public were not.

The most important thing was to start a new life, as opposed to being involved in politics. We had our Government-in-Exile and we read newspapers to see what was being said about Poland. We were all great patriots; after all, this was a patriotic emigration and we all wanted to return to Poland, but Poland no longer existed. Also it was very dangerous for us. Everyone had gone through so much; deportation to Russia, the German camps and the War.

I had English lessons on the transport ships and I used to go to the cinema in Scotland; then, I would look up key words. There was work but it depended on what kind of work and where. We were, in effect, homeless, living out of a suitcase in rented accommodation.

I did not think about going to war again; there were some who did, but when Churchill realized he had made a grave mistake and that there was the Iron Curtain, it was too late. Then England started to re-arm. I worked in an office where we designed plane parts so I had a lot of work and earned well. I had thought of going to the USA, and even had a sponsor, but changed my mind. I was also going to go to Canada but changed my mind about that as well. Some people emigrated to Canada, the USA, or South America in the hope of finding good positions. I worked and bought a house. I had the Polish Parish and so I started to feel good. But you are always a foreigner; when it came to the higher positions, you were discriminated against. Even if you had the same or higher qualifications, they would not hire you. But I had a good relationship with the English and am generally happy with my life there.

As for the impact of my experiences, I remember we had to beg for food so I now appreciate every crumb. I remember having to ask poor people for food, and how one poor woman who had very little said that she would give us what she could because her son, also a soldier, might be out there somewhere begging for food too. I always used to think that if I survived this then nothing would ever be as bad again.

Zygmunt Kopel
b. 1934, Mołodeczno
April 1940, deported to the Soviet Union
1942-47, Iran, Iraq, Palestine
1947-present, England

I remember an incident. I was travelling with my father to Rivenhall; my father was in uniform as he had no other clothing. The railway workers at Brandon Station told my father that he should be working just like they were and not travelling around in a uniform.

I went to English school in Wickham straight away, but it was not pleasant. The children in the schools would put swastikas on their sleeves and nobody told them off, yet, this was something that was not even allowed in Germany. I only had religion classes in Rivenhall. My sister went to Joseph Conrad College where, in 1948-49, there were older cadets and female volunteers. They took the English 'A' level.[207] When we lived as civilians in Bracknell, and there were very few Poles, people would approach us; if there was a larger group then people kept their distance as we seemed to be more exotic to them.

We had no money, but neither did the English. In Bracknell, we lived in a house with six or seven families. One family invited another and told them the schools were good. There were very few Poles but we did keep together. The priest would come from Reading; we had our Polish paper. In Rivenhall, we felt very safe. I remember a conversation with my father; he told me that we would definitely return to Poland whether it was in one year or 10. There were moments when we thought there might be a war, for example, during the Berlin Blockade in 1948, the Korean War in 1956, and during the 1950s unrest in Poland, then Hungary. We were terribly disappointed that the Americans

---

207   A level: Advanced Level General Certificate of Education, University entrance examinations, usually taken during the final year of high school.

did not help Hungary.[208]

The Polish hostels were either Nissen huts or barracks. The winters were very cold in 1947 and 1948. In Bodney, there was a very long barrack with a heater in the middle, so those who were on the ends of the barracks were very cold. I remember heating a piece of asbestos I had found in a rubbish dump and placing it on my feet to keep warm. In those days nobody knew that asbestos was so deadly. In Rivenhall, the Nissen huts, or *beczki*[209] as we called them, were divided into two; they were previously US or British Army camps. The Americans left very quickly. There were some German POWs in the country in 1948. That's when the last group left. I believe that they were deliberately kept as they provided cheap labor.

Jerzy Kozłowski

b. 1929, Łuck
February 1940, deported to the Soviet Union
1942-47, Iran, Palestine
1947-present, England

The Union representatives asked me for my Union card. I didn't have one so they threatened to go on strike if I was employed. The employer let me go. I found another job and was asked to start almost immediately.

When I told the employer my name he said that he would *"send me a letter in a few days."* When I confronted him about this change of heart, he said that this was a closed shop, but he suggested I turn up at work and we'd see what would happen. When I turned up for work there was a Union representative waiting for me at the gate. He asked if I was a member of the Union; I said that I supposed I was. He then asked for my Union card which, of course, I did not have. I said to him *"Were you born with a card in your mouth? Why won't you give me a chance to get one?"* I was allowed to stay for a 4-week trial period. I got my card and everything was OK.

---

208   The Hungarian Revolution, 23 October to 10 November 1956, was an unsuccessful revolt against the Stalinist regime in Hungary. The United Nations condemned the Soviet suppression of the revolt, but no military support was provided to the Hungarians.
209   *beczki* (Polish): barrels.

Roma Michniewicz King

b. 1939, Poland
1940, deported to the Soviet Union
1942-46, Persia, Lebanon, Egypt
1946-51, England
1951-59, New Zealand
1959-present, USA

Soldiers from the Polish Army could not get the jobs in England for which they were trained before the War; they were attorneys, architects, and the like, but they did not have the language and the ability to go into the work for which they were trained. In England, the Polish Forces were being retrained for something that would actually earn them money and enable them to support their families. A lot of them trained to be gardeners and construction workers; things they could do. My father was one of the officers assigned to the training camps receiving members of the Polish Army who came from Italy to be retrained. For example, our dearest friend, who was a captain in the Polish Navy, became the gardener at my boarding school. Just a couple of years ago, in Australia, he finally got honors and a medal for his role in the Baltic Sea. It's amazing the stories you come across.

**Figure 107. Roma Michniewicz King and her family,
England, 1946**

Lech Hałko

b. 1925, Warszawa
1944-45, Germany
1945-46, Czechoslovakia, Italy
1946-53, England
1953-present, Canada

Figure 108. Lech Hałko, USA, 2006

We knew from the press, and the radio that the Polish Government-in-Exile was active in London, but what could we do? We knew that we had been betrayed; the British didn't even allow us to march in the Victory Parade (in London, 1946). To this day they have not explained how General Sikorski, the Prime Minister of Poland's London-based Government-in-Exile and Commander-in-Chief of her armed forces, died; he was probably murdered.

At that time everyone loved Joe Stalin, so we were a thorn in the British Government's flesh. We were called 'fascists' because we were anti-Communist, or perhaps it's more appropriate to say that we did not accept the Communist occupation of Poland.

Bolesław Biega

b. 1922, Warszawa
1944-46, Germany
1946-50, England
1950-present, USA

I decided to go to the USA because things were difficult in England, not just for the Poles, but also for the British. Also, having worked for the US Army, I had made a lot of American friends. The challenge was persuading my family to come with me. There was a lot of resentment among the English of these hundreds of thousands of Poles coming to Britain and being supported by the taxpayer. I had personal experience of this. I had a decent job in London after I had completed my engineering degree, but you are always looking for something better. I followed up on an advertisement that I saw in the paper and the company didn't realize that I was Polish as I had no Polish accent. Everything went well; we had agreed on the salary and everything, but when I wrote on the form that I was born in Poland and that I was, in fact, Polish, the conversation suddenly ended.

RATIONING IN ENGLAND 1939-54

Before the War, Britain imported about 55 million tons of food annually from other countries. After war was declared in September 1939, German submarines began to torpedo British supply ships, so food imports decreased. In order to avoid food shortages, the British Government introduced a system of rationing. On 8 January, 1940, bacon, butter and sugar were rationed. Everyone was issued with a ration book containing coupons that had to be handed in to shops every time rationed food was bought. As well as the basic ration, everybody had 16 coupons each month that they could spend on what they wished.

Beginning of Rationing:
1939   gasoline
1940   bacon, butter, sugar, all meat, tea, margarine
1941   jelly (gelatin), cheese, clothing, eggs
1942   coal, rice, dried fruit, soap, tinned peas and tomatoes, coal, gas, electricity, candy, chocolate
1943   biscuits, sausages

End of Rationing:
1948   flour
1949   clothes
1950   canned and dried fruit, chocolate, biscuits, treacle, syrup, jelly (gelatin), mincemeat, soap
1952   tea
1954   candy, sugar

All food rationing ended by 1954

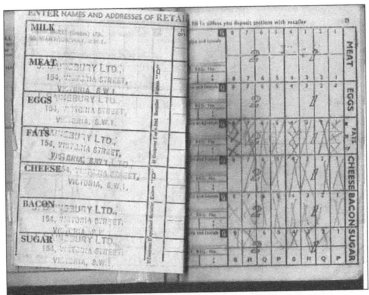

Figure 109. English rationing book,
belonging to Bolesław Wojciechowski, England, 1946

Stanisław Szuttenbach

b. 1929, Orany
July 1941, deported to the Soviet Union
1941-48, Iran, Iraq, Palestine, Egypt
1948-51, England
1951-present, USA

My family was re-united in England in 1948. My father traveled from Scotland, my mother and sister from Calvedon Camp, and I from the Mikołaj Kopernik School in Bottisham. After completing the Polish Resettlement Corps, my father got a job in England. There wasn't much choice of work; Poles had to take what they were offered. Those of us who had been in the Cadet School did not have to enter the Polish Resettlement Corps but were sent to civilian school so we could finish our education. My father wanted to leave England because living conditions were so hard, particularly in the Nissen huts; to get other housing was difficult because the English were given preference.

Personally, I did not experience any pressure to return to Poland but I was aware that the British Government was trying to get us to return. Conditions in England were difficult; there was rationing and a shortage of housing. The English wanted to get rid of the 'burden' that was the Second Corps, the First Corps, the Navy and the Air Force. It was easiest to tell us that they would give us transportation and that we should return to Poland to rebuild our country. That sounded like a very patriotic thing to do, but we knew what was waiting for us. Now we know just how many people returned and were shot or imprisoned for many years. Those who knew English were in a far better position to get a good job than those who had not ventured outside the Polish community. The idea of leaving a Polish camp, particularly for farmers or laborers who had come from the Kresy area, must have been a daunting prospect.

Figure 110. Stanisław Szuttenbach and friends,[210]
Stowell Park School, England, 1947

Communist officials from Poland came to the camps in Europe, especially in Germany and England, to convince people to return to Poland. My brother-in-law finished Polish University College and mentioned there were Communist 'plants' among the students.

We had re-established contact with our family in Poland by 1951 and, while it was difficult to identify precisely which letters were opened, we knew there was censorship. My cousin, who had been in the Home Army, told me during my visit to Poland in the 1960s that he was constantly asked about its activities. My family knew about the deportations to the Soviet Union.

I met my wife in Poland in the 1970s and she had difficulties with the FBI over getting permission to enter the USA because she had been a member of the Polish Scouts in post-War Poland; they viewed this as being a member of

---

210   Stanisław is standing on the left.

a Communist organization.[211] She explained that she had belonged so that she would have an opportunity to travel and that, being a student of physical fitness, this was a good organization to belong to. Eventually, they left her alone.

Kazimiera Miara Janota Bzowska
b. 1925, Tarnów
1942-46, Germany
1946-48, France
1948-present, England

**Figure 111. Kazimiera Miara Janota Bzowska,
Calveley Camp, England, 1948**

As for politics, there was the Government-in-Exile which lasted until 1990, when President Kaczorowski handed over the insignia of state to the new President, Lech Wałęsa. In all this time the Poles kept together, and they formed all these organizations. Some of the organizations are dying now, but many are still alive from their founding in 1948. We had Polish ministers; people who gave their lives to Poland. We had a lot of controversy here, as the exiled Polish politicians were in dispute with one another;[212] when there are two Poles,

---

211   Ironically, during the War, the Polish Scouts were viewed by the Germans as a subversive organization as the organization was closely involved with the Polish Home Army and Resistance. The Scouts played a very active role in the Warsaw Uprising.

212   The Council of Three (Polish: *Rada Trzech*) was created by the Polish Government-in-Exile in 1954 with prerogatives of the President of Poland. It consisted of three members of the Government chosen by the Council of National Unity, *(Rada Jedności Narodowej)*, the Parliament-in-Exile. It was created after President August Zaleski declined to leave his office after his 7-year term ended. It was dissolved in July 1972, following Zaleski's death, when the Council of Three recognized Zaleski's successor, Stanisław Ostrowski, who became the Third President of Poland-in-Exile.

you have three organizations. The Government-in-Exile was the keeper of Polish history and made sure that the world never forgot about the deportations to Siberia, about Katyń, and about conditions in Poland. It publicized this. Thanks to this Government, the world knew what was happening.

From the age of 14 to 20, I lived through a real nightmare. Perhaps, because of this, I became a different person in the sense that, for me, there are no surprises. I am very adaptable; if you give me dry bread, then it will taste good. I am grateful to see the sun each morning because there was a time in my life when I did not know if I would see the sun the next day. There are no cruel people, as I have seen worse. In my house there can be no shortage of food. I must always have extra of everything; I won't throw anything out because *"it may come in useful."* I learned this from times when nothing was available.

I had no school friends; I had no college friends, and I had no army friends because I was not in the army. The friendships I built in England were built after I got married but these are people you talk to about the present; you are not joined by memories of childhood, school, marriage, or the birth of your children. I was always on my own. I have a friend whom I met in a German labor camp; she lives in the USA and does not want to remember anything from the past; she is surprised that I remember so much. Yet this is what joins us, as this is when I met her. I want to have a hook to the past; she is this hook, my 'sister'. I was with her from the first day they put us into a cattle truck, slammed the door shut and took us to Germany. She is my 'sentimental' sister as I lived through the most difficult years of my life with her.

There are various groups in existence, such as the women who were in Stowell Park School, or in Tehran, or India, or Africa, or the men from the Cadet School in Palestine, or the Third Carpathian Artillery Brigade; they have a shared history and meet to this day. Someone who had my experiences of being alone as a 14-year-old child, being deported to a labor camp in Germany, moving from DP camp to DP camp in Germany, moving to France and living in an army camp while attending school and being alone in a Polish camp in England, was always alone and never part of a group.

Because we didn't know for a long time whether or not we were going back to Poland, we didn't try to settle. From the end of the War until 1950, at least, we lived out of our suitcases because we didn't know what would happen, or what we should do. We waited in the belief that we would eventually return to Poland.

Stefa Kowalczyk Bączkowska
b. 1924, Baby
1942-45, Germany
1945-46, Italy
1946-present, England

One day our history teacher came to see us with another man and asked if we wanted to continue to study and, if we did, he would ensure that we received scholarships. We were not, so he left. Some time later, an English official came to see us and asked if we had been approached by anyone offering us an opportunity to continue our studies. We said that our history teacher had approached us with another man, but that we had turned down his offer. We were informed that they had been trying to recruit us as agents so that we would carry information between the Communists in England and those in the Poland. They said that if we had such another visit to contact the British officials immediately.

The British were generally not well disposed towards us, though Anders worked hard to change this by pointing out the Polish military contribution to the Allied effort. Personally, I did not experience much animosity, but I know that others did. I went to Buckinghamshire Hospital and Nursing College in Aylesbury. I knew no English and had to learn quickly, but I knew anatomy very well, which helped a lot. The first year, we worked as orderlies on the wards so that we could improve our English. As I could not sleep during the day, it was very difficult for me to be on night duty, especially as I was generally weak; I only weighed 84 pounds at this time. I resigned from the nursing course and went to London where my friend, Danka, had a job as a seamstress; she said that there was work for me too.

I rented a room in Acton, West London. Those Poles who had arrived earlier were advertising for tenants in the Polish newspaper. We had one room with a heating stove. Polish organizations were already established in the area. I remember, when I met my husband, we used to go to Polish cafés and a Polish shop. I still pined after Poland and always wanted to return but, in 1950, I was told not to return. I was married in 1951 and widowed in 1964. My husband had gone through Russia so, as long as he was alive, there was no question of return.

After he died I thought again about returning with my young children. I got a British passport and went to Poland in 1966. When we crossed into Poland and I saw the haystacks I started crying and could not stop. My children could not understand why I was crying so much. In 2006, I was in Poland and went to a church to observe some children receive their First Holy Communion; it was where I had received my own. I started crying and could not stop. How can I explain this except that I was overcome by emotion and could not enter the church? Each time I stepped in, I started to cry again.

Jerzy Zubrzycki

b. 1920, Kraków

1940-41, Slovakia, Hungary, Yugoslavia, Italy, France

1941-55, England

1955-present, Australia

Figure 112. Jerzy Zubrzycki, Australia, 2008

Some money was set aside from the Polish resettlement funds to set up Polish University College as an external college of London University, preparing students for the University of London examinations. I applied for a job as a lecturer and worked as an assistant to Edmund Szczepanik[213] who, later, became Prime Minister of the exiled Polish Government in London.

We taught in English and the examinations were in English but the College was comprised entirely of Polish students. I didn't get much money to maintain my family (wife and two children), so I found a job on the night shift of the British Broadcasting Corporation at Bush House in London.[214] I was examined, tested, and worked at night reading the 3 AM and 4 AM news. This was a time when Polish broadcasts were jammed so that people could not listen, but the night was the best time to transmit a broadcast to Poland. I translated the news from English into Polish, slept a little in the basement of Bush House and, usually, went on to the library at the London School of Economics[215] (LSE) to work on my dissertation which was later published as a book, *Polish Immigrants in Britain: a Study of Adjustment.*[216]

---

213   Edward Franciszek Szczepanik, (1915-2005), was a Polish economist and the last Prime Minister of the Polish Government-in-Exile. He was an assistant professor at Polish University College in London from 1947-53.

214   Bush House, London, is the home of the BBC World Service Radio.

215   The London School of Economics is a specialist college of the University of London, England. Founded in 1895, it is an internationally renowned academic institution.

216   Zubrzycki, J. (1956). *Polish Immigrants in Britain: a study of adjustment. Studies in Social Life Vol. III.* The Hague: Martinus Nijhoff.

The English population was quite friendly, especially the English Catholics. There was a good network of Catholic organizations that helped people like me. There really was no time for politics; I had to study and write my thesis and work in radio to earn a living since my scholarship was very insignificant. But I learned a great deal about Polish organizations and associations by writing my thesis and, of course, I maintained these contacts. I was aware of the belief that some servicemen held about there being another world war. Scotland, especially, had a large Polish contingent who felt this way before they were sent off into civilian life. It didn't affect me personally. I wore my army uniform only during the first year of my university studies because I couldn't afford any other clothing.

During my early years at the LSE, I established a Polish Society which was very well received by the Director of the School. I was involved in many Polish circles, Catholic circles, and Polish scholars' circles in London. Being able to speak English made a great difference because I was able to go to university, get a book published and, finally, get a job in Australia.

After I was demobilized I maintained contact with my fellow British officers who were in the SOE. In 1949, after three or four years of teaching at University College,[217] I received a note from one of my fellow officers inviting me for an interview in the British Foreign Office; I was offered a job as the head of the Polish Desk in the Research Department of the British Foreign Office. At this time, I had applied for British citizenship which I was granted quite quickly and I worked for almost four years as a Desk Officer, then a Senior Researcher and, then, a Principal Researcher in charge of all of Eastern Europe. Eastern Europe was in my custody for research purposes during the Cold War, during a time of great tension. I couldn't publish very much unless it was anonymously; this was the nature of my work.

My long-term prospects, however, were bad because, not being born British, I could not advance in the British Foreign Service. I also wanted to be an academic. Luckily, in 1955, I received a note from one of my supervisors telling me of a position in Immigration Studies in the newly-founded University of Australia. I applied, was interviewed in London and, having already done some work on population studies, was offered the job in Canberra; the University is now the ranked 16th in the world.[218]

---

217   University College London, UCL, founded in 1826, is a member college of the University of London, ranked among the top ten universities in the world in 2008. http://i.cs.hku.hk/~tse/topten.html

218   Times Higher Education Rankings, the Australian National University was ranked 16th in the world in 2006 and 2007. http://www.timeshighereducation.co.uk/hybrid.asp?typeCode=144

The Polish Hostels (Camps)

"The rate at which the Poles have been absorbed into the community is illustrated by the following table showing the number of hostels and residents in them:

End December	Hostels/Housing Estates	Residents	End December	Hostels/Housing Estates	Residents
1948	37	16,429	1956	15	6,165
1949	27	13, 865	1959	9	2,980
1950	26	14,263	1962	5	1,103
1953	21	10,512	1964	2	728

It is clear that a hard core is now being reached; that many of the remaining residents will never be able to settle down in the community or absorb the British way of life. And it seems appropriate for the Board[219] to take stock of the situation and consider what their future policy should be." [220]

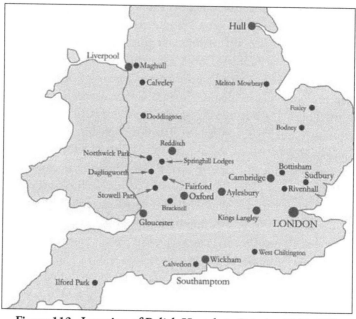

Figure 113. Location of Polish Hostels in Britain, 1945-70[221]

---

219   Board: The National Assistance Board, created by the National Assistance Act of 1948 to ensure those of insufficient means would not become destitute.

220   AST 18/88, *Issue of Monthly Statistics to members of the National Assistance Board showing employment position and number of residents in Polish hostels, 1950-1965.* National Archives, London, England. For a listing of over one thousand former POW camps, many of which became transitional or more permanent homes for Poles in England see: *www.islandfarm.fsnet.co.uk*

221   Hostels referenced in this work, as well as other places of residence.

Figure 114. Bolesław Wojciechowski's and Celina Kabala Wojciechowska's ID cards, 1946-49

Mieczysław Juny

b. 1913, Lwów
1939-45, Hungary, Yugoslavia, Greece, Lebanon,
Syria, Palestine, Egypt, Iraq, England,
South Africa, Sierra Leone, Scotland
1945-present, England

There were those who believed that there would be another war and that they would return to Poland with General Anders; we all had thought like this at one point. There was also the attitude of the English who feared that we would take their work and homes though, once they realized that this would not be the case, their attitude towards us changed. Companies would come to the camps to recruit workers or even set up factories and offices nearby. Those who got work at certain companies even got help with housing.

It is true that certain Poles got manual work, but this was a result of the problem with their speaking English. Eventually, they moved up to managerial positions but, initially, they had to do manual work. The National Assistance Board employed me as a Liaison Officer whose responsibility it was to help Poles adjust and find employment and, then, to close the camps. I lived in

Melton Mowbray, then Fairford Hostel and, until it closed in 1970, at Northwick Park Polish Families Camp.

The English wanted the Poles to settle within English communities and to assimilate, but housing was a problem. Also, the young English had returned from war and wanted to get married and have their own homes, so they had priority. After a while, the Poles began to leave the camps and become independent.

Figure 115. Mieczysław Juny *(on the left)*,
Fairford Polish Hostel, England, c1950

People decided for themselves whether or not to leave for another country. Nobody forced them to leave. Those who left usually had the assurance of jobs or family in the USA. Australia was very different because we had strong ties with the Australians during the War; the Carpathian Brigade replaced them in Tobruk, and they wanted us to come to Australia. But some Polish soldiers were given jobs in Tasmania, which caused some disappointment; this was not the heaven they thought they were going to, though life did improve later. Australia was better able than England to absorb large numbers of Poles. Poles also went to Brazil; I used to help people prepare their documents and get them ready for departure.

There were suicides, depression, and mental illness as a result of the ending of the War, and the English attitude of indifference to this did not help. People really did not know what to do with themselves. My job was to do what I could to remedy this situation and to help people accept that they would not be going back.

As for the Government-in-Exile, I had some contact, though more with the British Government as they were my employers. Also, those who lived in London had more contact with them. The Government-in-Exile established schools and was very active but this ended when the Poles realized that it would be wiser to send their children to English schools.

**Figure 116. Fairford Polish Hostel Primary
School, England, 1955**

Parents who sent their children to English schools found it was a great help to have their children fluent in English because they could help them as translators. In Fairford Hostel, the English school was too far away for the children to attend. The Polish schools organized in the camps were gradually shut down and children were moved to the local English schools. The Polish Government-in-Exile was responsible for schools in the camps for a few more years. Before a hostel was closed the children were all moved to local schools. I drove my daughter to the local English school even though a Polish school was available at Northwick Park Polish Families Camp.

Conditions in the camps were not the best. Initially, the biggest problems were housing and food. In 1951, people in Fairford Hostel started receiving ration books so they could feed themselves independently; the communal kitchens were closed. Housing in the barracks varied. Prior to 1948, some people had arrived through UNRRA. Some of these barracks were very large as they were previously army hospitals. The families who lived there had the worst situation as their rooms were divided only by blankets. Eventually, they were properly divided so that, by the time many hostels closed, the accommodation was fine; there was even central heating and some people did not want to leave.

Many people died. There were times when as many as five people died in a camp in one week. Those who died were usually invalids who had been injured during the War. Most of the people in the hostels in the early years were from the Army so the average age was between 30 and 35, though this had little impact on their mortality.

People found work in various ways but, usually, they looked for work near the hostel. They did not want to leave as they were afraid; the hostel was a place of safety and security. It was only when many resettled, and showed by example that it was safe, that others moved out.

When we knew that a hostel was due to be closed, we would encourage people to find work outside; those who could not find work were moved elsewhere, from Fairford Hostel to Daglingworth, from Daglingworth to Springhill Lodges, from Springhill Lodges to Northwick Park. I was never told to move people out in a certain amount of time; it was up to the firms. We went to the Unemployment Board to encourage firms to hire Poles; Poles were needed everywhere and they found work. At this time, the British also imported Italians to work in the mines; Poles took work which the English did not want. In Northwick Park there was a fish factory that employed 40 women. We never knew how long a hostel would last. We thought that Northwick Park would close sooner than it did, but it all depended on circumstances outside our control, like the availability of employment. It was particularly important for the children to move into an environment where they would spend the rest of their lives.

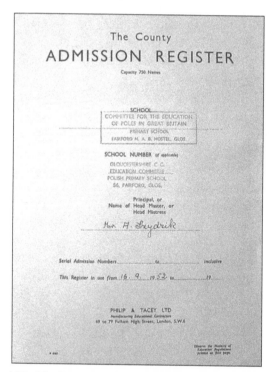

Figure 117. The Register of the Fairford Polish Hostel Primary School, England, 1952[222]

222   *Fairford Polish Hostel Primary School, The County Admission Register*, S141/1/1 Gloucestershire Archives, Gloucester, England.

I went from Fairford Hostel to Springhill Lodges in 1951; even then, there was talk of closing Fairford Hostel. The difference between these two was that Springhill had brick houses and not barracks, though cooking facilities were the same. Those who were in the few barracks were moved to houses. Northwick Park stayed open the longest; it was farthest away from sources of employment and required the least renovation to make it habitable. The children were in English schools in Chipping Camden, Moreton-in-the-Marsh and Blockley. What happened in the hostels was greatly influenced by what was happening outside.

We had no DPs in our camps; they were all Army people. We only had one DP, a Hungarian Gypsy who had escaped from Europe. Towards the end, hostel life was normalized though it was hoped people would not live out their lives there.

Celina Kabala Wojciechowska
b. 1924, Warszawa
1944-45, Germany, Austria
1945-46, Italy
1946-present, England

It was not known in England that the Polish Government-in-Exile was funding Polish schools for older students such as me. The Government had brought substantial resources with it when it left Poland in 1939. Those of us who were older were encouraged to leave school. Only the younger girls went to university; the rest went to work in hotels and as nurses. Had I not got married at this time, I would have returned to Poland.

In 1939, my husband had been studying law and diplomacy in Lwów hoping to become a trade attaché. In order to improve his French he spent the summer vacation of 1939 in France. When the War broke out he could not return home so he joined the Army in France. On the way to Scotland, he lived in various camps, and, eventually, fell ill in Scotland and spent 6 months in hospital during which time he studied English grammar. When his health improved, he wanted to return to the Army but was told, *"We have enough soldiers, but we'll need people like you to take leadership roles upon your return to Poland."* So, he went to Edinburgh University to study. After the War he held various positions but it was hard for a Pole to get work. My neighbor got work in a mine, but when the first group of Poles went down the mine all the English workers came up and went on strike.

Figure 118. Bolesław Wojciechowski, Chairman of the
Residents' Association, Fairford Polish Hostel, England, 1950

Figure 119. The Wojciechowski family
outside their barrack, Fairford Polish Hostel, England, 1952[223]

Figure 120. Bolesław Wojciechowski greeting
General Anders, Fairford Polish Hostel, England, 1952

---

223 Celina commented that the pipe on which she is sitting in the photograph was a hot water pipe, insulated with asbestos. She planted nasturtiums by the pipe and they grew to 6 feet in height: people would stop and wonder at their height and beauty.

Figure 121. Nissen huts, Northwick Park
Polish Families Camp, England

Figure 122. Springhill Lodges Hostel, England, visit from
General Anders, 1952

Figure 123. Bolesław Wojciechowski and Celina Kabala
Wojciechowska, Fairford Polish Hostel, England, 1949

My husband got a job as a translator, working on the sick bay in Fairford Polish Hostel. Out of the 1,500 Poles in Fairford Hostel, only three spoke English. Most of the residents were people who had escaped from Russia. I did not arrive in Fairford until 1949. The camp was initially managed by UNRAA and, then, by the British National Assistance Board. I think that the conditions for Poles in the camp were better than for those who lived in towns. At first, we had one room, then two, and then three. We had warm water and a communal kitchen. When we had the option of going 'on ration,' my husband wanted to stay with the communal kitchen but, when I saw how the food was served and how the server's sweat dripped into the potatoes, I said, *"We are going on rations."* Eventually, a shop opened in the hostel.

There was a pre-school and an elementary school in the hostel. I worked in the crèche and pre-school; we opened at 6:30 AM for all the children and, then, at 9 AM the older ones went to pre-school while the younger ones stayed with us. Most people worked in Swindon;[224] they left for work at 7 AM and returned at 7 PM. The elementary school was for children up to age 10. After that, they had to go the nearest English school. During the holidays, 150 older children would come to the hostel from Polish boarding schools such as Pitsford, a boarding school for girls.

The school in the hostel was taught by teachers from Poland, but these were not normal circumstances; the number of children was so small that they had to join classes of different ages. The textbooks were published in England and, also, in Palestine by the Polish Education Committee. I was always interested in Polish politics; if not for the Polish Government-in-Exile and the Poles in England, Poland would not have her freedom today as everything depended on the Poles in exile pressurizing western governments and supporting democratic movements in Poland. The fight for Poland's freedom was based in London and it is only now that people are beginning to acknowledge this.

General Anders was an icon; he gave spirit to us all. When the War ended, Churchill apparently told Anders, *"The war has ended; you can take your soldiers."*

People were encouraged to leave Fairford for the USA and Canada. I said to my husband that laborers were needed there and not intelligentsia, so what was he going to do there? There were many Ukrainians in Fairford because they had been in the Polish Army. Most of the Ukrainians moved to Reading. But we didn't differentiate between Ukrainians and Poles as we had all been together in the Army.

In 1959, we were told that the hostel was due to close. We always had work and the British were building new estates so people were moving out to live near their work. People moved from Fairford Hostel to other camps, or to

---

224   Distance from Fairford to Swindon is 10 miles.

Ilford Park where those who were too old or infirm to work were housed. My daughter's godfather went to Ilford Park, though we wanted him to move with us to town. He was worried about being a burden to us in his old age. He left the hostel before us, and said that he was glad, as he didn't have to watch us go. We always missed him.

In Swindon, the women worked in factories and the men in construction or in canal building. There were no vocational education classes in the hostel, only English classes. We started helping our families in Poland in 1949, but it was very hard as we also had nothing. My husband worked and I was at home with the children; for one of my friends' wedding, I went wearing a borrowed skirt. My family in Poland asked for nothing but my brother wrote to tell me that he had a pair of trousers made from my Army uniform.

Figure 124. The Crèche in Fairford Polish Hostel, England, 1949

Figure 125. The original Ilford Park Polish Home, Devon, England, 2006

Figure 126. The new Ilford Park Polish Home, Devon, England, 2006

My oldest daughter was born in the hostel; my second daughter, in Oxford. The hostel's maternity ward was closed in the early 1950s; it was substandard. The doctor there was only part-time so there were problems as he was sometimes absent when a woman gave birth. I remember that one woman was expecting; the baby was very large and she went into labor. Instead of taking her to the nearest hospital, they waited for the doctor to arrive by which time the baby had strangled itself with the umbilical cord. A few children died this way. My son died because my twins were born prematurely and he needed a respirator but there were none in the hostel.

When the Poles began to die, the local English Catholics were afraid that there would be no room left for them in the small Catholic cemetery on London Road. The elderly priest said that, if necessary, he would give up his own garden to accommodate the Poles; if the English did not agree, he said, he would go into a retirement home. So the burials of the Poles continued. The two Polish priests in the hostel were both survivors of Dachau concentration camp.

Young people left to go and study, so what could the rest do but leave? Raising children was good in the hostel. There was fresh air and there were places you could go for a walk; there was plenty of hot and cold water and nobody complained that a child was annoying them. The hostel was very safe. You would always find a few drunks, though; once, the English police knocked on the door looking for my husband. I thought I would faint but was told not to worry; some Poles had been in a fight and they were in need of a translator!

Now There Is A Plaque!

The bare field gives no sign,
no clue
of those whose lives were turned round
on this site.
Two waves of transient visitors
both groups here for healing,
before returning to the outside world.

Firstly, here
wounded American soldiers
were brought back to life, to health,
To fight again.
Or not-
whichever fate the skill
of the surgeon
and the fighting power of the body
could manage
and which politics dictated.
This hospital came and went.

More war-wounded
followed to fill the barracks:
families of Polish soldiers
war-allies, labelled 'aliens'-
this time with deeper,
invisible wounds.
This time,
this place healed
with the hope of normality,
restoring the civilian families
and former soldiers back to life,
enabling them to start a new, real life
after the nightmare journey of survival.
Till now,
no sign, no clue
remained here.
Not even a nail or splinter of glass.
The War was thus tidied away

out of pretty, honey-hued Fairford.
Till now, there was
no sign,
no clue
of the passing through
of the thin survivors
of the freezing death-chill
in the Siberian labour camps,
nor their skeletal hunger,
nor the wilting heat and disease
of African and Indian camps,
the seemingly never-ending camps
of their camp-freedom.
There was no tell-tale hint
of the brutality of their exile,
their near freezing to death
and the hell fire of war,
nor of their loss,
nor separation
from their own flesh and blood
from their farms,
their towns and villages
their soil
and homeland.

Hidden away
in barracks,
in the shadow of the village
they could laugh, eat, drink, dance,
be merry, meet life-long partners, marry,
have children, have hope
and a taster of normality.

The camp closed.
They left for the industry of Swindon,
And a bigger, alien world,
blending in, as seamlessly
as inconspicuously,
as they could.
The hospital

and its reincarnation
as the camp for displaced Poles,
closed for a second time:
it had now played its part
in healing the wounded.
Twice.

© **Alicja Świątek Christofides, 2009**[225]

Walter Orłowski

b. 1937, Pienacka
February 1940, deported to the Soviet Union
1942-47, Iran, Lebanon
1947-51, England
1951-present, USA

We were supposed to go to Africa, but my mother was too sick to travel so she was admitted into a hospital while we stayed in the orphanage. When she got better she took care of the children in the orphanage. My father was in the Army and we joined him in England in 1947. By this time, there were very few Poles left in Iran and Lebanon. My parents were in contact and my father was given a furlough to visit us in Lebanon, in 1946. My father continued to work for the British Army administration until we left for the USA in 1951. He was the only driver in Fairford Hostel with army rank.

I used to spend my summers in Fairford Hostel; during the school year I was in Bottisham. Fairford Hostel had two sections; the Nissen huts and another section that we called 'little Ukraine.' I remember, when the Americans came to hire Poles from the hostel, they looked so large to us. They were all MPs and had come to secure the camp.

Conditions in Fairford Hostel were not bad; the food was quite good, especially when you consider what we had had before, and there was enough for everyone. We had five grades in the elementary school and the teachers were

---

225   Alicja Świątek Christofides was born in Fairford in 1950 and lived there until 1955, at which time her family moved to Swindon. She worked with the Fairford History Society to place a commemorative plaque at the site of the hostel on May 30, 2009, the 50th anniversary of the closing of the camp in 1959.

all patriotically motivated to educate us. The British, in general, were very well disposed towards us but the Poles were somewhat hostile because the British Government (not the general public) was trying to force us to return to Poland. We never encountered any hostility by the public; they accepted us.

The threat of violence and abuse on the part of the Russians was always there, and the NKVD was, in effect, the government in Poland. The Russians were deporting Poles from Silesia as late as 1947. Many people do not realize this. The Polish Government in Poland essentially did what the NKVD told them to do. My father was offered a good position in France but he would not take it as he feared that the Russians would start a war in Europe. Some Poles had the illusion of there being a war to liberate Poland, but when the Poles found out the content of the Tehran and Yalta Conferences, they knew that their fate was sealed. The British put pressure on the Poles to accept its new eastern boundaries as early as 1943.

The Family Reunion

At two in the morning of February the tenth
The dream begins

It is misty, cold

From out of the impenetrable fog of the south
Floats a pale sad figure
Dressed in ethereal rags
Her face drawn, haggard
She is but forty years old
I come from my grave in Dubna, Tehran, she says
I am Janina, wife of Władysław
Mother of Jan, Zosia, and Danka
My body failed when starvation called
When the will to continue disappeared
In the exhausted lands, the endless rail tracks
Of the Russian lands.

From the west comes another ghost
A man, fifty, broken in heart
Eaten inside by the cancerous poison
A shroud wrapped around his hollow shoulders
His empty eyes look for four faces
I come from my grave in Haczow, Galicia, he says
Where they buried me at my family plot
After I passed away at the hospital in Zakopane
Waiting, always waiting for news of my stolen wife and children
Hiding, resisting, hiding, from the Red Army and the Nazis too
I am Władysław, husband of Janina
Father of my three long lost children, my jewels.

From the far west, from distant Scotland and England
Three aged figures emerge, hand in hand,
Two women and a man
Dressed in modern clothes, immaculate yet modest in style
They have shadows from the moon behind them
Which show teenage children's shapes

I am Jan. I am Zosia. I am Danka, say the three
And we are the children who never grew up
The old ones who lived the lost years
We are the three who blocked out our search
For Władysław our father, for Janina our mother
For to search was to know, and to know was to break down

And as the five spirits moved closer together
Janina's heartache lifted, her body regained its former shape
Władysław blossomed, the cancer gone, his face handsome
And Jan, Zosia and Danka threw off seven decades
To become once again, the teenage children of their shadows.
As the fog lightened, the mist rose
And they were home again
In the sunlight of the Kresy
And as the cows mooed and the pig grunted in the byre
They laughed at the world, and hugged each other once more
How they laughed until the end of time.

**Figure 127. Zosia and Danka Stepek,
Martin Stepek's aunts, Pahlevi, Iran, 1942**

CHAPTER 12

The Americas

Contextual Timeline

- 1939-45   15,000 Polish quota immigrants allowed in the USA; majority were professional middle class.

- 1945-48   17,000 came, 5-10% professional middle class, 70% farmers, the rest were young skilled and unskilled workers, average age 24-35, fairly well-educated, 92% Roman Catholic.

- 1948-52   Close to 140,000 Polish-born DPs and Polish veterans from Britain arrived in the USA.

- 1940-53   178,680 quota Polish-born immigrants arrived in the USA.

Because of Displaced Person Commission classification, these statistics include Ukrainians and Polish Jews as well as ethnic Poles. It is estimated that 40,000 were Polish Jews. They joined roughly 6 million Polish Americans, first generation and their offspring born in the USA. (1940 USA Census)[226]

Aniela Bechta-Crook
b. 1936, Borszczów
February 1940, deported to the Soviet Union
1942-49, Africa
1949-51, England
1951-61, Argentina
1961-68, USA
1968-present, New Zealand

In 1949 we were allowed to join my uncles who were now demobilized in England; we were assigned to Husbands Bosworth Polish Resettlement Camp in Leicestershire and housed in disused Nissen huts. My brother, Emil, and I

---

226   Jaroszyńska-Kirchmann, A. op. cit. p. 9.

began our formal education at boarding schools built especially for the children of Polish refugees. We did well; we loved the extensive variety of subjects and the company of other Polish youths. But, within two years, Mother announced that we were moving to Argentina to live with her brother who had settled there after the War.

My uncle and his Italian wife lived in a small house he'd built on the outskirts of Buenos Aires. When we got there, it felt like we had gone back in time. Argentina was ruled by Peron and his wife, Evita. After her death there was great political and economic instability. In a country with no social welfare or safety net, we had to find work to survive. Emil and I worked in factories while Mother was hired as a seamstress in a fashionable shop. Again, she helped her sister by sending coal and warm clothes through the Polish Assistance Bureau.

Within two years we had saved enough to buy a small plot of land, and built our own corrugated iron 'house'; Mother stopped working. I think she moved us to there because she longed to replicate her village life; having a garden with chickens, and geese for eiderdowns. It didn't worry her that we had no electricity or running water, or that the roof was leaking, or that the streets were muddy. She baked her own bread, made her own cheese and sewed our clothes. This was the life she had always known. We encountered some resentment for *"coming here to eat us out of our meat,"* but these were isolated incidents; Buenos Aires was very much a melting pot and we were just a few 'cabbage' leaves trying to keep afloat in it.

Like most immigrants, we immediately gravitated towards Polish groups. The Polish Club in our village of Llavallol had been established by pre-War economic migrants whose children were more Argentine than Polish, so we didn't have much in common. Eventually, the post-War ex-servicemen established a separate club in the city of Buenos Aires where 'newly-arrived' youths congregated. It was a happy atmosphere where friendships and romantic attachments blossomed. Some married, some moved to the USA or returned to Poland; others intermarried and remained in Argentina.

I was determined to leave factory work behind, so I improved my English at night school and trained as a stenographer. In time, I came to love Buenos Aires. I immersed myself in Latin culture and even dated a tango-loving Argentine; once again, I had to leave it all behind as, after a very long wait, my name finally came up for immigration to the USA. My aunt, in Boston, offered to sponsor me but indicated this was to be my last chance. At the age of 26, I said goodbye to my mother and brother, and went to a good job.

Although I found work immediately as a bilingual secretary in Boston, my dear aunt turned out to be so protective that I soon moved on to New

York. I lived in a women's hostel on 34th Street and worked in Times Square, experiencing freedom unknown to me until then. Within a year, I was able to sponsor my mother and brother to come to America, and rented an apartment in Brooklyn's Polish district. However, inner restlessness urged me to move again; this time, it was to beautiful San Francisco, where I trained as an insurance underwriter. Now aged 32, I thought I was destined to remain single when a visit to an English pub changed all that. In a quiet dart-room I found love; George was English but was long-settled in New Zealand and was visiting San Francisco as a researcher. After a day of walks and talks, and a few months corresponding, I traveled to New Zealand where we soon married and, once again, I was an immigrant. With the love of a caring man and the belief that I could survive anywhere, we set about making a new life for ourselves.

Meanwhile, Emil married and moved to San Francisco; our mother remained in New York among her Polish friends. She loved New Zealand but her roots were too deeply imbedded in the Polish culture and in the Catholic faith. She rests in peace in Our Lady of Częstochowa Cemetery in Doylestown, Pennsylvania.

After both my sons were born, I discovered a talent for teaching pre-school and, eventually, got to run my own kindergarten. The 20 years of nurturing the minds and bodies of those little children were the happiest years of my life. Maybe it had something to do with my own lost early childhood and being left in charge of my baby brother when Mother was out searching for food. To this day, I cannot bear to hear a child cry.

I returned to Poland after a 64-year absence; my birth place is now in the Ukraine and I was advised that, as a tourist, I should avoid it. I opted for a package tour that included Warszawa, Kraków and Zakopane. Our tour guide spoke quite angrily of the 'foreign capitalists' who were now leaving their own mark on Warszawa, the beautiful city that had been rebuilt with great sacrifice and determination after the War. Castles and places like Częstochowa were inundated with tourists and felt somewhat oppressive. Oświęcim, however, was eerily serene and brought home the enormity and magnitude of the suffering of millions. It wasn't until we drove to Zakopane and I saw cherry trees, cows, goats, geese and chickens roaming freely that I got a sense of my childhood, especially when the guide put on a CD of old Polish songs and we all joined in.

In 2008, I visited Uzbekistan, Turkmenistan, and Iran, and retraced our journey to freedom. Although I learned nothing about my father's fate, I found the people of Uzbekistan extremely friendly and helpful. With the help of the Polish Consulate in Tehran, I found my brother's grave on which I placed some red and white flowers and prayed for his tiny soul and those of others whose lives were cut short.

Figure 128. Aniela Bechta-Crook, Tehran Polish Cemetery, Iran, where her brother is buried, 2008[227]

Wojsław Milan Kamski

b. 1923, Lwów

1939-45, Romania, Iraq, Iran, Palestine, Italy

1945-51, England

1951-present, USA

Personally, I did not experience animosity towards Poles in the early 1950s. I got a job relatively easily because there was new technology (I was writing my dissertation on this subject) but, within a year, I discovered that others who were, basically, doing the same work were earning 30-40% more than I was. I decided I wasn't going to put up with that and I started looking for another position which I found easily. It was when I started working in a larger, more prominent American firm that I noticed a negative attitude towards Poles; the so-called 'Polish jokes' that depicted Poles as being stupid, uneducated, and dirty. I'll be honest with you; I think it was a deliberate attempt to stir up the Poles in order to obtain information about the Soviets, the Communists, and conditions in Soviet Russia.

---

227   The inscription reads *"In memory of Polish deportees, who, on their way to their homeland, rested in God for eternity, 1942-1944."*

Zdzisława Bilewicz Korniłowicz
b. 1926, Dolinów
February 1940, deported to the Soviet Union
1943-47, Iran, Palestine
1947-53, England
1953-present, USA

The 'older' Polonia in the United States did try to help the new arrivals, but they were expecting us to be poor people like they were upon their arrival to the USA. Instead, we were educated and landed on our feet quickly. They resented that we did not start with the worst of jobs as they had to.

There was miscommunication between the two groups for which we must take some blame as we considered the older Polonia to be uneducated. They were working-class people but the new arrivals failed to understand and recognize just what these earlier arrivals had achieved. They had arrived in the USA, often not knowing how to read and write but had managed to maintain their religion and establish Polish schools. They were very patriotic and faithful to Poland for several generations. I know that the 'new' Polonia presented itself as being more educated so there were many problems and miscommunications.

Figure 129. Zdzisława Bilewicz Korniłowicz
(third from the left) **and friends, USA, 2007**

I think we are to blame for a lot of this because we did not respect and understand what they had accomplished. They had wanted to help us, and we treated them as uneducated and ignorant. Eventually, all attempts at cooperation failed and the two groups set up their own separate organizations.

Witold Mazur

b. 1936, Kołodno
February 1940, deported to the Soviet Union
1942-48, Iran, Iraq, India, Africa
1948-58, England
1958-present, Canada

The older Polonia, the pre-World War II arrivals, was very resentful of the new arrivals; there was an ongoing verbal battle between the two of them all the time, even to this day. Personally, I think that when you have something and you lose it, not only did we lose our farms and our way of life, we also lost the land to which we were attached, and that left a permanent scar. We do not belong anywhere, and if you do not belong anywhere, you have no basis to make any plans. We were damaged goods. Going to Poland, to Warszawa or Kraków, is like going to Hawaii; there is no connection other than the language.

Anonymous (1)[228]

b. 1930, Wołyń
1940, deported to the Soviet Union
1941-45, Iran, India, Australia, New Zealand, USA, Mexico
1945-present, USA

I will tell you about the good side of the US Polonia. The older ladies from the Polish charities had a heart and they worked hard to help us settle down and find work. As for the American population as a whole (and forgive me for saying this), they didn't know history and geography. These were people who liked to laugh at you and who felt that they had to tell you Polish jokes. I said to them, *"Oh, more Polish insults?"* That stopped them.

Today, we have a wave of Jews recording their wartime experiences and it's difficult for us to say that we also had the same experiences. If you say anything they immediately ask, *"Are you a Jew?"* But I don't want to be placed in the category of victims. I am a survivor. What this taught me has rubbed off on my children; they got an education, and they are very well placed. In my mind, my work is completed.

---

228   Name withheld at interviewee's request.

Tadeusz Mączka

b. 1927, Tarnów
February 1940, deported to the Soviet Union
1942-46, Iran, Iraq, Palestine
1946-53, England
1953-present, Canada

Going to Canada from England was like going to heaven. In 1953, there was still rationing in England and there was hardly any food you could buy. I was really lucky as my landlady's son was a butcher and her daughter had a grocery store, so there was no problem with obtaining food. Still, English cooking... you know, going through Russia and the hunger, you'll eat anything now. I still don't like to waste food.

Figure 130. Tadeusz Mączka, Canada, 2006

Anita Paschwa-Kozicka

b. 1929, Rokitno
April 1940, deported to the Soviet Union
1942-46, Iran, India, Mexico
1946-present, USA

"I'm not going to be a Polish maid!" I went to bed every night in tears, repeating this to myself. *"I'll show you that I am an educated Polish person and not a Polish maid!"* They called us *"Polish maids"* as the orphanage had long been giving us away into service.

I criticize the older Polonia very much. When we arrived at the orphanage, the old ladies of the old Polonia, who were all working class, came to see us, to see what these Polish orphans looked like. I was of high school age. The whole class was standing in a circle and one of these women took a nickel and threw it in the center; she wanted to see which one of us would pick it up. When none of us picked it up, she said, *"Oh, so you're not hungry, you children from Poland, from Siberia. You don't want to pick up the money."* One of the girls said, *"This is not money, so why don't you take it and put it back into your pocket."*

**Figure 131. Anita Paschwa-Kozicka graduating
with her Master's Degree, USA, 1959**

"I want to leave you, dear reader, with the following thought:

I hope that reading my book has left you with a positive feeling about us Poles.

After so many years of suffering and longing for our Homeland, we still carry love for Poland in our hearts. I am hopeful that the pain brought on by reliving my past will serve everyone in a positive way, by showing how we should love and treasure the country in which we live....

I am hopeful that there will be more respect, love, and appreciation for your moms and dads, who are always there to help and give you all that is within their means and possibilities.

I have written this book with love and respect for my parents, teachers, for Poland, and for my adopted country, the United States."

Stella Synowiec-Tobis[229]

---

229 Synowiec-Tobis, S., op. cit., p.237

CHAPTER 13

Children of the Diaspora

This is a chapter that, when I started working on this book, I did not plan to write. However, the Internet is a great facilitator and I have met children of the émigrés who were writing poetry to acknowledge, preserve and publicize their parents' ordeals, such as John Guzłowski, Martin Stepek, and Hania Kaczanowska, or who have established websites, such as Zosia Hartman Biegus and Elżunia Gradosielska Olsson. And, there are those who asked me to interview their parents so that they could learn things that their parents found too painful to share with their children. Maybe there is a sequel to this book but, in the meantime, here is a chapter on the 'Children of the Diaspora.'

Figure 132. Children of Polish Christian Holocaust Survivors, USA, 2008[230]

---

230   Bożenna Urbanowicz Gilbride is second from the left.

In Praise of My Mother and Father

Belatedly I think of
You who
Brought me into this paradise of
Life and beauty and
Raised me from squealing bairn to
Precocious wean with great
Sacrifice and unending love even when your
Energies were completely emptied.

My mother who gave without seeking
Return and who worried
Needlessly about her ten strange
Offspring whose wild natures threw all
Hopes and predictions into the
Air and whose
Bizarre paths led everywhere but the path that she
Wanted but she took it all and
Never complained
But continued to pour out love
Like a vast donor of life.

My father whose energies
Overflowed, whether from nature or from
Survival of starvation, ethnic cleansing, and
Siberian winters of torture,
Near-fatal diseases and war zones
And yet emerged from it all with this matchless grit and
Won every battle against life's delusional obstacles
Fought and pushed and created and pulled us up
Roughly by the scruff of the neck and
Said life is hard and you must face it squarely and
Make of it all you can, and eventually I understood and
Try to love life with a similar passion.

To you both I bow my head in
Gratitude and love, for
In parenthood myself I understand a
Little of the burdens we were and

329

329

The love that you both offered.
Now when the end is on our minds, whether
Today or in twenty years time
It is timely to express homage.
And when life's energies start slipping away
Do not over-fight it and be fearful, nor
Fade into a shadow but
Measure your strengths and use them wisely to
Make peace with all beings and
With the huge content of your life,
And remember that you gave more than
Most, and that you gave your all to us, your
Children, who now, belatedly, express gratitude.

© **Martin Stepek, 2004**

Jurek Biegus

b. 1941, in the Soviet Union
April, 1940, his family was deported to the Soviet Union
1942-48, Iran, India, Africa
1948-present, England

My parents were from Tarnopol. My mother was deported in April 1940, while pregnant with me. My father had already been arrested and, later on, I found out that he had been murdered in Katyń. I don't know how I survived, given the infant mortality among deportees.

We sailed by ship from Mombasa, Kenya, to England. The ship was chartered by the IRO so all the passengers were refugees, like us; there were about 1,000 people. Initially, we lived in a transit camp outside Hull, then at Springhill Lodges, then Foxley and, finally, at Northwick Park. I was interviewed to go to a local English school but as my English was not good enough, I spent the first term in the Polish camp school. My mother recognized very early that there was no future in my going to a Polish school so she arranged for me to go to live with my aunt in Foxley Polish Camp and attend an English school in the town of Hereford. I failed the 11+ exam[231] so the choice was secondary

---

231   An examination taken at the age of 11 which determined whether or not a child would enter a grammar school, technical school, or secondary modern school; widely used in England, 1944-76.

school in either Hereford or in Springfield, so I went back to a school near Springfield Lodges for two terms. Eventually, the school decided that I should be at a grammar school and I transferred.

Figure 133. Christening of Jan Biegus, son of Jurek Biegus
(*back row, fifth from the left*), **and Zosia Hartman Biegus**
(*behind girl*), **Northwick Park Polish Families Camp, England, 1965**

After Springfield closed in 1956, we moved to Northwick Park. My mother lived in the camp even though she worked outside, because it was a comfortable place to live. She worked in a factory and had two children and my grandfather to maintain, and couldn't afford to buy a house; leaving the camp at that age would have been quite a wrench for her. The living conditions in the two camps were comparable. In Northwick Park we had half a 'barrel' at first and, then, got two rooms.

I didn't mind all the moving. As a child I thought it was quite wonderful. I certainly didn't see myself as disadvantaged in any way. I had a few toys and I remember receiving fruit at Christmas. My friends were almost exclusively Polish. We would come home from school to the camp and a Polish environment. The English children were quite keen to hear about my experiences in Africa, for example, and that made me feel that I had a contribution to make. We were very conscious of where we were and why. Whenever we got together with my aunt, we always talked about local and international politics. All my mother's friends were Polish. I left Northwick Park after my 'A' levels but my mother stayed for another 18 months, at which point she moved with a friend to a council flat232 in Redditch. The camp was being closed down so people were encouraged to move out.

My mother had been searching for news of my father since the end of the War; she had even written to Stalin and received no response. The first indication we had

---

232   council flat: public housing apartment.

that my father was dead was in 1949 when the Polish Army in Scotland sent us a list of Polish Officers missing from Starowiec which we found out, much later on, was one of the camps included in the Katyń massacre. I remember that my mother was always waiting for her husband to return, but I think that, after this letter, she must have known that there was very little chance of his being alive. My mother would always tell me that my father was alive and that he would come back. Perhaps it was a defense mechanism. She never sought to assimilate and spent her entire life in a Polish environment; in a way, she was always expecting to go back to Poland. There would be a war in two years, then three years, and then four years and, for a long time, she believed this. As a teenager I remember those types of conversations and how General Anders would lead them back to a free Poland.

There was a dichotomy between my mother and me; I was getting educated and saw things in practical terms, including my having a career in England but, on the other hand, I had a very powerfully nationalistic upbringing. I thought of Poland as a very special place to which we would eventually return. Recently my wife, Zosia, and I bought land in Poland that we think we might build on; deep down, we know that we probably won't. We live happily in England; we recognize that this is where we live, but we also have a plot of land in Poland. We go back every year to see our friends and family. It's a strange attitude.

My experiences broadened my perception of world affairs; I look at things differently. I tend not to believe governments and politicians. After all, our parents' generation was lied to and betrayed by various politicians. I am a little more cynical, perhaps. I think our children are the ones who have to find their roots. We had roots, back in Poland; we never felt we had come from 'nowhere'. When we arrived in England we had one tea chest of books, as my mother was responsible for closing down the school in Africa, and one chest of bedding and coats for the four of us. I am conscious that, until we went to England, I didn't know any children of my own age; they were either two years older or two years younger so, until we got to England, I didn't have any real friends.

Our two older children have been with us to Poland. The younger, born in 1972, is more Polish than we are. He reads a lot of Polish history and has a website for English fans of Polish soccer teams. He goes to Poland regularly for Polish football matches. He is always talking about setting up a business in Poland. If asked, they would say that they are English of Polish extraction. Their relatives in Poland see them as Polish.

I didn't ever feel that I was the victim of discrimination though, when I went to join the Royal Air Force, I was told that they appreciated everything that the Poles had done for them, but, as I was not born in England, I was not eligible to become an officer, only a private. I was, however, free to join the Army or Navy and seek promotion there.

**Figure 134. Corpus Christi Procession,
Melton Mowbray Hostel, England, c1950**

Krysia Bargiel
b. 1949, England
1959-present, USA

I was seven years old; we were in class, in a local Melton Mowbray school, when the teacher told all the Polish children to stand up. She then said, *"Go back to Poland; we don't want you here,"* and then let us sit down. The refugee experience formed who I am.

Halina Czerniejewska
b. 1950, Germany
1939, her father was a POW in Germany
1941-45, her father was a slave laborer in Germany
1942-45, her mother was a slave laborer in Germany
1945-52, her parents worked for UNRRA in Germany
1952-present, USA

My father was born near Poznań in western Poland and raised Catholic. As a young student he, as many others, was given a weapon to fight the Germans in the 1939 invasion. He was shot, sent home to recover and, later, sent to Dachau where all his fellow students died; he was on a detail that dumped their bodies into mass graves. He was released after more than a year and put into several labor camps from which he escaped. My mother, born in eastern Poland, was raised Russian Orthodox. She was born in an area that had changed rule many times. It is now in Belarus. In 1943, at age 16, she was taken to Germany by the Nazis to do farm work until the War ended. She met my father in Stokach DP camp, Germany; from 1945-52, my parents were both UNRRA employees who worked with displaced children. We emigrated to the United States when I was nearly two and my brother was three. We sailed on the ship, *General Langfitt*, arrived at Ellis Island and were settled in Toledo, Ohio.

Having the experiences of being a DP has given me more ambition. Maybe I would have had ambition either way, but I felt I had to prove something, even when I was little and was criticized for being... well, I was in grade school... those were the times of the 'Dumb Polack' jokes, and everybody thought it was quite funny to tell me them. It also made me more of a person with a world view, because I was exposed to news about places that other people never thought about. I was being told what was going on in Poland, I knew where Poland was, and I knew the history. My father had a lot of Polish pride and I was raised to be proud of Polish culture and customs.

Tata, And His Underwear!

Tata came from Poland, and was a handsome sort of man
He brought with him his culture to this new promised land.
He was always groomed and polished, with every hair in place
And when he walked, he moved with a special kind of grace.
A day's work left him smelling of railway diesel and tobacco smoke.
And our kisses on his cheek were met with a scratchy, stubble growth.
But when the day was over and he sat to read the news
His clothes were neatly pressed and he put on polished shoes.
He inhaled his cigarette smoke through a holder with grand finesse
And tipped back his glass of vodka, to relieve the day's stress.
He would never step out in public unless he took the time to dress
And always added a splash of cologne, if we were having guests.

When Tata died, we dressed him with tender, loving care.
But somehow we forgot to put on his underwear.
No one would know and that would be our secret to the grave
After all, Tata was a modest man and always very brave.
After his funeral, I awoke from a dream and saw my Tata standing there
He sadly asked, *"Verochka, where did you put my underwear?"*
Now you may think this is a joke, but I tell you this is true
And every time I dreamt of him, I asked what I could do.
When Mama got sick, just before she died, she asked to speak to me
And shared with me a special plan that was sure to set me free.
Before they closed her casket, I placed my gift inside her hands with care
In soft, powder blue tissue was a note tucked inside my Tata's underwear.
"Please Tat' forgive my oversight, I tried to do my best,
But today I can know that, finally, you are fully dressed."
A few days later I was watching sunlight pass through budding trees
As something brushed against my face with a softening breeze.
I looked up to see a powder blue tissue gently dancing in the air
As if to say, *"Verochka, I got your package, and everything was there!"*
I tried to catch the floating tissue as I knew this had to be a sign
But it willowed back into the clouds embraced by the warm sunshine.
I knew Tat' would be at heavens gate to greet Mama as she arrived
And now this was a blessing wrapped up in a giggling disguise.
I could go to sleep now and dream of my Tata's happy face
For now the looks of sadness were forever to be erased.

I share with you my wonderful memory and all that is true
Whether you believe me or not is entirely up to you!
And when the time comes that you lay your Tat' to rest
Make absolutely sure that you do your very best.
If by chance he's Polish and leaves this earth without his underwear
This will, without any doubt, be your personal cross to bear.
And for all of you who still have a Tat', kiss him on his stubbled cheek and
say:
"Today, I'm wishing you the Best and Happiest Father's Day."

© **Hania Kaczanowska, 2005**

Zosia Hartman Biegus

b. 1943, Germany
1940-45, both her parents were slave laborers in Germany
1945-48, they lived in Germany
1948-present, England

I think it is important for us to publicize our parents' history for their sake, so that it is not forgotten, because they went through a lot. We keep in touch with many Northwick Park people. My father was from Warszawa and my mother was from Pomorze. The whole family was taken out; my oldest brother was taken into the German Army from which he escaped. The rest were taken to Germany as slave laborers. My brother escaped from the German Army, to Yugoslavia, from where he went to join the Polish Army in Scotland. We lived in Germany, wherever the family was forced to work during the War. After the War we were in some camps in the English Zone, I believe. I was born in a little village in central Germany. Because my mother was born in western Poland, I believe the Germans kept the family together in order to Germanize us.

I remember my father talking about the 'third front', in other words, the 'third world war', but it didn't mean too much to me. When the War finished, UNRAA gathered all the displaced Poles and we were sent to some German town; General Maczek had his headquarters there so it was nicknamed 'Maczków.' My brother was already in England with the Army so he was able to bring us over with the first transport of civilians from Germany who then joined the Army personnel.

Figure 135. Zosia Hartman Biegus handing flowers to General Anders, Northwick Park Polish Families Camp, England, 1952

I remember that we helped the family in Poland, and we used to take parcels one-and-a-half miles across the fields to the post office in a pushchair or pram that my mother borrowed from other people. These parcels were not wrapped in paper; they were sewn in material. My father was sent to dig roads, which wasn't his line of work at all; he had been a teacher in Poland. He ended up teaching for the Royal Engineers. My mother, like everybody else, worked in a factory though, at first, she cooked meals in the camp's communal kitchen. Then, she became the caretaker of the local Polish school and, when they closed down the camp, she went back to the factory. She left the camp in 1968.

There was constant pressure in the 1960s for people to leave the camps. It was hard on my parents because of their language difficulties; they arrived in England in their forties and it was hard to learn English at that age. They were given a council house in Evesham. My father became a freelance journalist for the Polish newspaper. He used to travel to all the Polish camps and other Polish places and he wrote many articles. When the camps closed down he would go to the places to where the Poles had moved. The British didn't see the Poles as 'their problem' and did not think that they had an obligation to help. You could not get a council house unless you were a naturalized citizen and many of them were not; also, they could not afford to buy their own homes.

I never felt hostility or discrimination; it must have been there in the background because it is all documented. We were not allowed to speak Polish in the English school nor on the bus going back to the camp; it was forbidden and punishable. I was very much part of a clique in the camp; all my friends were Polish. I was five when we went to England, so I went to infant school not knowing a word of English; I spoke German. I cannot tell you how I learned English. There were new people arriving all the time and when I heard that there were people arriving from Africa, I imagined they would be black with curly hair!

Figure 136. Zosia's former home in Northwick Park Polish Families Camp, England, 2006

We had no water in our Nissen hut in Northwick Park. When you went on rations, unlike eating in the communal kitchen, you got a metal range in your hut to cook on. Even though my mother worked in the kitchen, we went on rations quite early. I remember sneaking into the kitchen with friends of mine who still ate in the communal kitchen. Life was hard, but people felt secure; being in the camp was a bit of stability. A number of families resisted leaving until the very last minute and were sent eviction notices. There is a big difference between what is in the documents in the Archives[233] and our view of the situation; we did not see ourselves as a 'problem,' whereas the British did. Some officials lost track of the reason as to why we were in England in the first place. Many English women who had married Polish men came to the Polish community for their social life and felt part of the Polish community. Some of these Polish husbands did not integrate into the English community. I never felt insecure in the camp; I didn't leave until I got married to Jurek Biegus.

Mamusia And The Red Scarf

I peeked into the dim-lit room and saw my *Babcia* kneeling in prayer.
The fireplace was crackling away and she had no idea I was there.
In candlelight she held a faded picture and a red scarf I had seen before
But they were always neatly tucked away into a special drawer.

I should have let her pray in silence but curiosity tweeked at me
What was the secret of the red scarf that no one else should see?
With the scarf she crossed herself as I had seen her do for years
And before I heard her fragile voice she wiped away her tears.

"Kochana Mamusiu, today is your birthday and it is a special day
For I am the same age now, as when you were taken away.
I pray for peaceful moments so your soul can heal with love
As you're surrounded by heavenly angels who take care of you above.

When I think of you, I am a young girl again, no sadness and no pain
People don't understand today and it is difficult to explain.
I still remember our happy lives, joy and laughter and then it ended.
And I still keep asking myself "Is this really what God intended?"

---

233   The National Archives, England.

First the war, then we lost Papa and then the train to a land of hell
I have tried to forget the grief we shared but still remember it well.
I remember days of cold and hunger and how you shared your bread
And every Polish prayer you whispered as you tucked me into bed.

No matter how tough the days became and we were filled with fright
You'd always smile and hug me and say "Everything will be alright."
I remember when you became ill and there was nothing I could do
We left you in the Uzbek *kolkhoz* and our neighbors took care of you.

One day the soldiers came and you told me I must leave with them.
You handed me 5 *rubles* and told me to hide them in my hem.
You tied the red scarf around my neck that Papa had given you
And told me it would keep me safe all the days through.

You blessed it with a mother's love and all you had to give
You pushed me into freedom's door so I would have a chance to live
Your vision engrained in my heart forever as we said goodbye
You promised we would see each other again and told me not to cry.

The trains were full and soldiers were doing their boarding checks
As one cried out "You child with the red scarf, you will be next."
They told me that you died and were buried the next day.
That wretched Uzbek soil holds no marker and no grave today.

Your spirit always lived within me and guided me thru the years,
And when I wore your red scarf I saw your reflection in the mirrors.
Somehow the scarf gave me comfort and is now ragged and torn
But that's from uplifting me in weakness all the times it was worn.

Even tho' its fibres are weak its memory is more precious than gold
For it represents a legacy to give to the young in remembering the old.

© **Hania Kaczanowska, 2006**

John Guzłowski
b. 1948, Germany
1940-45, his father was a slave laborer in Germany
1942-45, his mother was a slave laborer in Germany
1945-51, they lived in Germany
1951-present, USA

My father was living on a small farm west of Poznań when he was taken during a round-up in his village in 1940. He spent the next five years working in different areas and at different jobs. Towards the end of the War he was assigned to look for bodies in the rubble. My mother came from near Lwów; her father was a forest ranger so they lived in the woods. Her father died before the War and she was taken to Germany in 1942. The rest of her immediate family was killed in their home area.

Like my father, she was taken to Magdeburg where there was a central clearing facility for slave laborers. She, too, was sent to work where labor was needed though, in her case, her work was agricultural.

My parents met in a DP camp after the War. My father and uncle went looking for other members of the family in Germany. My mother and sister stayed behind. They found one of my aunts. My parents lived in DP camps and they mentioned that they were constantly moved from camp to camp. The sense I got from my mother is that it was a tremendously chaotic situation, and that there were hundreds of thousands of people there who didn't want to be there. My father was very skeptical about going back to Poland under the Communists; they tried to return once but were turned back at the border by armed Russian soldiers. He said that he was in a group and the Russians shot at them so they ran back into Germany. They had some options as to where to resettle, like Australia, Argentina or United States; it was quicker to get permission to move to the first two as there were fewer slots at the time for people going to the US. My mother didn't want to go to Australia or Argentina as she thought they were very hot countries. Her father had gone to the USA in 1910 and was hoping his family would join him but my grandmother refused. My parents talked about how conditions were hard at the very beginning when DP camps were first opened, and how there were still bodies lying around on the ground; when there was very little to eat, and when the water was bad. There didn't seem to be any organization to take care of these camps. They said little about the period after that.

I was three and my sister was five when we traveled to the USA. My earliest memories are that my mother made me a playsuit from silk from an American parachute that she had. I also remember a convoy of army trucks going back. I have vague memories of leaving Germany, of standing in long lines waiting to being inoculated.

We lived outside Buffalo, NY; my parents had been sponsored by a farmer. After they fulfilled their obligations to him they moved to Chicago and settled in a Polish area. My sister and I attended a school with a lot of Poles in it. The classes were partially in Polish and partially in English. I did not feel uncomfortable there at all but it was a different story outside the school as there was a lot of resentment against DPs from just about everybody. There was a lot of animosity. I remember a kid who called us *"DPs"* and began to hit us. We felt so embarrassed that we could not call out for our mother in Polish; we called to her in English but she did not understand so we were beaten up.

I remember telling kids that 'DP' did not stand for 'Dirty Polak'. I remember that when we first moved to Chicago my parents had a hard time finding an apartment because a lot of people would not rent to DPs. My parents socialized in a purely Polish community. It was like living in Poland. Most of the people on the street were Polish-American and the others were recent immigrants. In church, half of the masses were in Polish and half were in English. We had Polish newspapers, Polish films, and a very active Polish community.

**Figure 137. John Guzłowski's International Certificate
of Inoculation and Vaccination, 1951**

When I was a child, I thought that the problem was simply that we were Poles in a strange country. There were things that Americans could do and things that Poles could do. Americans could be happy; they could go to ballgames, museums, and movies. They could walk freely through the American world, whistling the song *Pennies from Heaven* as they walked and believe every word of its chorus, *"Every time it rains, it rains pennies from heaven."* Americans could go to restaurants and order food and not get into arguments with waiters or with other customers in the restaurant. They could go to picnics and not lose their children or their children's balloons. They could go to weddings and dance waltzes without falling down, without getting into fights, and without beating their children. Americans could laugh at the jokes on TV and know what they were about. They could smile and mean it, show love, concern, happiness, sorrow, sadness, and all at the right time.

Poles seemed to be hobbled. There were places we couldn't go; I actually believed this. When I was a boy growing up in Chicago, I never knew anyone who ever went to a professional ballgame. It was as if there were written restrictions; Poles could not go to ballgames, or museums, or fairs. I'm now sure much of this was simply the result of growing up in a working class neighborhood with working class parents. Who could afford a trip to a ballpark? But then, I had the feeling that Poles just didn't do such things; only Americans did.

And nothing ever seemed to go right. Washing machines would break down for no reason. Repairmen were always crooks or incompetent. Shirts, even brand new ones, would be stained or have a button missing. I remember, once, my mother went into a Woolworth's dime store and tried to haggle on the price of a toy. Of course, it didn't work. Nothing worked. It was hard karma. And there was no one to tell you how to change the hard karma and make it a little more malleable, a little softer. Everyone was in the same boat and trying to find some way to survive or keep afloat.[234]

There was a sense of animosity between the old and new Polonia. My father felt that older people were always putting on airs. My sister married a Polish-American. I always felt some sort of tension between my parents and my sister's in-laws. My parents approached the Red Cross to help locate their families. My father never became an US citizen; he always felt he was a Polish citizen. He was interested in conditions in Poland. He always participated in anti-Communist rallies in Humboldt Park, and took me with him. He was very concerned and angry about the conditions that the Soviets had imposed on Poland. I think that many hoped that there would be another war. He remembered seeing the Russian soldiers at the end of the War and said that he couldn't believe how badly equipped they were in comparison to American

---

234 The paragraphs above are from *Observations on being a DP*. These observations were originally written for an unpublished study of Polish immigrants by Danusha Goska. Copyright John Guzlowski, 2005.

troops. Therefore, he thought that the USA would win if there was a war. When I went to Poland in 1991, the Soviets were leaving on very antiquated tanks. I don't know what they ran on, they were making so much smoke. The flea markets were filled with Russian paraphernalia.

Figure 138. The Guzłowski family arriving in the USA, 1951

For a long time I thought the DP experience was behind me, but it is not. As I have grown older I am spending a lot of time writing and talking about my parents' experiences. It's like I am closer to it now than I was for the middle 30 years of my life. I had so much trouble being a DP in the USA, even in high school; it wasn't until college that I felt that I was moving away from the DP experience, that people didn't know that I was a DP and that I didn't have to think about myself in those ways. Even when I was in high school I was living in a Polish/Polish-American area so every day there were reminders of where I came from. I understand why people were suspicious of us. When we arrived in the United States, we looked strange. I remember, around 1955-56, a family from Germany moved next door. I remember looking at them, thinking that these people looked really strange; they were thin, they wore strange clothes, the little girls wore thick black stockings. It was summer yet she was wearing a woolen hat and jacket! They looked like immigrants. I think that kind of stuff goes on all the time; if someone looks different they are not treated with the respect they deserve. The experience made me very liberal politically; I identify with all kinds of immigrants and all kinds of people who are being treated unjustly. I identify very strongly with people like that and try to improve their conditions. Right now, I am working with literacy in the south of Georgia where we have an increasing Mexican population that doesn't have literacy skills. Being a DP gave me a sense of how people can be mistreated and looked down upon. I felt like I was a minority and I can identify with minorities. The people in the USA don't understand the post-War experience. It amazes me how many people say, *"I didn't know."* People know the Holocaust but they don't know about the aftermath of the War; the chaos, confusion, and the broken lives.

My mother and I were out buying a sofa for the living room in the late 1970s and I said, *"Hey Mom, how about this one over here."* She said *"I don't like anything with stripes."* Stripes reminded her of the camps. Their primary identify was that of being a slave laborer and a DP. They never got past that. My mother was not an open person who talked about these things; I only found out after she died, when her friends told me. My father would talk a lot about the War, going over and over images that disturbed him greatly. When I came to visit, he would start telling stories and my mother would leave the room; she didn't want to hear his stories yet again. I asked her if there was anyone to help them when they got to the States; she said that nobody was interested in helping. My father also mentioned that there was an awareness of the rank people had before the War, and who was an 'officer'. We had to address some people by their pre-War titles, especially if they had been in the military. My parents suffered for years from their experiences during and after the War. My father never forgot about it. When he was dying and in intensive care, he came out of a deep sleep terrified as he thought the nurses and doctors were the camp guards coming to beat him.

In 1999 I thought I had written everything there was to write about them and, yet, I have written twice as much about them since. I now write almost exclusively about my parents.

Liberation

She has the peasant's view of the world:
Disorder and chaos, roads that end
In marshy fields, chickens that begin
To bleed from the mouth for no reason.
Nobody makes movies of such lives,
She says, and begins to tell me the story
Of when the Americans first came,
Of the sergeant who stood with a suitcase
In the yard between the barracks.

He was shouting, screaming
They didn't know what he wanted
And feared him. One of the women
Came out (first, she hid her children
Under the bed) and then another.
They knew he wasn't a German
When fifteen of them stood in the yard.
He opened the suitcase, emptied
Its deutschemarks on the ground,
Said in broken German, "This is for you
Take it, this is the money they owe you."

And then the British came,
And put them in another camp,
Where the corpses still had not been buried,
Where the water was bad, where my mother
Got sick, where her stool was as red
As the beets she had to dig everyday.
And my father worked hard, sawing
The wood, getting ready for winter,
Like he did in Poland. He knew this work
And did it for her and the children,
My sister and me. But the British
Moved them again, to another camp,
And they had to leave the wood, even though
My father tried to carry some on his back
And it was cold in the new place, and some
Of the babies died, and my sister was very sick,
Maybe from drinking the dirty water.

© John Guzlowski, 2005

Mari Czeczerska Sutton

b. 1948, Germany
1940-45, her mother was a slave laborer in Germany
1945-51, they lived in Germany
1951-present, USA

Figure 139. Krystyna Czeczerska and Mari Czeczerska Sutton
(on the right), **Rosenheim, Germany, 1949**

My mother's family had a farm in Germany; there was a bunker on their farm where they hid in times of bombardments or German raids. One night, because my grandmother was sick, my mother did not hide in the bunker. The Germans burst into the house and took her in her night dress. She was 23 years old. She was taken to Dachau and a local farmer picked her for slave labor. My father, Jan Kurek, was the other slave laborer working on this farm, and this is how they met. When the War ended the German farmer offered my parents jobs on the farm as they needed help and two of their three sons had died during the War. However, they decided not to stay there and, instead, went to a DP camp. They decided not to return to Poland because word had reached them that Stalin was executing Polish people or deporting them to Siberia.

They lived in dilapidated, overcrowded barracks and they had to move around a lot as camps were being closed. My mother was in at least five different DP camps: Pfaffenhofen, Altenstadt, Grafenaschau, Rosenheim, Mittenwald, and, maybe, Augsberg and Ingolstadt.

In each DP camp there was a group of people who would go out and steal livestock and food. The IRO ignored this activity as they recognized that the DPs had insufficient food. Eventually the local people complained, so the IRO told the DPs that they had a certain amount of time in which to get food and then they could no longer steal. Despite this directive, my father and his good friend went on out to steal food again and were caught by soldiers; his friend was shot. Allegedly, his friend's dying words were, *"please take care of my wife and four children."* My father promised him he would do that. When he returned to the barracks he began to taking care of his friend's widow and her children, and abandoned us. He carried on stealing and was imprisoned. We did not see him again.

This was 1948. When my father disappeared, my mother was told that no country would take a single woman with two children and that she would have to return to Poland. Her transport was arranged but, because she was so frightened of returning, she decided to drown herself, my sister, and me in a nearby lake.

Figure 140. Julia Czeczerska, Germany, 1945

Fortunately she changed her mind; at the same time her transport to Poland was delayed by six weeks. Miraculously, in those six weeks she met and married my stepfather. He was originally from Lithuania; he was on the American payroll, helping to reconstruct Germany. He heard that any Lithuanian returning to reclaim their land would be imprisoned. The USA was the last country to take DPs who had to be sponsored by an organization, have a job and have a place to stay. We were sponsored by Catholic Charities. We were supposed to go to Detroit but, somehow, landed up in Colorado and began working on a farm. We eventually moved to Denver where my stepfather built cement vaults for Mount Auburn Cemetery. There were Poles in Denver and my mother joined the local Polish organizations that had been organized by the new immigrants; she made friends with people who were also DPs. We didn't think we were different from the locals and I noticed no discrimination until I heard some kid yell out, *"DPs, DPs"* in a very sneering way. This was 1956.

My mother never talked about her family in Poland until, in 2003, I started searching for them and, eventually, found my mother's brother by using the services of an ex-KGB officer.[235] I started looking for my birth-father in 1961 and spent the next 43 years looking or him. Needless to say, my mother didn't want me to find him.

I submitted all my documents to the Red Cross; I knew his whereabouts. In the end I found my father while the Red Cross had written to me saying they could not find him. I got a big lead from one of the local prisons which had a record of his arrest. I found his last place of residence before incarceration was Dachau. An attorney in Munich found his widow and we did a DNA test to prove he was my father. He had spent three years in prison and then met a woman from Yugoslavia and married her. He stayed in Germany and worked as a construction worker. The last time his family in Poland heard from him was in 1956 when he wrote asking for his birth certificate so that he could get married. He wrote that he was never coming back to Poland and they never heard from him again.

The search was a very slow process but the introduction of the Internet greatly speeded this up; without it I would not have found him. However, it was a disappointing experience finding the family. Although family, we had no shared memory. We may have wanted to start creating such memories but, by then, there was also the language barrier.

Danuta Janina Wojcik
b. 1951, Canada
1939-40, her father was in the Polish Army
1940-45, he was a slave laborer in Germany
1945-49, he lived in DP camps in Germany
1949-present, Canada

My father, Jan Wojcik, was from the Tarnów area, and was in the Polish Army, from 1937-40. He was captured by the Germans in February, 1940 and sent to forced labor in Germany. Poland was defeated and occupied by the Nazis. He was placed on a train in Rzeszów, and headed for Vienna. He attempted to escape but was caught by the Nazi police and their dogs. Interviewed by my

---

235   KGB: (Soviet) Committee for State Security.

sister, he said, *"I was put in prison with other men and they treated us badly. After two weeks I was deported to Austria, then to Germany, and placed on a farm. I was forced to work for several German farmers. The conditions that I had to endure were deplorable. The food we were given was unsuitable for human consumption; it was cabbage soup with worms. I had no freedom as I was always confined to the farm property. I recall I was able to find an old bicycle and I fixed it and it was taken away from me by the Nazi police. There were heavy restrictions on laborers moving about. The quarters I was placed in were not suitable: no blankets, no pillows, and I slept on boards. There was no heat in the winter; the living conditions I had were unbearable. Also the clothing was not adequate; we were given no socks, only old wooden shoes that did not fit properly. I also had to wear the tag that identified me as a Pole, the letter 'P'. My proud Polish heritage was always mocked and there was a lot of name-calling and abuse. I had to get up early in the morning to clear and work the fields, and take care of the animals from dusk to dawn, through summer and winter, for five years."*

**Figure 141. Jan Wojcik, father of Danuta Wojcik,
in his Cavalry uniform, Poland, 1937**

**Figure 142. Jan Wojcik, as a German slave laborer,
wearing his letter 'P', Germany, 1940**

He told me the army would not supply enough food to eat and that, sometimes, they had to eat horses. He said there was a shortage of ammunition. I would sit on his knee and he would tell me stories. I wish I could remember them.

Figure 143. German workbook, front cover, Germany, 1940

In 1944, he met my mother; they lived together and my sister was born in September 1945. My mom told me that they did not get married until 1947 because it was hard to find a priest in the camps. Their wedding rings were made from melted German *marks*. The men and women would go out all day to work and would leave their children in daycare. The parents would return from work and, sometimes, their children were missing because they had been kidnapped for Germanization. My mother was from Węgierka. They had everybody listed and came knocking on the door; they took her and her sisters. They left my grandparents and young uncle behind.

My father moved to Manitoba, Canada, where he worked in a sugar-beet refinery. Mother stayed behind in IRO Fort Amberg until he was able to sponsor her to join him. He met several men on the ship and made lifelong friends. The conditions in Manitoba were good. His roommate also sponsored his family to come, so the two families came together. The accommodation was at the refinery. He was received warmly and, after they completed their year's contract, they found accommodation and work in a Polish section of Winnipeg. There was a church there that welcomed all immigrants. By 1953, my father had his own house.

**Figure 144. Workbook belonging to Danuta's mother,
Zofia Cicirko, Germany[236]**

My mother traveled over to Canada during the harshest winter ever. She became pregnant with me and they rented a duplex; we were already in our new home when she got pregnant with my brother who was born in 1953. After the birth of my brother, my mother and her friends worked the evening shift in the local hospital where she stayed for 35 years. My father took care of us in the evenings. We grew up in a very tight Polish community.

---

236 Jan Wojcik served with *5 Pułk Strzelców Konnych*, (the Fifth Mounted Rifles). He was captured by the Germans; from October 1939 to 1940, he was in Przeworsk and Landshut POW camps. Regulations under the Geneva Convention were not followed and POWs were sent to various forced labor camps. The first date on Jan's workbook is March 9, 1940. From September 1940 to September 1943 he worked for various farmers in Karpham, Bavaria; 1943-45, he worked for Alois Fischer, wagonmaker, Karpham, Bavaria. After the War he worked in security: 1946-47 as an UN-RRA policeman in Poking, near Passau; 1947-1948, Camp Supervision Guard, APO 403 US-Army; 1948-49 road builder in Weiden in der Oberpfalz, Bavaria; in 1949, the family emigrated to Canada.

Figure 145. Danuta Wojcik's mother, Zofia Cicirko
(first on the right), **and her sister, Irena, Germany, 1946**

Figure 146. Irena Wojcik, Slubsing DP Camp, Germany, 1946

They had some contact with family in Poland and, when my mother died in 2005, my father asked me to go to Poland. He was planning to go in 1995 but my mother had her first stroke so they could not travel. On Mother's side, two sisters had gone to the USA; one was in Chicago and the other was in the Boston area. When the German Army took them away, they were separated and, although they were in different camps, they kept writing and exchanging pictures. My mom found her sisters and brother through the Red Cross. She never saw her brother again. I went to the Ukraine, to my mother's village, knocking on doors hoping to find my uncle. Unfortunately he had died in 1971 and, having married a lady 20 years his senior, had no children. I keep in contact with his neighbors. It was a wonderful meeting as I often wondered what had happened to him; I was told that he, Jan, was left alone and the house burned down. He used to sleep on the grave of his mother who had died in 1943. In his teens he met a woman from the Ukraine and he went with her. He wrote to my mother but only one letter reached her. The neighbors would write for him as he only knew Russian and Ukrainian, not Polish. He wanted to be reconnected with his sisters but it never happened. My grandfather came home from the War and lived with neighbors. He was resettled in 1947[237] as he was Greek Orthodox Catholic; after Stalin's death, he was able to return to his village. Lots of Poles began to return to their homes at this time. I remember he used to write to my mother, and she was going to bring him to Canada. Unfortunately he died in 1958, the same year my mother became a Canadian citizen.

I started a search for all the Wojciks I could find, including an uncle in France. I contacted a woman in France whose name was Wojcik. When she went

Figure 147. Irena Wojcik's kindergarten class, Germany, 1949

---

237   Operation Wisła: (Polish: *Akcja Wisła*) was the code name for the 1947 deportation of southeast Poland's Ukrainian, Boyko and Lemko populations, carried out by the Polish Communist authorities. About 200,000 people, mostly of Ukrainian ethnicity and resident in southeastern Poland, were forcibly resettled to the 'Recovered Territories' in the north and west of the country. The operation was named after the Vistula River, *Wisła* (Polish).

to get some glasses, the clerk said that his name was also Wojcik and they shared their stories. She mentioned that she'd received a letter from Canada. He told her to bring him the letter; it turned out that she was married to my first cousin.

It was wonderful to meet my family in Poland. In my dad's village I have second cousins, and I am best friends with their children because they are all my age. When I visit they don't ever want me to leave. A lady from my dad's village told me what it was like in wartime Poland. She said it was awful; bombs were flying and there was no food. They made holes in the ground and slept in them for safety.

Rita Miller

b. 1946, Germany
1942-49, her mother was in Germany
1949-present, her mother lives in Canada
1951-present, Rita lives in the USA

My mother left Poland in 1942 when she was taken as a slave laborer by the Nazis. They wanted to take her mother as well but she refused to go and was put into jail for a couple of weeks. My mother volunteered to go, since there were still children at home and her mother could not be spared. She said that the soldiers put her in the back of a truck with nothing, no clothes; I am not sure if she was fed. She was taken to a farm in Saalfelden, Austria, where she milked cows and worked in the fields. I believe she was treated well by the farm owners. Her family sent her cards and letters; she also wrote to them. My mother didn't see her parents again; she didn't return to Poland until the 1970's, by which time they had passed away.

After the War, my mother was billeted in Flandernkaserne, an old Army barracks. While there, she met my father who had been an SS soldier. They had a relationship and I was born. I had my mother's name; she did not name him on my birth certificate but, later, when I was due to go to the States, he was contacted and his name was written on my birth certificate. My mother met his family, including his mother, my *Oma*[238], who was an impoverished widow. My father was, basically, a cruel man; I remember some of his actions, including trying to drown me in a tub when I was about three.

My mother left me with my *Oma* and went to Canada. No one ever heard from her again. When I was five, the authorities took me from my *Oma* and

---

238   *Oma* (German): Grandma.

put me in a camp in Munich until I was flown to the US. I do not remember that part of my life, but I remember my *Oma* as a loving person. I had always thought she was my mother until I received the papers explaining it all and describing me as an abandoned child. I was adopted by a family in Iowa and have lived there ever since. My relatives hesitated to tell me much about my father because they didn't want me to feel bad. However, to an extent, I do remember him although I did not put the name 'father' to my memories.

I was taken away because my father did not support me, and because my mother had abandoned me. My *Oma* was a poor widow and, as this was immediately after the War, things were really difficult. She took in laundry for people, and I can remember being left alone at a young age while she went to bake bread at the community bake house. She was very, very loving to me. Finally my *Oma* could no longer provide for me, so she went to the authorities to ask for help to make my father support me. The authorities came to our home, saw the poverty, and told *Oma* she must surrender me. She refused, so they said they would take me by force if necessary; the entire family (minus my father and mother, of course) went along to the place where they were told to deliver me.

Years later, I found my German *Tante*[239] during my search for my father who, through an interpreter, told me what had happened. She said I was crying and screaming and the entire family wept when I left. I don't remember that, although I do remember quite a few other things. I am not sure how long I was in the DP camp and I don't know the name of it but I think it was full, mainly, of orphaned children waiting to go to the States. I flew on the *Flying Tiger*, an old army plane; this was the last transport under the immigration quota.

We flew to New York and I was in an orphanage there until my journey to Davenport, Iowa. I was sponsored by Catholic Charities and went to St. Vincent's Home. I can remember the trip to Burlington with my adoptive parents. I was a chatterbox and was fascinated by the sights. We lived near the school which was run by nuns. There were about eight of us immigrant children from various countries, mainly Italy, Latvia, and Russia, and from German DP camps. I was the only ethnic German/Pole. We were treated like celebrities and I got a big head, I think. I was reading in English sooner than anyone else in my class and was very bright so they made much of me. Of course, in later years, the other kids caught up and I ceased to be special. I had a younger sister, also adopted from an American orphanage, and an older brother who was the birth child of my adoptive parents. I remember being afraid of him; now I know it was because he was tall and dark, and reminded me of my father who had been cruel.

My uncle in Poland called my cousin in Canada and told her about me.

---

239   *Tante* (German): Aunt.

She called me and I could not believe my ears, especially when she said my mother was still alive. She is in a nursing home in Canada, near Toronto. My cousin and I hit it off immediately and she promised to tell my mother about me. Naturally, I thought she and I had been separated and she had been grieving for me all her life. Not so. At first she denied having any children, then, she relented and admitted she'd had a daughter who died. My cousin could see that she was lying. I was heartbroken. Finally, I called her at the home and, after I broke down and cried, she admitted to being my mother. I was still elated, and hoped to win her over. I sent her gifts and cards and called frequently. Sometimes she would talk very mean, or hang up on me. Of course, I knew dementia sometimes does that to people but my cousin finally told me some stories that confirmed that this was not all due to dementia. My cousin sent pictures and I almost fainted; my mother and I look so much alike. I have a wedding picture of her, all decked out in a white dress with a long trailing veil. At the time of her wedding, I was 4 years old and lived in poverty in Germany. Please pardon me but I am still a bit bitter and heartbroken.

My cousin invited me to come to Canada. In 2004, my daughter, brother-in-law and I, took the train to Buffalo; my cousin met us and drove us to Mississagua. It was difficult because I have a disorder that makes walking difficult and I use a cane; I am heavy and was worried about how they would receive me. However, we became immediate friends and they showed us the most wonderful hospitality. My mother's friends invited us to dinner and prepared the most wonderful meal with all Polish foods.

I had sent away for my immigration records from Homeland Security, and the packet came the same day that my cousin sent me some shoes, purses and a coat that had belonged to my mother. I stroked the items like they were my mother; I was just thrilled to touch things that she had owned. However, I opened the package from Homeland Security and learned that my mother and father had abandoned me, and I was in the care of a German woman before being sent to the States. Who was she? I learned about my mother's history from my cousins and my German relatives, whom I also found. My Tante is my mother's age and supplied the details of my early life. All my relatives are kind and wonderful; it is my parents who were not. My mother did tell me that her life began in Canada. She only went back to Poland once, and she never said a word about having a child. When I went to meet her I was hoping for a hug and some affection, but I didn't get it. She was angry that I came and 'ruined' everything.

My cousins and I keep in touch, and I have a great affection for them. One of them made a trip to Poland and took pictures of the home place and the surrounding area. My mother came from very simple people, and she wanted them to think she was rich in Canada. I do not understand that kind of deception and haughty attitude. She did not care about my feelings; she only wanted her reputation to remain unsullied. She spent time in Ludwigsburg, too, before going on the ship, *Marine Shark,* that took her to Canada. She worked as a domestic help for a year and, then, worked in a factory. She was a hard worker, and I think my work ethic comes from that side of the family because my father liked to live off others.

The German woman who had cared for me turned out to be my grandmother. My *Tante* was able to give me the story of my mother and father, and told me also about my early years. Some of my memories were exact; *Tante* was amazed that I could remember so much. I also scanned my passport picture from 1952, and it was the same one that was in their family album. It was all overwhelming and I was overcome for a long, long time. My *Tante* told me that, after the War, my father had to hide out in the woods and had no clothing or food. I then asked, was he in the SS? My relatives reluctantly told me, *"yes."* I was so ashamed. Actually, I had always been fascinated with World War II stories and read many books about that time. When I read that the SS would drown people on the banks of rivers, I was chilled because my father had tried to drown me. In my heart I knew that he was evil. Coincidentally, I learned the name of my father's wife and wrote to her, and included my e-mail. Soon I had an e-mail from a woman who was my half-sister! I was so happy to find a sister. However, we do not speak one another's language so it's hard to communicate. My sister told me that our father was cruel and beat her and her mother and did not support them. She had no good memories of him at all. Our father is now dead; he died in a Salvation Army-type shelter.

My cousin did not experience the War as she is only 40 years old. Her father, however, was a young boy at the time, and told her the story of how my mother had decided to go to be a work prisoner instead of her mother. She also told me that her mother's sister had been taken; she suffered with leg problems all her life and returned to Poland. Her father has been dead for a number of years; it seems that people do not wish to talk about those years. My mother talked about those times once, but my cousin didn't pay much attention because she was a kid and was not all that interested.

My mother married a Pole from the Ukraine. He was in the Polish Home Army and was decorated. I have a picture of him and my mother taken on Katyń Day, in Toronto. He was a very nice person, I am told. I was actually surprised to find that my mother had moved to Canada as I thought she had gone back to Poland. I did not realize the state of post-War Poland. I think my mother went to Canada because they had places for the immigrants and jobs for them as domestic help. My mother did tell me that she hated her position and left as soon as her year of bondage was over. She did not like her employers; the husband was a doctor.

Sometimes my mother would be pleasant when I called, other times she was horrible and would hang up on me. She always told me, she was a good-looking woman. There was never a word of regret about leaving me. She was very active in the Polish community in Canada. To me, it was very absorbing to be around her friends and culture. In Iowa, it was the custom to forget the past and not talk about anything. My adoptive parents did not encourage me to remember anything. I have a few memories of things they told me, but not many. Most of my relatives are deceased. It makes me sad to be in this time of my life when the answers have mostly been buried.

I've tried to learn all I could about my Polish side, and have learned a few words but I find it difficult. German comes easier because my adoptive parents had German backgrounds; my maternal grandfather had come from Germany in the early 1900s, so he could speak to me and translate. I feel bad about missing out on my Polish heritage. I did memorize the words of *Sto Lat*[240] to sing to my cousin on her birthday. I still feel like a displaced person, even though I consider myself an American. I am also a German and a Pole. But, to a certain degree, I am always on the outside looking in.

Barbara Gryszel Masgula
b. 1964, USA
March 1940, her mother was deported to the Soviet Union
1942-47, her mother was in Iran, Africa
1947-52, her mother was in England
1952-present, USA

When I was in the fifth grade, we were instructed to write an essay about a family member. I chose my mother's father, Maksymilian Rozner. I wrote about him being was killed at Katyń. This was 1973. My teacher gave me an 'F' for my essay and told the class that I had made it all up! She called me a liar because, she said, what I had written was *"not true."* Some time, in the 1980s, I read an article about the Katyń Massacre, and flashed back to the fifth grade. That teacher made me believe that my mother had lied to me. I felt so very sad for that teacher. I do not think the Katyń Massacre or what our parents and relatives went through will ever be taught in our classrooms! History repeats itself as massacres are happening over and over.

---

240   *Sto Lat*: (Polish): *Hundred Years,* the song sung at birthdays, wishing the celebrant a hundred years of life.

Polscy Chłopcy[241]

"Lest We Forget" was boldly printed on the card
To honour those who died for their countries while standing guard.
They were men and boys, young and old, weak and strong,
And each one was to be remembered with patriotic song.

As long as I can remember, Nov. 11th was your special day.
You shined up your war medals and donned your beret.
As veterans paid tribute with wreaths of poppies upon the square,
You proudly saluted the heavens to all the soldiers there.

With old trembling hands you held your card and thought to years gone by.
And every time the trumpets roared, I saw the tears that filled your eyes.
What were you thinking that brought you such pain?
Were you remembering Polscy Chłopcy that died in vain?

Or were you thinking of your own sorrow and how this all began
Because of greed and hatred, best expressed by man.
Were your tears for your little village and all that was once yours?
Or were your tears for the broken dreams snatched away by war.

Germany was creating havoc and Poland knew there might be trouble in sight
But she was assured there would be help, if she needed to fight.
Great America and England promised if needed they'd rise to the plate
But instead sat silent while Poland's defeat became your fate.

Were your tears for the broken promises made man to man?
Or for how meaningless had become the shake of one's hand?
Germans abounded from the west and the army was ready for almighty war
But as they were pushed back, from the east came something more.

On Sept 17, 1939, the Rusks like hungry vultures awaiting their prey
Swarmed all around you with bayonets and for being Polish, you'd pay.
They occupied quickly and took Lwów, Wilno and Lutck
What did a young peasant boy know of promises the Nazis had made to the
Rusks?

---

241   *Polscy Chłopcy* (Polish): Polish Boys.

In the cold of winter, they knocked on Kresyland doors ripping people from
their sleep
And yelled, "you have an hour to pack, don't waste the time to weep!"
Old people and children were herded like cattle into the snow
And guns blasted loudly at those who said, "I won't go!"

Sleds and wagons carried you to the nearest railway stations
Thus beginning for Kresowiacy, heartless and cruel deportations.
Crammed into frozen boxcars with little food and hardly room to lay
They prayed "Święty Boże i Matko Boska,[242] please show us the way!"

After shuffling you into prison, black raven trucks and a windowless train
They said "Comrades don't cry, save your tears for future pain!"
We will send you Polscy Chłopcy to Archangel and Siberia
If hunger doesn't kill you, there'll be scurvy, typhoid and diphtheria

Oh God they were right when they said that God created heaven and the
devil created Archangel.

Temperatures so cold, you couldn't bear your skin,
And if you dared spit, it froze in the wind.
Newspapers and rags gently wrapped around your feet
But be damned if you'd let your spirit be beat.

With backbreaking labour you crushed rocks for their roads
Swinging axes and shovels load after load.
For a grueling days work they fed you 700 grams of bread
Anything less and you'da soon been dead.

At night, with barely enough clothing to warm your bones
You fell fast asleep only to dream of more stones.
And who'da thought in this land of Godforsaken ice
Millions of bedbugs and those bastardly lice.

On barges and boats they shuffled you around
Then rumours of freedom started to abound.
Dirty ol' Stalin had found himself in a fix,
As his good buddy Hitler pulled out a few more tricks.

---

242   "*Święty Boże i Matko Boska...*" (Polish): "Holy God and Mother of God..."

Stalin said "Polscy Chłopcy, try to understand,
This wasn't about you, I just wanted your land.
We'll toast to freedom, and with a new Polish Army we'll work side by side.
Forget about all those men who died!"

So with release cards and empty stomachs he set you free
You headed south where the army was supposed to be.
Sikorski and Anders waited for the Polish Army to regroup
As thousands of you half-starved and sick arrived for bread and soup.

Were your tears for all the women and children you passed on the road
Each one beyond their years, showing scars of their merciless load?
Did you cry for the corpses they callously threw into the wind?
Or ask if this was punishment for man who had sinned?

The Brits gave you uniforms and a white Polish eagle to wear
on your shoulder
General Anders restored your faith and put things in order.
Stalin held back your bread and insisted that Polscy Chłopcy be sent to the front.
Anders refused because he knew on Stalin he could no longer count.

Anders moved his army to Persia in order for Polscy Chłopcy to survive.
The Caspian Sea carried you to Pahlevi, some barely alive.
With wounded souls and bodies frail
Thousands were left behind and missed the last sail.

Were you thinking of this when you choked back the tears?
Knowing how much they continued to suffer for many more years.
You became a proud soldier in Polish Second Corps
And fought in Monte Cassino with much determined force.

Pulled from rags in Russia, Polscy Chłopcy passed the test
They became a great army and certainly one of the best.
Polish blood soaked the soil from your countrymen that laid dead
Amongst the shattered poppies that were already red.

Polscy Chłopcy stood proud and still
As they placed their country's flag upon the captured hill.
The white eagle soared with victorious delight
For all the exiled soldiers who had won their fight.

The world celebrated with victory parades and promised fences to mend
But Polscy Chłopcy were not invited to attend.
Great America and England let Stalin take your land
So what exactly you had fought for was hard to understand.

To appease the Communists you were again deported and pushed aside
With spirits crushed and broken hearts, valiant soldiers cried.
Instead of paying you tribute they made you search for home in a new place
While they demobilized your army just to save face.

Did you weep for your family for whom you would never again see?
Or the loss of their freedoms, while you were in a new land and free?
Were your tears for Polscy Chłopcy as they were being called DPs
Or for the suggestions that you change your Polish name and drop the "ski"?

You remained proud to your heritage and kept your name.
This was all you had left and it bore you no shame.
On Rememberance Day, you stood alone as you remembered those who died
Because there were no Polscy Chłopcy to share your memories at your side.

There was no one here that had shared your footsteps from the past.
And many of the young never cared to ask.
They had never been to war, and they didn't understand
What it really meant to lose one's land.

Today I stand alone, holding your polished medals at your grave,
And I thank you with all my heart for being so brave.
I thank you for the Polish heritage that you passed on to me
And for raising me in a country where I am blessed to be free.

For Polscy Chłopcy, I will scatter red poppies in the wind, just for you
And I will do my best to my heritage be true.
And when the trumpets roar, I too, will salute the skies
For now I finally understand the tears in your eyes.

Written in memory of my father Kazimierz Kaczanowski

© Hania Kaczanowska, 2003

Teresa Stolarczyk Marshall

b. 1946, Germany
1940-45, her parents were slave laborers in Germany
1945-47, they lived in Germany
1947-present, England

Figure 148. Teresa Stolarcyzk Marshall and her mother, Juliana Łabińska Stolarczyk, Haydon Park Camp, England, 1949

I remember always being very poor, having very few belongings, and always moving from place to place until we finally bought our house in Bradford, England. We were a very close family as we had no one else: no grandparents, uncles or aunts. My parents, Juliana and Józef, were very friendly with all the other Polish people they met. Many of their friends from Haydon Park went to Bradford for work so they met again later.

I remember that there was resentment of Polish refugees. Occasionally my mother was called *"a bloody foreigner"* and, I remember, when I was about eight and simply playing out in the street, a man in a nearby house also called me this.

I spoke very little English when I went to school. We were lucky that, by chance one day, my father met one of his Army friends in the local park. This man had an English wife and we lived with them for a while. Auntie Mary, as we called her, taught my mother a little English and showed her how to shop. We stayed good friends all our lives.

My parents' experiences had an enormous impact on their lives. They were always sad that they were not really 'at home.' My mother always wanted to see her mother and to find her home and she cried almost every day. My father had to be very tough and had to cope. He had no one to teach him how to do things at home; he just had to learn.

They had a positive outlook on life in that they chose to come to England and were determined to make a good life for themselves. They were always anxious to be honest and hardworking and never to be a burden to anyone. They were wary of the police and authorities as there was always the fear that they could be sent back to Poland. They struggled with English all their lives, especially complicated forms, but I always helped them with these.

My father's mother seemed to accept that he had gone to England for a better life. I searched for the family in Poland and, in 2005, I found my mother's step-brother, Pavlo, living in what is now the Ukraine. He had been searching for her all his life. He thought that if she was alive she would return so he wanted to know what had happened to her. During the War he was told to destroy all contact with her, or his fate would be the same; that of deportation to Germany for slave labor. As the contact was broken, my mother was told that all her family was dead. So, my mother's family did not know that she was, in fact, alive and well in England. Only two years earlier, in 2004, Pavlo's granddaughter had been to Germany to search for my mother again.

I feel greatly for their very hard young lives, to the point that it is very painful for me.

Anonymous (2)

b. 1951, Canada
1940, each of her parents was deported to the Soviet Union
1942-49, her mother was in Iran, India and Africa; her father was in Iran and Italy
1949, they both emigrated to Canada

Each of my parents was deported to Russia in 1940 and met in Melton Mowbray Camp, England, after my father had seen service in Italy and my mother had been in Iran, India and Africa. The two families emigrated to Canada between 1948 and 1949, sponsored by relatives. I know very little about my father's experiences as he rarely speaks about them. However, I do know that my mother loved her life in Africa; she was sad to leave. I have run a support group for senior Polish women for 17 years. One of the group went back for a visit to Africa because she missed it so much and because she thought of it as her 'home.' Tehran was hard because so many were very ill, but Africa was different.

In Melton Mowbray, my mother trained to be a seamstress and, as she was raised in camps, communal life appealed to her. She socialized in the Polish community, founding a Polish scout troop in her Canadian hometown. Polish was my first language; I thought that the whole world spoke Polish. I thought that speaking in English to the dentist was part of dentistry! Everywhere else, in the shops and on the streets, you heard Polish. My mother even met Polish people she knew from Africa.

Relationships with the 'old' Polonia were difficult; their language, educational level and expectations were different. The older ones were almost bitter that the new arrivals got some help. My parents socialized with the veterans, mostly, as they had a lot more in common with them. The old Polonia also had a hard time believing the stories that the new immigrants told them of the deportations and the camps. It happens today; new arrivals from Poland, who were never taught about the deportations in Soviet-occupied Poland, have commented that films like *A Forgotten Odyssey*[243] are just propaganda. I have women in my therapy group who returned to Poland after the Amnesty and were branded as 'traitors' because they were in Russia during the War. People who do not know of the deportations believe the time spent in Russia was voluntary.

Being the daughter of Poles had a profound impact on me. I suffered culture shock growing up in my own country; the question of identify, dual identity, multiple identity, and awareness of the possibility of war. Even in kindergarten, when a plane would fly overhead I would dive for cover. I was afraid of planes for many, many years. I've also had issues around food, never wasting any and worrying that there would be enough. I've worked on it but it's still there. I go grocery shopping and I still buy two of everything. I still experience 'soul pain.' I was always aware that war could happen at any time and that I could come home and find that my family might be gone. I think: *"where did I learn that?"* Well, it's clear where it came from, and it helps me work with other people.

At one point I got angry with my parents because they had not taught me English. What use was Polish? I stopped using it. Then, a new girl who spoke no English came to my school; the teacher asked me to help; then, I saw it could be useful. The old and new Polonia kept apart, and it was not until the young people started dating that the two groups started working together. Up until Pierre Trudeau's policy of multi-culturalism in the 1960s it was difficult if your language, food and clothes were different. It wasn't bad; you just didn't fit in. I had friends but never close friends, and these were always from immigrant groups. There is something about being the first generation, born to parents who are war survivors, that bonds you together. And, now, the children of my generation are creating friendships with one another. I have felt like an outsider all my life and others have mentioned having the same feeling. When I am in Poland they call me Canadian; when I'm in Canada they refer to me as *"the Polish one."* It's a gift to get more objectivity that way.

---

243 Written and directed by Jagna Wright. (2000) *A Forgotten Odyssey, The untold story of 1,700,000 Poles deported to Siberia in 1940.*

**Figure 149. Anon's (2) aunt, grandfather and
mother, Tehran, Iran, 1943**

My cousin, who lives in my father's old home in Poland, will not talk
about what happened. He says, *"It's too awful to talk about."* But I was not as
interested then as I am now in what happened and did not ask too many questions. Since we have reached middle age, I think we have reached an awareness
of what our parents went through, and explore it more. After I showed *A Forgotten Odyssey,* a group of us got together to talk about what it meant to grow
up as the 'Siberian kids'. My parents don't think I should have been impacted
by their experiences as in their eyes I've had the best of everything. Sometimes,
my mother will look at me and ask, *"Where did you learn that? I could not have
taught you that,"* things like parenting skills, buying a house, going to school,
and attending things in the wider community. She sees us as existing in a different reality to hers.

When I show my mother the poems I have written about my grandmother,
and talk about my longing for her, she does not understand it at all; she says
that she had almost forgotten her maiden name, but that the poem is 'nice.'
Maybe this is too big for her, as when working with the women in my therapy
group they have told me bluntly that they don't have the capacity for the
insight that I have. They tell me it's 'my job'. They have opened up more to me
than to their own children. Even my mother will open up more to someone
else, even when I'm there. It's easier to open up to someone else than to your

own family. They have no idea what impact their experiences have had on their children. In those days, they did not recognize Post Traumatic Stress Syndrome; there was no help offered to them, they just had to carry on. But many men in Canada slept with a gun by their bed. Some of the Polish veterans I know hit the bottle to cope with their experiences. Many of the older women attribute their current physical problems to the suffering they endured during and immediately after the War.

Figure 150. Anon's (2) father, returning to his home in Poland in the 1970s and seeing the trees he had planted before the War

A Poem dedicated to my grandmother, 1888-1942
born Suszno,
died Kazakhstan, on the way to freedom from Siberia

Hearts broke
To leave you behind in Chok Pak
Lying by the side of the train track,
Wife and mother who'd sacrificed
So much for family
That my heart too
is touched by you
Despite all this time and space
distant

From your life on earth.
There are no photos,
no mementos
Of you, *Babcia*,
Other than the love and wisdom
How often I have tried
To piece together an image of you,
Studying your children's faces as they age,
Carried by your husband and children.

Anonymous (2), 2006

Mama,
I have to go.
It was a tiny whisper,
it wouldn't call
the attention
of guards.
There's nowhere to go, Kasiu,
just hold on.
Kasia tensed her brow
and clenched her teeth.
She tried to think
of other things.
Away from the confines
of the frigid, putrid cattle-car
that had held them for ten days,
they could almost
enjoy
this movement
through open space
by sleigh
were it not
for the severity
of their destination.
The silence fell hard
around them.
There was only the sound of hooves
and the shhhhh-shhhhh of runners
gliding across Siberian snow.

Mama,
I can't anymore.
The whisper
had become a whimper.
What was a ten-year-old to do?
The convoy of sleighs
would not stop.
The forest was thick,
night
was falling.
Mama,

I have to go,
I can't hold on anymore!
She was crying now.

Her knees shook.
Then go here,
where you are, my child,
go here.

Kasia watched him, hopefully.
Suddenly,
she felt
Mama's breath
fall hard upon her shoulder

Kasia, I have to go.
No! Mama, just hold on!
There's nowhere to go without you!
I can't,
I can't
hold on
any longer, my child...
and her body fell heavily
against Kasia's twelve-year-old shoulder.

Tata,
with pita bread
already broken
into pieces
to share,
arrived
too
late.

Hers
were not the only clothes
soaked and frozen on that journey.
The barracks exuded that scent
for weeks, seasons,
ages.
The shame stayed longer.

Loss
of control
of any kind
in front of guards
is lethal.

Years later,
when they left
that awful place,
it would take many days more
to reach freedom.
At the distant station,
they waited for the crowded train.
Hope rose, hard and sure.
The fragile sun
dared
whisper across their cheeks.

Tata found new, green onions!
Dear ones, eat,
she said softly.
What about you, Mama?
She smiled. *I can wait, my child.*
They were the sweetest onions of Kasia's life;
all future onions would be measured against these.

Their names were not on the list
but they boarded the train anyway.
What shall I do with your onion, Mama?
Hold it, my child.
Kasia held it tenderly,
this precious sign of Spring,
of new life.

When the train stopped
Tata jumped out
to exchange their last rags
for bread.

Mama, we can't leave you here!

Go, my child, go...
You will be freed by this train
you will be warmed by sun again
you will miss me, I know, but

Your heart will hold me
Though my body stays here

Your heart will hold me
As you move through the years

Your daughter will know me
As if I were near

And I will send love
to balance the fear.

Anonymous (2), 2007

AFTERWORD

The stories have been told; and yet, not told. There is too much to tell. There is not the space. There is not the emotional stamina to tell everything that befell our parents, grandparents, uncles, aunts. And there is so much we do not know, and may never know. There is so much lost that is precious to us.

But we can protect that which exists. Hidden for decades in university archives, in Polish clubs and museums strewn across the world, in drawers, photo albums, diaries, are sacred things, precious glimpses, mosaic pieces that help us to understand.

To understand what? To be honest we don't really know. Only this; that our Polish ancestry matters to us at a heart level that is difficult to translate into words; that the trauma that the people closest to us in our lives endured and survived needs to be aired, expressed, embraced, and most of all shared; shared with hundreds of thousands of other children of Siberiaks.

Out there in a hundred countries, in every continent, are middle-aged men and women who feel a gap in their lives, a gnawing hunger for an understanding of what befell their mother or father when they were young, in some cases when they were tiny babies or toddlers.

To understand ourselves too; to piece together legacy; to try to draw as many of the facts, personal, historical, political, military, and geographical, in order to see how this barrage of new detail resides also inside of us, is in our bloodstream; most deeply, is in our hearts. And we long to know where we fit with our past, with the pain and loss, and love and recovery that is our Polish legacy.

To this end we, a small group who don't really know each other but where it matters, know each other intimately, are seeking to pull together every fibre of documentation, film, photography, scrawled note, bureaucratic office report, that relates to the facts and fate of the Kresy-Siberiaks. We aim to digitize all of these documents, make them accessible to our fellow… we don't have a label for what we are, for we are the children of the Kresy-Siberiaks, and we don't need a label. We know what we are.

We will collate from around the world everything there is that relates to the Kresy-Siberia odyssey, and make these available at a Kresy-Siberia virtual museum. As new discoveries are made these will be added to the Museum. When, in the mysterious, unpredictable way it happens, a son or daughter (and, soon, grandsons and grand-daughters) awakens to their remarkable tragic heritage, they will find our virtual museum, and there they will find answers. They will find truths about themselves. And truths about the astonishing people of the Kresy. From these truths they will grow as people because it is impossible to know what happened to our Polish ancestors without it enriching our lives.

Over time we hope to make it a thing of the past to do as we had to do. To find ourselves, isolated searchers for details, trawling obscure websites, emailing strangers in institutions we had never heard of, in countries we had never visited, on the hunch of another stranger who said that, just maybe, there might be a document relating to your father in such and such a place. To wait, sometimes over a year, to receive an answer yet, miraculously, after a year something arrives in the mail from a place you had forgotten you had contacted so long ago, and it contains a personal handwritten note from your grandfather or aunt written in the 1930s or 1940s. And you cry just to have a copy of such a document in your hands.

We hope to make available these treasures without the blind searching, without the waiting, the hoping, the loss of hope. We want, in a hundred years and more, generations of young people of Kresy descent to know of our museum, to show it to their friends at school, to their teachers, and say this is my history, this is what my great-great grandmother endured, survived, overcame. Because the expulsion and brutalisation of the people of the Kresy, our parents and other relatives, their travails, heroism, strength, beauty and recovery, and their deaths, tortures, hungers, illnesses, exhaustion; this whole epic sweep of a crucial moment of human history is not known to the world. And we, the children of the survivors, are determined that it will not be forgotten, that it will be known, that it will never be forgotten. We love our Polish families, we love the family we never were able to touch, hold, know; we love these people and we will honour them best by ensuring that their lives and their legacy will live through our efforts.

**Martin Stepek, on behalf of the Kresy-Siberia Group
and in recognition of all descendants of survivors of
Nazi and Stalinist Oppression, 2008**

History is still being written

History is still being written
Each of you has a pen in hand
And is writing a chapter with every thought, word, and action
In what direction are you writing humanity?

© Martin Stepek, 2007

BIBLIOGRAPHY

Interviews:

Anonymous (1), (2006, October). (B. Wojciechowska, Interviewer)

Anonymous (2), (2006, September 29). (B. Wojciechowska, Interviewer)

Bączyński, K. (2006, August). (B. Wojciechowska, Interviewer)

Bączkowska, S. (2006, August). (B. Wojciechowska, Interviewer)

Bargiel, K. (2006, June). (B. Wojciechowska, Interviewer)

Bechta-Crook, A. (2006, July). (B. Wojciechowska, Interviewer)

Biega, B. (2006, October). (B. Wojciechowska, Interviewer)

Biegus, J. (2006, August). (B. Wojciechowska, Interviewer)

Biegus, Z. (2006, August). (B. Wojciechowska, Interviewer)

Bik, B. (2006, July). (B. Wojciechowska, Interviewer)

Bik, V. (2006, June). (B. Wojciechowska, Interviewer)

Bitner, J. (2006, July). (B. Wojciechowska, Interviewer)

Blacha, J. (2006, July). (B. Wojciechowska, Interviewer)

Chojnacka, E. (2006, July). (B. Wojciechowska, Interviewer)

Ciupak, J. (2007, October). (B. Wojciechowska, Interviewer)

Czerniejewski, H. (2006, August). (B. Wojciechowska, Interviewer)

Fleming, P. T. (2006, July). (B. Wojciechowska, Interviewer)

Gradosielska, D. (2006, August). (B. Wojciechowska, Interviewer)

Guzłowski, J. (2006, July). (B. Wojciechowska, Interviewer)

Hałko, L. (2006, May). (B. Wojciechowska, Interviewer)

Haszlakiewicz, Z. (2006, May). (B. Wojciechowska, Interviewer)

Hayward (Siennicki) G. (2006, July). (B. Wojciechowska, Interviewer)

Herzog, F. (2006, October). (B. Wojciechowska, Interviewer)

Herzog, K. (2006, October). (B. Wojciechowska, Interviewer)

Janota Bzowska, K. M. (2006, August). (B. Wojciechowska, Interviewer)

Jopek (Jopeck), H. (2006, October). (B. Wojciechowska, Interviewer)

Jopek (Jopeck), H. (2006, October). (B. Wojciechowska, Interviewer)

Juny, M. (2006, July). (B. Wojciechowska, Interviewer)

Kałwa, J. (2006, October). (B. Wojciechowska, Interviewer)

Kazimierski, A. (2006, September). (B. Wojciechowska, Interviewer)

King, R. (2006, July). (B. Wojciechowska, Interviewer)

Kopel, Z. (2006, August). (B. Wojciechowska, Interviewer)

Korniłowicz, Z. (2007, September). (B. Wojciechowska, Interviewer)

Kozłowski, J. (2006, August). (B. Wojciechowska, Interviewer)

Kuczyński, E. (2006, November). miscellaneous.

Larkowski, W. (2006, June). (B. Wojciechowska, Interviewer)

Lesczuk, C. (2006, August). (B. Wojciechowska, Interviewer)

Lipiński, R. (2006, June). (B. Wojciechowska, Interviewer)

Mączka, S. (2006, August). (B. Wojciechowska, Interviewer)

Mączka, T. (2006, June). (B. Wojciechowska, Interviewer)

Marshall, T, (2006, July). (B. Wojciechowska, Interviewer)

Masgula, B. (2009, April). (B. Wojciechowska, Interviewer)

Mazur, W. (2006, October). (B. Wojciechowska, Interviewer)

Milan-Kamski, W. M. (2006, July). (B. Wojciechowska, Interviewer)

Milewski, S. (2006, October). (B. Wojciechowska, Interviewer)

Miller, R. (2006, July). (B. Wojciechowska, Interviewer)

Orłowska, H. (2007, July). (B. Wojciechowska, Interviewer)

Orłowski, W. (2006, July). (B. Wojciechowska, Interviewer)

Paschwa-Kozicka, A. (2006, July). (B. Wojciechowska, Interviewer)

Piasecka, J. K. (2006, S). (B. Wojciechowska, Interviewer)

Płowy, J. (2006, October). (B. Wojciechowska, Interviewer)

Poślinska, H. (2006, September). (B. Wojciechowska, Interviewer)

Poślinski, J. (2006, May). (B. Wojciechowska, Interviewer)

Rasiej, K. (2006, July). (B. Wojciechowska, Interviewer)

Rasiej, M. (2006, July). (B. Wojciechowska, Interviewer)

Remmert, A. (2006, June). (B. Wojciechowska, Interviewer)

Sagen, S. (2006, June). (B. Wojciechowska, Interviewer)

Skulski, R. (2006, May). (B. Wojciechowska, Interviewer)

Sławinski, A. K. (2006, August). (B. Wojciechowska, Interviewer)

Sutton, M. (2006, July). (B. Wojciechowska, Interviewer)

Synowiec-Tobis, S. (2006, August). (B. Wojciechowska, Interviewer)

Szklarz, M. (2006, July). (B. Wojciechowska, Interviewer)

Szkudłapski, J. (2006, August). (B. Wojciechowska, Interviewer)

Szlachetko, D. (2006, August). (B. Wojciechowska, Interviewer)

Szuttenbach, S. (2006, December). (B. Wojciechowska, Interviewer)

Szydło, D. (2006, August). (B. Wojciechowska, Interviewer)

Szydło, K. (2006, August). (B. Wojciechowska, Interviewer)

Szymel, A. (2007, September). (B. Wojciechowska, Interviewer)

Topolski, A. (2006, July). (B. Wojciechowska, Interviewer)

Trzcinska-Croydon, L. (2006, May). (B. Wojciechowska, Interviewer)

Urbanowicz Gilbride, B. (2006, July). (B. Wojciechowska, Interviewer)

Wardzala, J. (2006, May). (B. Wojciechowska, Interviewer)

Wojciechowska, C. (2006, August). (B. Wojciechowska, Interviewer)

Wojcik, D. (2007, November). (B. Wojciechowska, Interviewer)

Woźniak, S. (2006, August). (B. Wojciechowska, Interviewer)

Zdanowicz, A. (2008, February). (B. Wojciechowska, Interviewer)

Films:

(Adamski, 2004) *The Betrayal of Poland.*

(Baginski, Jewsiewicki & Walkowski, 1997). *Kroniki Powstania Warszawskiego (Chronicle of the Warsaw Uprising).*

(Batty, 2004). *The Battle for Warsaw. The Nazi Annihilation of Poland's Historic Capital.*

(Owens & Sikora, 1991). *Katyń. Slaughter and Silence.*

(Wajda, 2007). *Katyń.*

(Wright, 2000). *A Forgotten Odyssey. The untold story of 1,700,000 Poles deported to Siberia in 1940.*

Published sources:

Adamaczyk, M. W. (2004). *When God Looked the Other Way. An Odyssey of War, Exile, and Redemption.* Chicago: The University of Chicago Press.

Adamski, J. (1972). *Historia dla klasy 4 liceum ogólnokształacego (History for general high school 4th class).* Warszawa: Wydawnictwa Szkolne i Pedagogiczne (Warsaw: School and Pedagogical Publications).

Adamski, J. & Chmiel, L. (1985). *Czasy Ludzie Wydarzenia. Część 4 od roku 1939 (Times, People and Events. Part 4 from 1939).* Warszawa: Wydawnictwa Szkolne i Pedagogiczne (Warsaw: School and Pedagogical Publications).

Lt.-General W. Anders, C. (1949). *An Army in Exile.* Nashville: The Battery Press.

Anti-Polish Sentiment. (n.d.). Retrieved 2008, from http://en.wikipedia.org/wiki/Anti-Polish_sentiment

Armia Polska We Francji. The Polish Army in France. (n.d.). Retrieved 2008, from Polonia Today Online: http://poloniatoday.com/images/record2-2.jpg

Berger, J. & Schneider, S. *Forced Labor under the Third Reich. Parts 1 and 2.* (1999). Nathan Associates, Inc. Retrieved 2008, from http://www.nathaninc.com/?downloadid=72

Biega, B. C. (1996). *Thirteen Is My Lucky Number.* North Brunswick: Syrena Press.

Bevin, E. Speech in the House of Commons. Hansard, House of Commons Parliamentary Debates, UK. March 20, 1946.

Catholic Breaks with Polish-Jewish Dialogue Group. (2003, 5 5). Retrieved 2008, from http://www.sfpol.com/holocaust.html

Cienciala, A. M., Lebedeva, N. S., & Materski, W. eds. (2007). *Katyń. A Crime Without Punishment.* New Haven & London: Yale University Press.

Davies, N. (2003). *Rising '44. The Battle for Warsaw.* USA, Penguin Books.

Davies, N., Sword, K. S., & Ciechanowski, J. (1989). *The Formation of the Polish Community in Great Britain, 1939-50.* London: University of London.

Fishman, C. ed. (2007). *Blood to Remember: American Poets on the Holocaust.* St. Louis: Time Being Books.

Gradosielska, D. *My Life in Exile 1939-1946.* (n.d.). Retrieved 2008, from Tales of the Deported 1940-46: www.kresy.co.uk/memories.html

Gumkowski, J. (1961). *Poland Under Nazi Occupation.* Warsaw: Polonia Publishing House.

Guzłowski, J. (2007). *Language of Mules.* Bowling Green: Steel Toe Books.

Guzłowski, J. (2007). *Lightning and Ashes.* Bowling Green: Steel Toe Books.

Hałko, L. (1999). *Kotwica Herbem Wybranym (The Anchor is the Chosen Emblem).* Warszawa: Wydawnictwo Askon (Askon Publishers).

Hautzig, E. (1968). *The Endless Steppe. Growing Up in Siberia.* New York: Harper Collins Publishers Inc.

Henderson, D. ed. (2001). *The Lion and the Eagle. Polish Second World War Veterans in Scotland.* Dunfermline: Cualann Press.

Herbert, U. (1997). *Hitler's Foreign Workers. Enforced Foreign Labor in Germany under the Third Reich.* Cambridge, Cambridge University Press.

Hoffman, J. (2001). *Stalin's War of Extermination, 1941-1945.* Alabama: Theses & Dissertations Press.

Hope, M. (2000). *Polish Deportees in the Soviet Union. Original of Post-War Settlement in Great Britain.* London: Veritas Foundation Publication Centre.

Hulme, K. (1953). *The Wild Place.* New York: Cardinal Books.

Jaroszewski, Z. ed. (1993). *Zagłada Psychicznie Chorych w Polsce, 1939-1945 (Extermination of Mental Hospital Patients in Poland, 1939-1945).* Warszawa: Polskie Towarzystwo Psychiatryczne (Warsaw: Polish Psychiatry Society) and Komisja Nauk Historii Psychiatrii Polskiej (Academic Commission of the History of Polish Psychiatry).

Jaroszyńska-Kirchmann, A. D. (2004). *The Exile Mission.* Athens: Ohio University Press.

Jurgielewicz, E. B. (n.d.). *To Arms in the Ranks of the Home Army.* Retrieved 2008, from Warsaw Uprising, Augsut 1 - October 2: http://www.warsawuprising.com/poster.htm

Kaczanowska, H. (2008). *Kawałek Chleba.* Retrieved 2008, http://groups.yahoo.com/group/Kresy-Siberia/message/31594.

Kaczanowska, H. (2006). *Mamusia and her Red Scarf.* Retrieved 2008, from ESWO Roots: http://www.eswo.org/roots/index.htm

Kaczanowska, H. (2003). *Polscy Chłopcy.* Retrieved 2008, from Kresy-Siberia: Message: Polscy Chlopcy.

Kaczanowska, H. (2005). *Tata, and his Underwear!* Retrieved 2008, from Kresy-Siberia: Message: Re: T: http://groups.yahoo.com/group/Kresy-Siberia/message/15930

Kaczanowska, H. (2007). *The Light of the Candle.* Retrieved 2008, from ESWO Blog: http://blog.eswo.org

Kaczorowska, T. (2007). *Children of the Katyń Massacre.* Jefferson: McFarland.

Karski, J. (1944). *Story of a Secret State.* Cambridge: Houghton Mifflin.

Katyń Massacre. (n.d.). Retrieved 2008, from Russia World War: http://lietuvos.net/istorija/communism/

Kaz-Ostaszewicz, K. (1984). *Długie Drogi Syberii (The Long Roads of Siberia).* London: Poets' and Painters' Press.

Korbonski, S. (1956). *Fighting Warsaw. The Story of the Polish Underground State.* Rev. Ed. New York: Hippocrene Books, Inc.

Dr. Stanisław Milewski Wins International Acclaim for Textbook On Vitreoretinal Surgery. The Kosciuszko Foundation Newsletter. Volume LVI, No.2, summer 2006.

Kosinski, J. (1976). *The Painted Bird.* New York, Houghton Mifflin Co.

Kozłowski, J. (2001). *Junacka Szkoła Kadetów, 1942-1947 (Junacy Cadet School, 1942-1945).* London, Zwiazwk Junackiej Szkoly Kadetów (Association of the Junacy Cadet School).

Kramek, H. (1990). *Refugees' Trails.* Venice: John Kramek.

Kresy-Siberia Group. (n.d.). Retrieved 2008 from Kresy Siberia Group: http://www.kresy-siberia.org/books/memoirs.html

Król, T. (1996). *How Destiny and Fate Placed the Króls in America.* Rochester: unpublished.

Królikowski, L. (2001). *Stolen Childhood: A Saga of Polish War Children.* New York: Publishing House: Authors Choice Press.

Krzysztoporska, M. (1981). *Pamiętnik Matki: 1940-1942.* London: Veritas Publishers.

Księga Pamiątkowa Junackiej Szkoły Kadetów (JSK) 1942-1948,. (2000). Londyn .

Lachocki, E. (1996). *No Return.* New Smyrna Beach: Luthers Publishers.

Lachocki, Niziol, G. (1999). Niezapomniane Jutro (Not Forgotten Tomorrow). Lawrenceville: Brunswick Publishing.

Lane, D. (1970). *Politics and Society in the USSR.* London: Weidenfeld & Nicolson, first edition.

Lucairs, E. (2002). Retrieved 2006, from Poland's Holocaust: http://holocaustforgotten.com/Lucaire.htm

Lukas, R. C. (1994). *Did the Children Cry? Hitler's War Against Jewish and Polish Children, 1939-45.* New York: Hippocrene Books.

Lukas, R. C. (1997). *Forgotten Holocaust. The Poles Under German Occupation, 1939-1944.* Rev. Ed. New York: Hippocrene Books.

Lukas, R. C. ed. (2004). *Forgotten Survivors. Polish Christians Remember the Nazi Occupation.* Lawrence: University Press of Kansas.

Mączka, T, The Fish Lake Garlic Man. (n.d.). Retrieved 2008, from http://www.pecounty.on.ca/government/corporate_services/pdf/TedMaczka.pdf

Mickiewicz, A. (1834). *Pan Tadeusz, or the Last Foray in Lithuania: a History of the Nobility in the Years 1811 and 1812 in Twelve Books of Verse.* Paris.

Miedza-Tomaszewski, S. (n.d.). 'To Arms! In the AK Ranks'. Retrieved 2008, from Warsaw Uprising 1994, August 1 - October 2; 2004-2005 Project InPosterum: http://www.warsawuprising.com/poster.htm

Moor-Jankowski, J. (2004-2008 Project InPosterum. Photo courtesy of the Polish American Congress, Washington Metropolitan Area Division). *Warsaw Uprising, 1944.* Retrieved 2006, from Holocaust of non-Jewish Poles in World War II: http://www.warsawuprising.com/paper/jankowski1.htm

O'Driscoll, B. (2007). *Zmów Zdrowaske. Historia Marii i Jerzeja Giertychowa (Say a Hail Mary. The history of Maria and George Giertych).* Radom: Polskie Wydawnictwo Encyklopedyczne (Radom: Polish Encyclopedic Publishers).

Olson, L. & Cloud, S. (2004). *A Question of Honor. The Kosciuszko Squadron: Forgotten Heroes of World War II.* New York: Vintage Books.

Ostaszewski, J. (1945). *Powstanie Warszawskie (The Warsaw Uprising).* Rome: no publisher cited.

Ostrowski, M. (n.d.). *Retrieved May 2006, from 'To Return To Poland Or Not To Return- The Dilemma Facing The Polish Armed Forces At The End Of The Second World War:* www.angelfire.com/ok2/polisharmy

Pancewicz, B. (1985). *Harcerstwo w Afryce, 1941-1949 (Scouting in Africa, 1941-1949).* Londyn: Harcerska Komisja Historyczna (London: Scouting Historical Commission).

Park, K. B. (2000). *Drogami Swiata do Stowell Park (By the World's Roads to Stowell Park).* Sussex: Caldra House.

Paschwa-Kozicka, A. (1996). *My Flight to Freedom.* Chicago: Panorama Publishing Company.

Polish Cemeteries in Iran. (n.d.). Retrieved 2008, from Poland Iran 2008: http://polandiran.blogspot.com/2007/09/polish-cemeteries-in-iran.html

Piotrowski, T. (2004). *The Polish Deportees of World War One.* Jefferson: McFarland & Company.

Polish Independent Carpathian Rifle Brigade. (n.d.). Retrieved 2007, from Polish Independent Carpathian Rifle Brigade: http://en.wikipedia.org/wiki/Polish_Independent_Carpathian_Brigade

Porajska, B. (1988). *From the Steppes to the Savannah. The true story of a family and their survival against all odds.* GB: Coronet Books.

Pratt, D & S. (2003). *The Spirit of Penley: The 20th Century in Photographs.* Ashbourne Landmark Publishing Ltd.

Proch, F. J. (1985). *Poland's Way of the Cross, 1939-1945.* New York: Polstar Publishing Corp.

Rusinek, M. (1946). *Z Barykady w Doline Głodu (From the Barricade to the Valley of Hunger)*. Warszawa: Wydawnictwo Eugeniusza Kuthana (Warsaw: Eugene Kuthan Publisher).

Russian Propaganda Poster. (n.d.). Retrieved from K: http://en.wikipedia.org/wiki/kolkhoz

Sagan, S. J. (1982). *Food Carriers Out!* Toronto.

Sokolowski, H. (n.d.). *Invasion Map*. Retrieved 2008, from The Soviet Invasion of Poland during World War II: http://felsztyn.tripod.com/id19.html

Soviet Propaganda Poster, (1941). *Rescue Europe from the Fetters of Fascist Enslavement*. Retrieved 2007, from Graphic witness: http://www.graphicwitness.org/undone/rp18.jpg

Spieglman, A. *Maus: A Survivor's Tale*. New York, Pantheon Books, 1996.

Stachura, P. D. ed. (2004). *The Poles in Britain, 1940-2000: from Betrayal to Assimilation*. London: Frank Cass Publishers.

Stepek, M. (n.d.). Retrieved 2008, from Polish Legacy Poems: http://polishlegacypoems.blogspot.com

Subritzky-Kusza, M. (1996). *History of the Polish Government (In Exile), 1939-1990*. Papakura: 'Three Feathers' Publishing Co.

Sword, K. with Davies, N. & Ciechanowski, J. (1989). *The Formation of the Polish Community in Great Britain, 1939-1950*. Great Britain: School of Slavonic and East European Studies, University of London, Caldra House Ltd.

Synowiec-Tobis, S. (2002). *The Fulfillment of Visionary Return*. Rev. Ed. Chicago: ARTPOL Printing.

Szatsznajder, J. (1989). *Drogi do Polski (Roads to Poland)*. Wrocław: Klub Motorowy 'Rzemieslnik (Wrocław: Rzemeslnik Motor Club).

Szcześniak, A. L. (1989). *Historia Polska i Swiat Naszego Wieku od Roku 1939 (History of Poland the World in our Century from 1939)*. Warszawa: Wydawnictwa Szkolne i Pedagogiczne (School and Pedagogical Publications).

Szydło, K. (2008). *Na Zołnierskim Szlaku - Dzienniczek Karpatczyka*. The Fast Print Bookshop.

Szulakowska, H. (2005, November 29). *Corporal Antoni Szulakowski, Signal-man with the Anti-tank Airlanding Battery Independent Polish Parachute Brigade.* Retrieved 2008, from WW2 People's War: http://www.bbc.co.uk/ww2-peopleswar/stories/67a7382667.shtml

Topolski, A. (2001). *Without Vodka. Adventures in Wartime Russia.* South Royalton: Steerforth Press.

Trzcinska-Croydon, L. (2004). *The Labyrinth of Dangerous Hours. A Memoir of the Second World War.* Toronto: University of Toronto Press.

Wasilewska, E. (1970). *The Silver Madonna.* New York: The John Day Company.

Wyman, M. (1989). *DPs. Europe's Displaced Persons, 1945-1951.* Ithaca and London: Cornell University Press.

Zamoyski, A. (1995). *The Forgotten Few. The Polish Air Force in the Second World War.* Rev. Ed. Barnsley: Pen & Sword Books Limited.

Zubrzycki, J. (1956). *Polish Immigrants in Britain: a study of adjustment. Studies in Social Life Vol. III.* The Hague: Martinus Nijhoff.

Zygadło, M. (2001). *Lying Down With The Dogs. A Personal Portrait of a Polish Exile.* Aberdour: Inyx Publishing.

Unpublished sources:

Second Lt. Adam Truszkowski, ex-POW, interrogation report to British authorities. (n.d.) HS4/21, M19/MS/BM/173/3, No. 13, 5th June, 1945. National Archives, England.

Copy of statement of Polish women from the dissolved concentration camp from Ravensbruck. (1945). HS4/21, M19/MS/BM/173/3. National Archives, England.

Christofides, A. S. (2009). *Now there is a plaque!* England: unpublished.

Interrogation of British Junior NCOs and Privates (ex-POWs) evacuated through Russia and arriving in the UK, May 7, 1945. (1945). HS4/21, M19/MS/BM/173/3, National Archives, England.

Interrogation Reports. Warsaw Uprising, Polish Civil Population, Jawiszowice, Maydanek, Ravensbruck Concentration Camps. (1945). HS4/21 File Number Special Operations Executive, Poland. Box number 616. National Archives, England.

Franczak, H. (2006, January). Correspondence with Helena Hayden.

Jędrzejczak, W. (2000). *Kredenza Miłości, (Love's Credenza)*. Hectorville: unpublished.

Łaskiewicz, A. S. (n.d.). *My Wartime Experiences (1939-45) and Beyond.* England: unpublished.

Mączka, S. (2006). *Memoirs.* England: unpublished.

Miccheli, J. (2006, June). miscellaneous. USA.

Pankiewicz, J. *Autobiography.* Colchester: unpublished.

Question of Poles in India, 1947. Mr. Calwell, the Australian Minister for Immigration. Extract from Mr. Hankey's minute. (n.d.). FO 371/66266. Political Departments: General Correspondence from 1906-1966. National Archives, England.

Sawicki, W. (2007-08). Canada: unpublished.

Sgt. Joanna H. Douglas, Interrogation Report to British Authorities. (n.d.). HS4/21, M19/MS/BM/173/3, No. 13, 5th June, 1945. National Archives, England.

Stolarczyk Marshall, T. (2006, December). miscellaneous. England.

Szukalowska, U. (2006). *Life at Melton Mowbray Polish Refugee Camp*, 1957-58. England: unpublished.

The County Admission Register. Gloucestershire C.C. Education Committee. Polish Primary School, 56, Fairford Hostel, Glocs. (1952, 8 16). Gloucestershire Record Office, Gloucester, England.

Times Higher Education Rankings. (2007). *Times Higher Education Supplement.* http://www.timeshighereducation.co.uk/hybrid.asp?typeCode=144

Index

CPSIA information can be obtained
at www.ICGtesting.com
Printed in the USA
FSHW01n1241151018
53025FS